ENGLISH, SCOTTISH AND IRISH

TABLE GLASS

1   Goblet with gilded rim; enamelled in red, azure, and gold; compound white opaque-twist stem

ENGLISH, SCOTTISH AND IRISH TABLE GLASS

From the Sixteenth Century to 1820

By

G. Bernard Hughes

BRAMHALL HOUSE · NEW YORK

This edition published by Bramhall House,
a division of Clarkson N. Potter, Inc.,
by arrangement with B. T. Batsford Ltd.
(A)

In ever-appreciative memory
of
HER MAJESTY QUEEN MARY

who graciously accepted dedication of this work upon its
commencement and whose informed and sustained interest
was a constant encouragement throughout its preparation

PREFACE

IN PREPARING THIS WORK I have examined more than 10,000 specimens of English table glass. Many of these are in the Royal and other private collections, and others in the sale rooms. Others again are in museums, but these so far as my own observations are concerned, are seldom adequately labelled and access for the purpose of examination is difficult. In combination with this wide survey of fine old specimens, I have had unusually close association with the technical side of the work, having had the opportunity of observing for a government department many of the processes by which the old craft has developed into the great glass industry of today. I have always been astonished at the apparent lack of fundamental knowledge among many glass collectors concerning the industrial processes, manual and mechanical, which have been used to produce the exquisite specimens in their cabinets.

It is essential that collectors should possess a general understanding as to how old table glass was made. Such knowledge assists greatly in dating specimens and in distinguishing the genuine from the forgery. Authentic historical facts relating to flint-glass manufacture are invaluable in defining the general characteristics which it is possible to find in the work produced at different periods during the centuries under consideration.

A study of technical treatises imposes a tax on time and patience however. For this reason I have outlined fundamental manufacturing processes without introducing a confusion of technical details. An explanatory glossary of terms used has been included.

As far as possible throughout I have retained the original terms. For instance, the contemporaneous name flint-glass has always been used in reference to glass containing lead oxide as its characteristic ingredient, in preference to the twentieth-century term 'lead crystal'. Similarly, I have preferred the contemporaneous use of the term tint to the misleading word colour for those elusive shades which the old glassmen tried so hard to eradicate from their 'clear white metal' and which are now so highly regarded among collectors.

Student-collectors are often bewildered by the array of stylistic attributes found in almost any collection of glass. Most pieces will fit into the classifications outlined here. The dates given indicate the period during which the feature in question was most fashionable, but it must be realised that certain styles continued in production long after they had been abandoned in fashionable London. For instance, drinking-glasses with drawn stems and trumpet bowls are shown in engravings published from the time of Queen Anne until after the death of George IV.

Among many works of reference consulted throughout the preparation of this book I should like to refer briefly to a long series of authenticated, well-illustrated articles which appeared in *The Queen Newspaper*, a weekly journal of which I was editor-in-chief. These articles did outstanding work in encouraging collectors of old English table glass. My omission of reference to Newcastle glasses is deliberate.

New Romney
1955

G. BERNARD HUGHES

CONTENTS

LIST OF ILLUSTRATIONS

ENGLISH, SCOTTISH
AND IRISH
TABLE GLASS

CHAPTER ONE

EARLY HISTORY

T HE JEWEL-BEAUTY OF GLASS first caught the imagination of the Syrians 4,500 years ago and was cherished as a living art through the centuries that followed. Excavations in the Euphrates region have disclosed remnants of glass-furnaces worked by these ancient craftsmen. Here, near Baghdad, was found the earliest-known piece of table glass — a cylinder of light blue glass strangely free from flaws.

That great Egyptologist, Sir Flinders Petrie, considered that all glass used in Egypt before 1500 B.C. should be attributed to Syria. Not until then did the Egyptians begin to make simple drinking-vessels, founding an industry which was to bring world-fame to the glass-houses of Alexandria. The oldest preserved specimen of Egyptian table glass is a small goblet dating from 1450 B.C. inscribed with the name of the reigning Pharaoh and ornamented with two bands of yellow.

Egyptian glass was prepared in shallow, trough-shaped clay crucibles containing about five pounds of the basic materials, sand and vegetable-ash or soda from their salt lakes. Priests were consulted before the glassmen lit fires in the primitive hearth pits, and the ingredients fused to an accompaniment of noisy ceremonial and incantations.

The glass bowls and bottles in which these Egyptians left food and wine for their dead were made by the sand-core method. This consisted of building up a core of sand on a wooden or metal rod around which was modelled the molten glass. When the glass cooled, rod and core were both removed. By this laborious process the inhabitants of the Nile basin manufactured the unguent containers in which they exported eastern cosmetics across the Mediterranean.

The art of producing hollow-ware such as bowls, cups, and dishes, in one operation, by pressing molten glass into open moulds, was developed by an Egyptian slave some three thousand years ago. The Phoenicians, however, made the most significant discovery of all, about a thousand years later, when they began blowing plastic glass into hollow shapes on the end of metal blowpipes, using elaborately incised moulds to shape the inflated material into decorative forms. The news quickly reached Egypt where already the most ancient form of translucent glass had been superseded for several centuries by transparent uncoloured glass. Within a few years — between 50 and 20 B.C. — Egyptian glassmen were blowing an endless variety of hollow vessels, shaping them with tools exactly as is done by twentieth-century craftsmen.

After Egypt had fallen beneath the might of Imperial Rome, a large part of Egyptian tribute was in the form of glass. At the command of Augustus Caesar glittering prizes were offered to Egyptian glass-blowers as rewards for establishing what was to become a prosperous industry on the Tiber. Fantastic sums were paid by Nero (A.D. 54–58) for exquisitely wrought articles of fragile glass, and at the same time sturdy glass drinking-goblets were sold in the Roman markets for a copper coin. The Romans evolved nothing new in glass drinking-vessels, contenting themselves with the perfect form of the Grecian goblet, almost identical in shape with the present-day brandy inhaler. But they did vastly elaborate form and decoration, with the result that their luxury glass captured the trade of the entire western world. Simple cutting and engraving decorated the surface of Roman glass. When not intentionally coloured, the domestic glass displayed a blue-green or green tint, the hue deepening in proportion to the quantity of iron in the sand. After two centuries of experiments, the glassmen learned that they could neutralize these green tints by adding manganese. They also found that certain proportions of this chemical coloured their work with a violet hue, and copper a dull red.

So successful was the enterprise that by A.D. 220 extra taxes were levied upon members of the Roman guild of glass-makers, while the fire hazard of their innumerable furnaces became so dangerous to the overcrowded city that the industry was concentrated into a single district.

Even in those days private collections of glass were noteworthy enough to warrant exhibition in the Roman Forum. Here were shown the finest local examples of transparent glass and decorative millefiori work in company with prized antiques from Greece, Persian glass enriched with gold, ancient glass from India and China. Nor was the trade confined to the rich. In Equpt, a small Roman-Egyptian town, archaeologists have unearthed one humble home containing thirty-seven glass vessels, some stored in jars, others leaning against the walls. The collection included eight oval dishes, sixteen bowls, two drinking-cups, two wine-flasks, and five conical lamps.

Glass-blowing, like many other branches of industrial art, radiated from Rome to the Roman colonies. Several furnaces are known to have been

26

operating in Britain during the Roman occupation. At Wilderspool, Warrington, on the sandy Mersey estuary, not ten miles from St. Helens, a centre of the modern glass industry, excavations among the foundations of a Roman glass-house have revealed pieces of crucible, fragments of cut-glass, and a wheel for cutting. Roman cutting consisted of intersecting grooves in association with shallow facets.

The Britons continued glass-making after the Roman withdrawal, producing ware of bluish-green tints; the word glass is actually derived from the Celtic 'glas' meaning bluish-green. The Bishop of Mayence sent a number of glass-blowers to England in A.D. 678, but there are no records of their work. Anglo-Saxon drinking-glasses included simple bowl-shaped cups; conical and trumpet-shaped tumblers ornamented with raised patterns in glass thread-work, and deep beakers decorated with projecting claws.

The recognized centre of the English glass industry, then and for the next thousand years, was Chiddingfold in Surrey. Here window-glass was manufactured as well as coarse, deep green glass-ware for domestic use; no technical improvements occurred until Elizabethan days. Drinking-glasses of the tumbler type and other domestic ware were made by glassmen moving from place to place near natural deposits of glass-sand in search of forest timber and the plants of bracken and glasswort from which to make their potash. Beech was their favourite fuel, the side of a wooded hill their favourite site. Turner's *Herbal*, 1568, refers to bracken as 'glaswede because the ash of it serve to make glass with'.

Glass-houses were one-man establishments until the 1560's, each consisting of a single furnace producing one type of article. Masters kept their formulae secret, employing four servants to do the manual work under personal supervision. Letters dated 1587 concerning the glass-house at Knole record that 'they worke night and day, bout only whyles the founder is tempering his mettell, on the one side of the furnes Valyan and Ferris doe worke, on the other side Brussell and the younger man'. Such master glassmen styled themselves 'gentlemen glass-blowers', paying royalties to landowners for permission to burn dried forest wood for their furnaces (fig. 2).

With the Renaissance came the brilliant flowering of the Venetian artist-craftsmen who developed a fragile, lightweight glass displaying a smoothness and clarity hitherto unknown. The metal also took colour well and table-ware might be decorated with gilding and filigree work. Soon the exquisitely designed masterpieces of Venice graced every royal table in Europe and were in demand wherever expensive glass could be afforded.

27

The Grand Council of the Venetian Republic granted liberties and rights to glassmen approaching the rights of nobility. Jealous of foreign spies, the Grand Council 'exiled' these valuable operatives to the island of Murano, the better to guard their trade secrets, for the theft of which the Republic had a range of punishments varying from a term in the galley to death at the hand of a trained assassin.

The three-piece drinking-glass, consisting of bowl, stem, and foot, was developed and an extensive trade was carried on with England. Because of distance and breakage during transport Venetian glasses were costly luxuries: Henry VIII possessed a celebrated collection of some three hundred pieces of exquisite glass from Murano. Thomas Deloney, writing in 1597, mentioned Henry VIII as 'being sat with the chiefest of the Council about him and after a delicate dinner a sumptuous banquet was brought in, served all in glasses'. The banquet of the period was a course of sweetmeats, fruit, and wine, served after the principal course or dinner.

Spasmodic attempts were made to persuade Venetians to manufacture drinking-glasses in England. This ambition remained unfulfilled until Jean Carré, a glass-maker from Arras and Antwerp, arrived in London during 1565 with the intention of setting up round furnaces, such as were used at Murano, for the manufacture of window-glass and vessels of clear glass. Glass furnaces in England were long, low buildings measuring about 16 feet long by 6 to 8 feet in height. Crucibles were cylindrical, measuring about 2 feet in height, 18 inches at the mouth, with a 16-inch base, and 2 inches thick. After negotiations with the Crown occupying almost two years, he was licensed to make 'glass for glazing such as is made in France, Burgundy, and Lorraine' and permitted to establish a glass-house at Alford in Sussex. Having been refused a licence for the manufacture of drinking-vessels in the Venetian style, he appears to have set up an illicit furnace in the deep Fernfold woodlands near Loxwood, Sussex. Excavations on the site have disclosed numerous glass fragments of a clear metal tinged blue-green with a fine surface displaying Venetian characteristics. Goblets with knopped stems, tumblers with *rigaree* bases, and footed quaffing-glasses with finely moulded bowls have been recovered from the debris of nearly four centuries ago.

Late in 1570 Carré — having apparently been granted a licence — was operating a glass-house in the Crutched Friars, London, making glass vessels in the Venetian style. Here he employed several glassmen from Murano under the supervision of Jacob Verzelini. Carré must therefore be considered England's earliest maker of delicate Venetian glass. When he died in May 1572 the glass-house came under the full control of Verzelini who quickly placed the business on a commercially successful footing. A disastrous fire destroyed the glass-house in 1575 and almost at once Verzelini opened a branch in Broad Street while the Crutched Friars was being rebuilt: this he continued operating until his retirement. In December of the same year, despite violent opposition from the glass-sellers, Queen Elizabeth I then granted him a twenty-one-year monopoly to make Anglo-Venetian glass, the agreement stipulating that the drinking-glasses should be as cheap or cheaper than those imported from Murano; that no similar glasses should be made within Elizabeth's dominions by other glass-makers; that Englishmen should be taught the craft. Penalties for infringing the licence were £200 for each furnace and 10s. for each glass, half of the fines reverting to the Crown, one-quarter each to Verzelini and the informer. Soon Verzelini was appointed Glass-maker to the Queen, employing about twenty expert glassmen and many labourers at his furnaces. He retired in 1592, a very rich man.

Several of Verzelini's glasses (fig. 4), elaborately engraved with the diamond-point, still exist, carefully preserved as precious evidence of that enterprising period in English glass-making. The metal is clouded by innumerable minute bubbles and discoloured with various hues including a brownish shade, pale smoke-grey, and greyish-green. Records suggest the engraving to have been the work of Anthony de Lisley (figs. 5–7), a decorating retailer, who bought blanks from Verzelini.

Elizabethan drinking-glasses in fine metal were copies of stemmed cups in silver, everyday drinking-vessels of the rich. Verzelini shaped his glasses as like these as conveniently possible, avoiding the fantastic decoration of Venice. The amount of Venetian glass imported at this time may be judged by Stowe's remark that 'before 1575 there were fifty households in London supported by selling Venetian glass'. Such glasses entered the homes of gentry and yeomen the country over and were protected from damage by 'cages'. These occur among the furniture entries of many inventories such as that of Thomas Morton, 1581, 'a joyned caij for glasses xx^d', and of Matthew White, Durham, 1586, 'j glasse cage, with glasses . . . '.

Non-resinous wood, 'split to the size of a small man's wrist', 4 feet long and dried in ovens until it could be lighted from a candle, was used to heat the furnaces. Lack of wood was always a major problem with Verzelini and his contemporaries. Experiments with coal were carried out in 1586, but any advantage was heavily outbalanced by the smoky tint of the finished metal. Twenty-five years passed before Sir William Slingsby patented a coal-burning furnace, and four years later, in 1615, a 'Royal Proclamation Touching Glasses' prohibited the use of wood as a fuel for glass-making.

This embargo on the burning of wood appears not to have been concerned in conserving supplies, for its use continued until late in the eighteenth century. Its intention was to assist the monopolist in squeezing unlicensed furnaces out of business owing to inability to obtain coal in remote areas. In 1618 Sir Robert Mansell obtained 'letters of assistance' giving him permission to destroy all non-coal-burning glass-houses, although by 1624 only five of his many glass-houses operated coal-burning furnaces.

It was, however, the 'melting furnacye' invented by Captain Thornesse Franke and patented in 1635 that transformed the industry. Glass-furnaces were now housed in structures called 'howls' which, according to the patent, 'by contracting the ayre and causing and bringing in wynd into the sayd furnaces wch shall make the fyers burne with as much vyolence as any blast whatsoever'. This produced a draught enabling the ingredients to be fused with 'more than a full third parts of the fewell now vsed and with much less labour and farre shorter tyme'. Crucibles were slightly enlarged and for the first time were covered to protect the 'batch' from smoke fumes. The cumulative effect of these improvements was to cheapen glass, but impurities from the raw materials still gave the metal a colour varying from light sea-green to deep brownish-olive.

Sir Jerome Bowes, financier and former Ambassador to Russia, acquired the Verzelini glass-house in 1592 when Queen Elizabeth renewed the monopoly for a further twelve years. She also extended its scope by giving Bowes the exclusive right to import 'Venetian glass for Noblemen within Her Majesty's Realm'. For this privilege he paid the Queen 200 marks a year, the monopoly continuing until 1614 when James I granted an additional licence to a group of financiers in return for a yearly rent of £1,000 and a contract to use only Scottish coal at their glass-houses.

The Duke of Rutland's MSS. at Belvoir contain numerous sidelights on the use of Anglo-Venetian table glass in wealthy households at this period. References to glass plates 'with graven rims', which in 1602 cost 6s. 2d. a dozen, occur frequently until 1615, suggesting that decorative glass plates were a fashionable table appointment. One entry reads: '4 Julii 1598: Item for sweete meates at dyner when my Lady was there, and hyre of glass plates.' The hiring of 'feast vessels' in glass and pewter was a profitable occupation: an entry for 10th June 1600 records that drinking-glasses for a dinner in London were hired at a cost of 11s. 6d.

Accounts dated 17th August 1599 refer to '12 drinking-glasses, 4 with covers and 2 were very long'. These cost 35s. 6d., with a box for packing 2s. and 6d. extra for carriage. Three years later 39s. was paid for '5 Venice drincking glasses with covers, 8 others uncovered and one for oyle and vinegere', and three dozen 'glasse fruyte dishes' cost 18s. In 1604 the cost of '6 Venice Glasses wyne 18/-; 4 beere glasses 10/-; 2 ordinary glasses wyne 12d.' and in 1614 a dozen 'Venice glasses sent to Belvoir' cost £1. 13s.

Vice-Admiral Sir Robert Mansell, M.P. for King's Lynn, with several business associates including 'Lord Pembroke and other prime lords of the Court', acquired the glass monopoly during 1618, paying the king £1,500 a year. Lady Mansell, daughter of the Earl of Worcester, acted as 'director of glass-houses', controlling productive establishments operating in some twenty centres throughout the country. Within five years Mansell eliminated his co-partners and secured a new licence giving him complete control of England's glass industry. This power he used to organize the trade on a rational basis.

An outstanding example of Mansell's business acumen is provided by his handling of the alkali problem. He built substantial ash-houses at strategic points throughout the country. A considerable seasonal trade had long existed in the burning of bracken, glasswort, and other plants, the resulting alkali or potash being pressed into blocks and sold in the nearest glass-house centre. Mansell's agents now placed firm orders for potash which was stored in ash-houses built with stout stone walls and floors. Bacon, writing in 1626, mentions that 'they crush the ashes into lumps and so sell them to the Venetians for their glasse works'. Makers of fine table glass at that time and for another half-century were known as Venetians, the wares they manufactured being known as 'Venice glasses'.

The Earl of Middleton's Collection of MSS. contains references to the ash or 'asse', as well as a few sidelights upon the manufacture of English drinking-glasses during the days of James I. A document written by Robert Fosbroke, dated 1617 and entitled 'Observations for Glasse', explains that a case of window-glass was a horse-load, 'which at the rate of 200 weight to a horse-load, is a tenth of a tun'. He continues, 'wiche asse [ash of witch hazel] beanstraw asse and green fearne asse are all good. Peas-straw asse and gorse asse are not so good. Dry ferne is nott good. Two good workmen will make 16 or 18 case of glasse weeklie. For the nomber of coales and quantite of asse, they must be proportioned according to the bigness of the forness. Broad-glasse spendeth more coales and asse, quantitie for quantitie, than drinking glasse dothe. The forness for drinking glasse spendeth above 20 strikes [bushels] of asse weeklie, and about 10 or 11 loades of coales.

'The making of 80 tun of glasse yerelie will spend above 6 tun of coales weeklie . . . the fornesses will cost about £20 a piece, butt you are to proportion your rent according to the ground where they are sett, for all that ground is wast.' Then 'a conjectur all aiming att the proffitt and charge of glasse making' shows that a single furnace made '80 tuns of glasse yerelie, which, at 16/- a case, that is, £8 a tun, is £640. The costs are rent of furniss £10; wages of five men £100; asse £50, coales £125; sand £6. 13. 4; carriage to London £80; and total £371. 13. 4.' Green drinking-glasses were sold at twenty to the dozen pieces. It should be remembered in reviewing these figures that seventeenth- and eighteenth-century glass-furnaces stood idle for at least three months of every year.

Fine drinking-vessels, almost Venetian in appearance and technique, highly prized and costly luxuries, continued to be made at the Crutched Friars glass-house under Mansell's control. Elsewhere he or his licensees manufactured coarse drinking-glasses and table-ware, window-glass, mirror-plate, and bottles. In 1624 Mansell informed the House of Commons that 4,000 workers were employed by the glass industry.

Mansell exercised his monopolistic rights to the full. On 30th July 1641, for instance, he 'sent Richard Batson into custody without a hearing for buying 129 chests of imported glasses'. But at the same time the great nobles and merchant princes could legitimately buy fine glass for their own use direct from Antwerp or Murano. Any glassman making unlicensed ware was imprisoned and his furnaces confiscated.

The manufacture of fine drinking-vessels appears to have been almost abandoned during the Commonwealth, although domestic glass continued to be made in quantities large enough to prompt Cromwell to impose a tax. Mansell retired upon the forfeiture of monopolies, leaving a legacy of sturdy industrial efficiency but little, if any, improvement in the quality of Anglo-Venetian glass.

Thorpe[1] details three principal types of drinking-glass stems as emanating from the Crutched Friars glass-house during the monopoly regime:

1 Hollow, mould-blown stems which might be decorated with masks or festoons or with both introduced alternately. Until 1635.

2 Hollow, mould-blown urn-shaped stems with vertical bands of ladder patterning. From about 1590.

3 Hollow but much thicker blown stems, the upper part shorter, the lower part slimmer and taller and lacking decorative moulding. From about 1615.

[1] *English Glass* by W. A. Thorpe, 1935.

2 'From Sand Pit to Glass Furnace', a miniature in grisaille from the fifteenth-century manuscript *The Buke of John Maundeville*

4 Earliest example of dated English table-glass, made by Jacob Verzelini in London with engraving attributed to Anthony de Lisley: dated 1577

3 Venetian glass painted with red, blue, green, and yellow enamels: stem bears London hallmark 1527 (?)

GOBLETS WITH SILVER-GILT FEET VICED ON

5–7 Two engraved betrothal or marriage goblets made in London by Jacob Verzelini:
top, dated 1578; *lower*, dated 1586

8–12   Diamond-engraved Anglo-Venetian glass dating from 1582 to 1663

Masks or mascarons were much favoured by the Venetian glass-makers and their English imitators: these were small blobs of applied glass stamped while hot with faces of men or animals.

Table glass was being sold in sets during the reign of Charles I. Howell refers to this in a letter dated 1645, remarking that 'she desires you to send her a compleat cupboard of the best christal glasses'. Large households stored table glass in the goblet office attached to the buttery and in the charge of a liveried goblet boy whose duties included carrying a serving-bottle and a salver of goblets among assembled guests, a service noted a century later (fig. 33).

With the Restoration it became every glass-maker's ambition to produce wares stronger and more translucent than those of his competitors. At the same time certain London merchants began to reap rich rewards by importing Venetian glass without restriction.

This Venetian glass was extremely fragile. To display clarity to the full it was blown very thin for, like the Roman glass 1,500 years earlier, it contained a straw-coloured tinge, conspicuous in stem knops but scarcely perceptible elsewhere. This metal was worked at a low temperature, cooling quickly and requiring great speed in manipulation. Although very complicated forms were produced, Venetian soda-glass lacked the lustre of the beautiful glass-of-lead which was shortly to replace it on the tables of Englishmen.

Within three months of Charles II's arrival in London, during 1660, a lime-soda glass known as *christall de roache,* or rock crystal, was produced by John de la Cam, a Master Doctor Ordinary to the King of France and friend of the second Duke of Buckingham who financed a glass-house in the Charterhouse Yard to the extent of £6,000. In 1662 Thomas Tilston of London was granted a patent permitting him sole use of a process for 'makeing christall glasse' invented by Martin Clifford and Thomas Paulden and said to be ' a new manufacture not formerly used or practiced in this naçon'. A year later this, too, came under Buckingham's control. Tilston's crystal is said to have been a clearer metal than any formerly made though still colour-tinged. It was the finest glass to appear so far in England, and profitable export markets were quickly opened. The well-known 'Royal Oak' glass (figs. 11 and 12), dated 1663, is one of the few existing specimens from Buckingham's glass-houses. The thin metal is pale greenish-brown in tint, devoid of brilliancy, entirely lacking the clear, pellucid quality soon to distinguish English glass. John Worlidge in his book on *Cider,* 1675, noted that fine French or Dutch glass was more transparent than the English.

37

Even by 1670 transparency had improved, but the Worshipful Company of Glass-sellers, incorporated during 1664 with autocratic powers over glass manufacturers and retailers in London, was far from satisfied with the quality of this English crystal. These arbiters of design and fashion demanded that glass manufacturers should experiment until a 'bright, cleer and whit sound Mettall' was produced. The Glass-sellers, assisted by a group of English scientists, including Robert Boyle and Christopher Merret, financed experiments. This policy resulted in George Ravenscroft evolving the English flint-glass which was soon to monopolize the table-glass trade of the world.

Figure 1

Goblet enamelled with the arms of Richard Lowndes, Member of Parliament for Buckinghamshire, 1742. Rich red, azure, and gold, in a rococo cartouche meticulously painted in white enamel. The bucket bowl, supported by a compound white opaque-twist stem, has a gilded rim of a diameter equal to that of the stout plain foot which is almost flat beneath, hollowed, and, like the bowl, shows distinct striae. 1760–80. Height 8½ inches.

In the Corning Museum of Glass

Figure 2

'From Sand Pit to Glass Furnace', a miniature in grisaille from the fifteenth-century manuscript *The Buke of John Maundevill*. The hole being dug at the top of the picture is the source of sand. This is carried to the glass-house where, combined with soda ash and other chemicals, it is made into molten glass. In the foreground a glass-worker is seen dipping the end of his blowpipe into the pot of glass, and its small capacity is to be noted. Next to him the plastic metal is being blown and roughly shaped upon a stone slab. The annealing kiln is seen to the left.

In the British Museum (Additional MS. 24189, F.16)

Figures 3 and 4

GOBLETS WITH FEET 'VICED ON'

(3) Bowl of Venetian glass painted with enamels in brilliant red, blue, green, and yellow, with a short stem composed of two ribbed knops to which is attached a pedestal foot of silver gilt. This bears a London hallmark believed to be that of 1527. The inventory of Henry VIII's glass in 1542 shows that he possessed such a glass, and references to silver-gilt feet 'viced on' are found throughout the sixteenth century. This example is used each year on the inauguration of the new Master of the Founders' Company, by whose permission it is reproduced here.

(4) The earliest piece of dated English glass on record, blown at the glass-house of Jacob Verzelini in London; the diamond-point engraving is attributed to Anthony de Lisley. The decoration includes a hunting-scene, two panels with initials, and the date 1577. Stem and foot are of fruit-wood and silver.

In the Corning Museum of Glass

Figures 5–7

BETROTHAL OR MARRIAGE GOBLETS

Made in soda-glass by Jacob Verzelini and diamond-engraved by Anthony de Lisley. (5, 6) Metal of greyish-green tint containing minute air bubbles; deep funnel bowl; hollow-blown, fluted stem between two small knops; low pedestal foot with narrow upward fold. Decorated with hunting-scene frieze showing a running stag and a unicorn chased by two collared hounds, each separated by a tree; a deep wavy band; and a band of arabesque with three open panels inscribed in hatched characters AT, RT, 1578, each pair of letters linked by a lover's knot. Height 8¼ inches.

By courtesy of Messrs Delomosne & Son Ltd

(7) Metal of pale smoky-grey tint and full of minute air bubbles; oviform bowl, short stem with hollow-blown fluted knop on a plain foot engraved with petals. The bowl is divided horizontally into three sections with double trails of clear glass, each edged with a thread of opaque white glass. The frieze is engraved with arabesques, interspersed with three panels, one inscribed with the letters GS joined by a lover's knot, and two with the date 1586: the central band inscribed with the motto of the Pewterers' Company: IN: GOD: IS: AL: MI: TRVST: The bowl rim and stem knop show evidence of contemporaneous gilding. Height 5¾ inches.

In the British Museum

CHAPTER TWO

THE DEVELOPMENT OF FLINT-GLASS
1660–1734

WHEN KING CHARLES II returned from exile in 1660 he and his courtiers brought with them from France and Holland a wealth of new ideas, new crafts, new fashions. It was a period of extravagant living in flamboyant houses, but it was a period, too, of eager experiment, with English craftsmen turning their inherent skill and ingenuity to produce wholly new refinements in dress, in furniture, and in the sumptuous presentation of food and drink.

Many fashions of that day were shortlived, but others established for England a reputation that extended throughout the Continent and continued for more than a hundred years. Of these, none was more notable than the introduction of what has come to be known to collectors as flint-glass, and to the present-day trade as lead crystal, a lustrous, sparkling material from which late-seventeenth-century glass-blowers fashioned handsome goblets and serving-bottles, unrivalled alike for their clarity and their sheen. Most highly prized among these are the few bearing seals impressed with the mark of a raven's head — proven products of George Ravenscroft, the first maker of flint-glass (figs. 13, 14, 15, 17 and 19).

George Ravenscroft (1618–81) was in the prime of life when the monarchy was restored. Although he himself received no court appointment — his younger brother became a Privy Councillor — he was closely associated with such brilliant minds as Sir Isaac Newton, Sir Christopher Wren, and Sir Samuel Morland, the King's Master Mechanic. He made a niche for himself as a prosperous merchant in the vastly increased traffic with the Continent and in the course of his trade with Venice many fabulously lovely goods passed through his warehouses. Among them were consignments of the exquisitely fashioned glass for which the island of Murano had long been celebrated. These were so heartbreakingly fragile as to challenge him to meet the ever-increasing demand for fine table-ware in glass of his own making.

41

English glass manufacture in and for seven miles around London was dominated by the Worshipful Company of Glass-sellers. When, in the summer of 1673, Ravenscroft erected a small glass-house in the Savoy, London, it was with the encouraging knowledge that this powerful Company was specifically urging manufacturers to meet the needs of the period with a 'bright, cleer, and whit sound mettall'. He operated one furnace with two chairs and two master workmen with their assistants. The fireclay used by Ravenscroft for his melting-pots came from Stourbridge. He paid a Mr Gray sevenpence a bushel on the spot and was responsible for the cost of carriage by canal to Bewdley, by river to Bristol, and thence by sea to London.

Turning naturally to Venice for advice, Ravenscroft not only employed Venetian technicians, but substituted for sand in his formula, crushed and calcined flint prepared from white marble river pebbles imported from Northern Italy, and instead of soda used refined potash from Spain. Robert Hooke, visiting Ravenscroft's glass-house in July of the same year, observed quantities of 'calcined flints as white as flour', reputedly free from the impurities found in the sand normally used in English glass-houses. Wren inspected, too, the mill in which the flints were pulverized 'after heating and quenching often'.

Within a few months Ravenscroft notified the Glass-sellers that he had achieved his object, and was able to produce 'fine Chrystaline Glasses in semblance of Rock Christall for beer, wine and other uses'.[1]

At once he petitioned the King to grant him a patent under the Statute of Monopolies. The attorney-general reported that the ingredients of Ravenscroft's glass were not used elsewhere in the kingdom and that the ware produced in this medium was as good as, if not better than, similar articles imported from Venice. Charles II then issued a seven-year patent, No. 176, dating from 16th May 1674. The Glass-sellers' Company thereupon agreed to buy his entire output for three years, a contract renewed in 1677.

Flint was, however, by no means a new ingredient to the English glass-makers. White marble pebbles from the Ticino and other rivers of Northern Italy had been used in the glass-houses of Murano from about 1560, and the Venetians long controlled this source of pure silica. The Venetian ambassador in England wrote to the Doge of Venice during 1620 that refugee glass-workers from Murano had instructed English workers in the preparation of flint and 'their crystal has now attained a beauty not sensibly inferior, but quite equal to that of Murano'. A few months later Sir Robert Mansell

[1] *The History of the Glass-sellers' Company* by Sydney Young, F.S.A., 1913.

informed Parliament that the fine table-ware made at his London glass-house included in its composition 'calcined pebbles of flint, powdered and sifted'.

Flint-glass, then, was no novelty to either English or Venetian glassmen when reintroduced by Ravenscroft in 1674: the flux, however, differed from that formerly used. The new glass was termed 'fflint crystalline', and it is interesting to note that the man himself came of an old and distinguished family from Flint in North Wales.

The Duke of Bedford's collection of family household bills[1] belonging to this period include about four hundred priced and dated references to domestic glass-ware. The purchase of 'fflint-crystalline' is first recorded on 25th April 1674, a few days before the patent was issued. In the same month the Glass-sellers' Company undertook to market Ravencroft's entire output, provided only that he worked to their designs. Ravenscroft's good fortune, however, was shortlived. Within a few months of manufacture the glass gradually devitrified, losing its transparency — a defect known to collectors as crizzling.

By the autumn of 1675, however, with the aid of oxide of lead he had created a new glass of a density and refractive brilliance previously unknown. This glass, tinged with a dark hue, was easier to work than his earlier metal. The lead made it heavier, softer, and more easily scratched. Hollow-ware, if flicked with thumb and finger, emitted the resonant ring that distinguished it from other glass which might be similar in appearance.

Ravenscroft's glass-of-lead was no sudden invention, but the culmination of a series of experiments no doubt inspired by a formula to be found in A. Neri's textbook *L'arte Vetraria*, published in Florence during 1612 and translated into English by Christopher Merret exactly half a century later. The sixty-fourth chapter states that 'glass-of-lead, known to few, is the finest and noblest glass of all others at this day, made in the furnace'.

The Glass-sellers' Company certified Ravenscroft's new glass as successfully withstanding their tests with the added 'distinction of sound enabling it to be discerned by any person'. On 18th September 1675 they issued a 'License of Consent' and Ravenscroft announced his glass-of-lead as 'improved fflint glass'.

Doctor Plot visited the Savoy glass-house during the spring of the following year and observed 'a sort of pebble glass, which is harder, more

[1] W. A. Thorpe, 'Woburn Abbey Glass-sellers' Bills', *Journal of the Society of Glass Technology*, 1938.

durable, and whiter than any from Venice, and will not crizel, but will endure the severest trials whatever, to be known from the former glass by a Seal set purposely upon them'. This seal was originally intended to distinguish the glass-of-lead from earlier products of the Savoy glass-house, but was continued with the approval of the Glass-sellers to enable Ravenscroft's glass to be recognized 'from all others that shall be made in resemblance of the said glasses'. The seal was a small glass disc impressed with the raven's head as borne on the Ravenscroft coat of arms (fig. 14).

Such marked glasses were sold in March 1676 to the Duke of Bedford by the glass dealer Thomas Apthorpe who described them as 'new fflint wine glasses M^{rd} 16/-'. The qualification 'new' was omitted from similar entries made after 1676. The new glass was soon in widespread use, for the household account book of Sarah Fell, Swarthsmoor Hall, Northumberland, shows that on 30th April 1677 she paid for 'one flint glasse & a vinig^r cruett 3/-', and 10d. for two ordinary glasses. A month later she paid 1s. for a vinegar cruet, thus showing that flint-glass was approximately five times more expensive than soda-glass at the period. The metal of the few sealed glasses still remaining is slightly clouded and displays many microscopic air bubbles known as seeds (fig. 19).

Seals were applied to the productions of at least two other flint-glass makers at this period: Henry Holden, glass-maker to the king from 1683, had authority to seal his ware with the King's arms; the Duke of Buckingham impressed his crest, the lion and coronet.

An old deed in the possession of the Glass-sellers' Company and quoted by Sydney Young lists the prices and weights agreed between Ravenscroft and the Company.

		a piece
Beer glasses ribbed & plain	7 oz.	1 - 6
Claret wine glasses ribbed & plain	5 oz.	1 - 0
Sacke glasses ribbed & plain	4 oz.	10^d
Castors ,, ,,	3 oz.	8^d
Brandy glasses ,, ,,	2 oz.	6^d
Beer Glasses nipt diamond wais	8 oz.	1 - 8
Claret glasses ,, ,, ,,	5½ oz.	1 - 3
Sack glasses ,, ,, ,,	4 oz.	1 - 0

Purled glasses for both beer & wine priced at same rates as nipt.

Diamond Crewitts of a pint ribbed & plain				a piece
with stoppers in them	9 oz.	for	2 -	0
¾ pint crewitts of same sort with stoppers in them	7 oz.	for	1 -	6
½ pint crewitts of same sort with stoppers in them	5 oz.	for	1 -	0
Quart ribbed bottles	16 oz.	for	3 -	0
Pint bottles of the same	10 oz.	for	2 -	0
Half pint bottles of the same	8 oz.	for	1 -	6
¼ pint bottles of the same	5 oz.	for	1 -	0
Quart bottles all over nipt diamond wais	16 oz.	for	4 -	0
Pint bottles of the same sort	10 oz.	for	2 -	6
½ pint bottles of the same sort				
Quarterne Bottles of the same sort	6 oz.	for	1 -	3

All and every of the said sorts of bottles to have stoppers fitted to them and given in to the rates aforesaid and also handles if required.

All covers for drinking or Sullibub glasses ribbed and plain shall be delivert at 3/- per lb., diamond or purled at 4/- per lb., and Extraordinary work at 5/- per lb. And all purled glasses bottles crewitts that shall be purled to be at the same rates as if they were diamond.

Extraordinary work was characterized by the application of elaborate trailing to moulded bowl bases and by stems enriched with pinched ornament such as strawberry prunts (figs. 14, 15 and 206 to 208).

A few days after the expiry of his patent in 1681 Ravenscroft died, thus ending an agreement with the Glass-sellers' Company which had enabled them virtually to dictate the forms into which the new metal might be shaped. In doing so they were always directly influenced by Venetian design and tended to treat molten flint-glass as if it were of the same consistency as the quick-cooling soda-glass to which they had been accustomed, each glass being blown from a single gathering of metal. In flint-glass, however, it was essential to take four gatherings of metal, one on top of the other. The result was heavy, thick-sectioned hollow-ware. This was usually sold by weight and the glass-sellers therefore had a financial incentive for making table-glass heavy and ponderous. Noble goblets with flaring bowls rounded at the deep solid base, on massive baluster stems rising from heavy feet, became fashionable and were at once christened 'tallboys'. D'Urfey, writing in 1694, noted the demand for glass tallboys (figs. 37 to 40).

Shortly after Ravenscroft's death two qualities of flint-glass were made, known first as thick and thin, and from the mid-1680's as double and single flint-glass. For long authorities have misinterpreted these terms, stating that they distinguish between the number of gathers taken up on the blowing iron, although contemporary descriptions for almost a century to come are consistent in stating that four gathers were taken.

They have overlooked the fact that double flint-glass contained a much greater amount of lead oxide than the single flint-glass. The latter, being of a thinner consistency, could be blown to a section approximately half that of the much more durable double flint-glass hollow-ware. These two qualities were advertised continuously until early in the nineteenth century when technical developments made the distinction unnecessary. A goblet of single flint-glass was lighter in weight, without 'veins', and of greater clarity than one of double flint-glass.

A dozen wineglasses in single flint-glass at fourteen to the dozen weighed less than a dozen of equal size and shape in double flint-glass at twelve to the dozen. Cullet, widely advertised for at 3d. a pound, implied double flint-glass: advertisements for single flint-glass cullet were infrequent, as it was comparatively scarce, and was valued at little more than half the price of double flint-glass. Comprehensive among several such advertisements noted is one quoted by Westropp from *Faulkiner's Dublin Journal*, January 1746, which ended: 'N.B. All double flint wineglasses, decanters, water-glasses and saucers at seven pence per lb. weight, the single flint at two shillings and four pence, fourteen to the dozen. . . . In exchange will be allowed for double flint broken glass twopence halfpenny per lb. and for single one penny halfpenny per lb.'

By the mid-1680's flint-glass was being made by individual London and provincial glassmen lacking expert knowledge of the process: such information was not divulged in published patents until after 1720. There were twenty-seven flint-glass houses operating in 1696, nine of them in London. Each was feeling its way experimentally with lead oxide and other chemicals producing variations in weight and clarity of metal, for nothing approaching standardization of ingredients in quality or quantity had been reached. Meanwhile metal varied considerably in weight and tint.

While flint-glass was enjoying the limelight of high patronage, the English crystal which it replaced became relegated to the kitchen and known merely as crystal. By 1683 the crystal was being described as 'ordinary glass' and hawked around the countryside at cut prices by pedlars and chapmen in defiance of the law of 1664 which gave to the glass-sellers a monopoly in the sale of 'Glasses, Looking-glasses, Hour glasses, stone pots or earthenware bottles'. Crystal, which was made by the old-fashioned frit process, continued in considerable production until the late 1730's, a wide range of household ware being marketed, including the newly fashionable stemmed glasses for beer.

Flint-glass, the most practical glass known up to that time, gave to England domination of world glass-markets throughout the Georgian era. Even Venice, the home of elegance and creation, found it necessary to copy the sturdy English designs of the late seventeenth century, but the lustre, sheer weight, and clarity of the metal were important assets which she failed to reproduce.

A petition presented to Parliament in 1695 records that 'the makers of Flint Glasses have long since beaten out all foreigners merely by making a better glass and underselling them'. At this time more than one-third of the English glass output was being exported. The petition also gives an insight into the poor quality of annealing. The glass-sellers, of whom there were 140 in the London area alone, anticipated that about 15 per cent of their stock would 'break and fly' while lying on their shelves. The periodical *Apollo* for 1708 describes flying as 'a Misfortune attending all those that deal in glass: flint glass cracks with a sound like that of a small bell and for no apparent reason'. An experienced storekeeper might expect 3 per cent of casualties in moving a consignment and if unskilled in the work might lose one in every twelve pieces handled. Further breakage might be anticipated during transport. Glass was carried in panniers strapped to the flanks of pack-horses moving in single file in the charge of an armed guard. No method had yet been discovered for preventing flint-glass from 'breaking and flying'. So that customers should receive intact the actual number required glass-men packed services 25 per cent more than ordered.

Flint-glass fresh from the hands of the blower was exceedingly brittle and unable to bear sudden changes of temperature or slight surface shocks without fracture. It was therefore essential to toughen the glass by annealing, that is, raising it to a high temperature and then cooling it gradually.

Annealing at this time was carried out in an oven built above the melting-chamber and operated on waste heat reaching it through small flues, known as linnet holes, connected with the furnace below. In the early Georgian era separate kilns began to be used for annealing flint-glass. The kiln was filled with glass-ware and when annealing temperature was reached the door was opened, slightly at first, and then a little wider, and finally the back was opened to cause a draught. The glass was then allowed to cool slowly during the night.

There is nothing to indicate that flint-glass domestic ware, as opposed to fine table glass, was produced in quantity earlier than the late 1730's,

47

although considerable numbers of coarse green-glass vessels and 'ordinary glass' (crystal) were made in forms resembling the fine glass. Francis Buckley has suggested that this crystal was made in the provinces as late as 1770. Not until the 1780's did the annual production of flint-glass domestic ware exceed that of fine flint-glass intended for the gentry.

So far there had been no competition from abroad. Then in 1772 M. Libaude received a state gratuity of 1,200 livres in recognition of his services to France in discovering the secret of making English flint-glass. Manufacture does not appear to have met with immediate success, however, for the *Reports of the Juries* in connection with the Great Exhibition of 1851 record that flint-glass comparable with the English product was first manufactured abroad in 1784 at a small glass-house in St. Cloud, France.

The term flint-glass was invariably employed in statutes and legal documents until after 1850, although pulverized calcined flints appear to have been used seldom after about 1730 owing to the high cost of preparation.

Flint-grinding was an important process in the manufacture of early flint-glass. The calcined flints were ground in a horse-powered mill, invented by John Tyzacke in 1691. This had two stones moving upon a marble bottom edged with sloping boards to retain the powder. The crushed flint was then sifted through a buckram bag shaped like a shirt-sleeve. John Houghton[1] in 1696 described this as 'a convenience for the workman, 'tis done in a close bin, with only two holes for him to put his arms in and shake the bag about; whatsoever material is not small enough to sift through is brought again to the mill to be new ground'. An improved machine was patented in 1732 by Thomas Benson.

To the collector of flint-glass, tint and striae distinctive to the experienced eye are of importance. Tint is important in the recognition of seventeenth- and eighteenth-century flint-glass, varying according to the quality of the metal, its period, and place of manufacture. The term does not imply colour in the sense that a hue such as green or blue is seen upon casual examination: it is a residual colour-tinge inherent in the ingredients composing the metal. This is best observed in a drinking-glass by placing it upon a white cloth and inspecting the bowl and stem junction. If a piece of modern glass is placed beside it, the entire fabric of the old glass will show darkly against the cloth — considerably darker than the new.

The term tint is not used in reference to metal of tavern or domestic quality, but to fine flint-glass. Even the costly 'extraordinary work' of the

[1] *A Collection of Letters for the Improvement of Husbandry and Trade*, London, 1681–3 and 1692–1703.

1680's had a bluish-white tint. By 1690 glass technicians were beginning to realize that the colourless metal of their dreams necessitated raw materials of absolute purity. The research that then began resulted in the eventual removal of impurities, but flint-glass was never tint-free during the collector's period.

In the flint-glass made earlier than about 1690 a scarcely perceptible dull-green tint, imparted to the metal by iron, the commonest and most dangerous impurity, is visible upon close inspection at the base of the bowl. To clear the metal a decolorizer was necessary, and oxide of manganese was used for this purpose. Manganese was, however, a difficult mineral to handle. When too much was added the glass became slightly pink and the small amount needed for decolorizing could not then be easily distributed evenly throughout the melting-pot. Moreover, it was liable to contain traces of cobalt and nickel and even when measured accurately might give the glass a greyish tone.

Shortly after 1700 it was realized that the fragments of glass which had been in contact with either the blowing-iron or the punty, 'from which there always remaineth iron', should not be utilized as cullet and 'thrown into the pots of crystal for they will make it black'. Another step had been taken towards tint elimination.

During the first half of the eighteenth century the tints displayed by flint-glass included yellow, steely-blue, violet, brown; all probably caused by residual impurities in the ingredients used. Buckley refers specifically to the peculiar purple tint of Bristol, the yellow and grey tints of the Stourbridge–Dudley area, and the light bluish tint of the north country. Each glass-house developed its own formula, so that various qualities of metal might be made simultaneously in the same district.

Eighteenth-century flint-glass might still be disfigured by red and black specks within its fabric, the result of imperfect fusion between lead and silica. Particles of white silica and other impurities known as stones were also likely to be visible. The metal might also contain groups of air bubbles, so minute that they resembled dust specks, and were known as 'seeds'. Such seeds indicate manufacture at a glass-house experiencing difficulty in raising the furnace temperature high enough to eliminate all the tiny bubbles of air trapped among the grains of the raw materials. These microscopic globules rose but slowly through the viscous mass, many never reaching the surface. Increased furnace heat was essential for the successful removal of both specks and seeds, thus producing glass of greater clarity. This was partially accomplished by the introduction of the Hessian bellows,

49

known in England as Savory's double hand-bellows, first applied experimentally to a London glass-house furnace in 1705 and improved by D. Papin. These bellows contained an interior fan furnishing greater blast than was formerly possible, bringing the furnace fire to greater heat and enabling higher fusing temperatures to be achieved. The Savory bellows were standard equipment in London glass-houses by 1710, enabling a full-bodied, dark, clear, lustrous glass to be manufactured though the intensity of its dark hue was never consistent. This glass feels almost greasy to the touch.

Some of the green-tinted and dark-tinted flint-glass table-ware made during the eighteenth century shows well-defined striae, that is, apparent undulating markings within the metal (fig. 92). They are perfectly vitrified and as transparent as any other part of the glass. Striae are very pronounced in green-tinted metal of the seventeenth century. Cords — slight striae which may be felt with the fingertips on the surface of the glass — were similarly caused by using metal which was of uneven composition because insufficiently molten. These defects, known to glassmen at the time as 'veins', may be found in double flint-glass throughout the collector's period. As late as 1830 the Society of Arts offered a gold medal to anyone who should 'invent a process for making flint-glass free from veins, as dense and as transparent as the best now in use'.

50

Figures 8-12

ANGLO-VENETIAN GLASS DATING FROM 1582 TO 1663

(8) Beaker with a silver base viced on and diamond-point engraved with the arms of Smith of Oldhaugh, Cheshire, and of Altensteig, Nuremberg; inscribed 'William Smith Maie 30th 1582'.

In the Victoria and Albert Museum

(9) Flute of the type made at Sir Robert Mansell's glass-house in London; bowl and folded foot decorated with diamond-point engraving; hollow urn-shaped mould-blown stem.

In the Victoria and Albert Museum

(10) Goblet with straight-sided bowl engraved in diamond-point with a stag-hunting scene and applied moulding of vertical flutes, on a blown baluster and collared stem with folded foot engraved with flower sprays. Height 8¼ inches.

By courtesy of Messrs Christie, Manson and Woods Ltd

(11, 12) Two views of the Royal Oak goblet dated 1663; made of light, almost colourless metal and weighing only three ounces. Bucket bowl on blown knop stem; diamond-engraved with portrait bust of Charles II in stylised oak tree and inscribed 'Royal Oak', also a royal coat of arms; further engraved with portraits of Charles II and his Queen Katharine of Braganza. Height 5⅜ inches.

Formerly in the Bles Collection

Figures 13-15

RAVENSCROFT GLASS

(13) A pair of Ravenscroft bowls with deep foot rims and displaying the crizzling recorded as being present on his early issues of flint-glass. Both are diamond-point engraved in commemoration of the marriage between Butler Buggin and Winifred Burnett, 17th July 1676. The bowls are ornamented with scrollwork, flowers and foliage, and flying-dragon crests of the Buggin family. The crest in full is engraved on the right-hand bowl: the same coat of arms impaled with that of his wife appears on the other bowl, together with an engraver's cypher. Height 4 inches, diameter 5 inches.

By courtesy of Mr W. G. T. Burne

(14, 15) Two romers, free from crizzling, and bearing (lower front of stems) the raven's-head seals of George Ravenscroft, Savoy Glass-house, London. Incurved bowls, ribbed hollow pedestal feet with folded edges; thick hollow stems vertically ribbed and decorated with six strawberry prunts. Wavy collars conceal the bowl-stem junctions. 1678–81.

Left: Bowl vertically ribbed. Height 6½ inches.

In the Victoria and Albert Museum

Right: Bowl with pinched trellis ('nipt diamond wais') decoration. Height 7 $\frac{5}{16}$ inches.

Sold in 1946 to Messrs Cecil Davis Ltd for 620 guineas;
now in the Corning Museum of Glass

Figures 16–18

EARLY FLINT-GLASS MADE DURING THE 1680's

(16) Sweetmeat glass with flat bowl with vertical sides and base moulded with gadrooning; incised stem with collar above, flat folded foot. Height 4¾ inches.

Formerly in the Bles Collection

(17) Sealed Ravenscroft jug of crizzled metal, with boldly ribbed bowl and pedestal foot joined by a four-lobed hollow knop between thin collars. The foot and lip rims are folded and the handle twisted; the raven's-head seal is fixed to the handle terminal. Height 9 inches.

In the Victoria and Albert Museum

(18) Badly crizzled salver with flat circular plate on hollow pedestal foot; rims of plate and foot are folded.

In the Corning Museum of Glass

Figures 19, 20

(19) Ravenscroft bowl with moulded base and folded rim, and an applied raven's-head seal. 1676–80.

In the Cecil Higgins Museum, Bedford

(20) Bowl with incurved sides engraved with a hunting-scene in diamond-point, and inscribed 'Gabriell Stephens 1706'.

In the Cecil Higgins Museum, Bedford

13   The Buggin bowls dated 17th July 1676

14, 15   Two sealed romers with hollow stems

RAVENSCROFT GLASS

16–18 Flint-glass made during the 1680's, including a sealed Ravenscroft jug

19   Ravenscroft bowl with an applied raven's-head seal

20   Bowl diamond-engraved with hunting scene and dated 1706

21–23 Goblets of flint-glass made under the influence of Venetian design
during the 1680's

24 Loving-cup and covered bowl with body bases worked in relief: early George II

25 Spouted posset cups

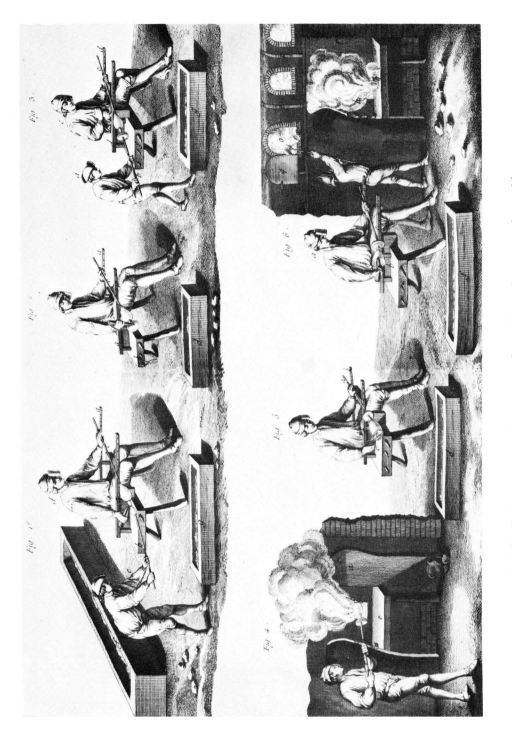

26 The final processes in the making of an eighteenth-century glass goblet

27　William Parker's trade card illustrating fashionable facet-cut glass of the 1760's

28   Maydwell and Windle's trade card illustrating a manually driven glass-cutting machine, and cut-glass of the early 1770's

Figures 21–3

EARLY FLINT-GLASS MADE DURING THE 1680's UNDER THE INFLUENCE OF VENETIAN DESIGN AND PROCESSES

(21) Covered goblet with base of bowl pinched with trellis decoration in relief, and encircled above with trailed decoration and strawberry prunts, large and small alternately. The lid is similarly decorated, and has a crown finial on a cushion knop. The stem consists of two hollow knops separated by mereses on a flat, folded foot.

(22) Goblet with decoration pinched in relief; blown baluster stem decorated with fringe-work and strawberry prunts; on a folded foot.

(23) Goblet, its decoration pinched in relief, with hollow knop encircled by strawberry prunts on a hollow baluster stem; folded foot.

All in the Brooklyn Museum

Figures 24, 25

(24) *Left:* Loving-cup with waisted bowl on short knopped stem rising from a highly domed and moulded foot; base of body worked in relief, and trailed decoration encircling the waist. Early George II.
   Right: Covered bowl similarly decorated with ball finial to cover. Early George II.

In the Victoria and Albert Museum

(25) Spouted posset cups, each with a pair of swan-neck handles — the covers are missing.
   Left: With curved plain body, moulded ring foot, and swan-neck spout; *c.* 1720; Height 6 inches.
   Right: Of slightly crizzled glass, with the handles set low on the body, the base of which is moulded with gadroon decoration and has a high kick; the spout is flattened; *c.* 1680. Height 3½ inches.

By courtesy of Mr Howard Phillips

CHAPTER THREE

THE DEVELOPMENT OF FLINT-GLASS
1734–1820

SO FAR the flint-glass industry had consisted of numerous small glass-houses, technical reasons compelling them to use melting-pots of limited capacity and seldom much larger than a kitchen bucket. Six of these were heated in a single round furnace. Then, in 1734, Humphrey Perrott of Bristol perfected a furnace producing a much fiercer heat than had formerly been deemed possible. Patent No. 545 records that Perrott 'followed the Trade and Mystery of a Glass Maker who for some years has been endeavouring to make a finer Metal than heretofore'. The Perrott furnace was notable for its inclusion of 'Double Bottom Potts for the better Melting, Preparing, and Preserving all sorts of Glass Wares, which furnace is contrived in a new Manner with Artificial Draughts to it, whereby to force the heat of the Fire the sooner to perform its Office . . . by Feeding it with Fewell at Teasing Holes which will much reduce the Expense of Coal'. This furnace, providing a vastly increased temperature, enabled much larger pots to be used, and produced a smoother metal, less dark than formerly.

The Universal Dictionary of Arts and Sciences, 1751, estimated the cost of such a furnace as £3,500, and noted that it seldom lasted three years and required lengthy refitting every three months. Each working furnace was built beneath a brick cone 90 feet high and 50 feet in diameter at ground level, smoke and gases escaping through an opening at the top. The furnace itself measured 6 feet in height and 10 feet in diameter, and was divided into three vaulted sections.

Such a furnace contained eight or more pots, and by 1748 each might contain as much as 1,500 pounds of glass. On these were placed crucibles called piling-pots, each capable of holding about 100 pounds of 'a finer and more nice metal, fit for the nicest works'. This fine-quality glass is referred to in several technical works of the period and is definite proof that qualities of metal might vary inside individual glass-houses. Some writers on glass-collecting deny this possibility. Furthermore, the metal at the top of the pot was of a poorer quality than that below and under the name of tale glass was sold at a cheaper rate.

The Universal Dictionary of Arts and Sciences in 1751 also described the wide use in English glass-houses of the tunnel leer, 'about five or six yards long, where the vessels are annealed or cooled . . . the glasses are put in with a fork and set on the floor or bottom, but they are drawn out in iron pans, called fraches, through the leer to cool by degrees, so that they are quite cold by the time they reach the mouth of the leer, which enters the room where the glasses are to be stored'. Authorities have previously stated that the tunnel leer was introduced to English glass-houses in 1780 by George Ensall of Stourbridge. The term leer is taken from the German *leer ofen*, meaning 'empty furnace'.

Annealing flint-glass by this method so toughened the metal that its working life was considerably lengthened. It did not now 'fly' whilst in stock or crack for no apparent reason, and breakage in transport became less frequent. Such tenacious metal enabled cutting to be carried out on double flint-glass in much deeper relief than formerly, with reduced danger of fracture at the wheel. During the 1740's it was found that a second journey through the tunnel increased surface brilliance and improved the tint of thick flint-glass intended for cutting. This appears to have been introduced by Brent and Lowe, 'At ye Old Barge House, opposite The Temple in the County of Surry', whose trade card, issued in 1748 and now in the collection of Sir Ambrose Heal, states that 'all glass made at this House is Double Anneal'd; no other has had conveniences for that purpose though the most effectual way to make it durable and fit for exportation'.

The annealing tunnel by then was a long, low, narrow-vaulted arch of brickwork, heated at the entrance by a firebox on either side. A chimney near the other end caused a strong draught which drew flames and heat some distance down the arch. At the exit the temperature was little warmer than elsewhere in the store-room. The glass was loaded on flat iron pans hooked together in a continuous train and slowly drawn through the tunnel on rollers. A hand-operated winch in the store-room moved the train, allowing it to be loaded at the entrance, pan by pan. The pan might be allowed as little as two or as much as four hours to pass through the leer.

Until Josiah Wedgwood invented the pyrometer in 1784, the temperature in the leer was a matter of chance, depending largely upon the heat of the glass when entering the tunnel, and the direction of the wind. The leer-man judged the temperature by observing the time taken by a wad of paper, tossed into the tunnel entrance, to burst into flames. The Excise Act of 1810 imposed a yearly licence of £100 on each annealing tunnel. Because some glass-makers were still using the less costly annealing oven, to the detriment of the trade, it was also made compulsory to anneal all flint-glass by the tunnel method.

Perrott's patent enabled him to 'vend the new invention', and before his monopoly expired in 1748 several of his furnaces were operating in Bristol, London, Newcastle, and Stourbridge. Glass-houses now became dangerous places to work in owing to the greater size of the crucibles without any corresponding improvement in their quality. These crucibles were made on the premises, owing to the danger of imperceptible fracture when transported by carrier's cart along cobble-paved roads. The specification of patent No. 929, 1769, concerning glass-house furnaces records that workers were frequently burned or crushed to death, and their lives continually endangered by 'the collapse of the clay pots, the metal running to waste'. This is stated to be the only reason why glass was so expensive, the loss in time and material exceeding £250.

The intense, more uniform, heat produced by the new furnace enabled the raw materials to be fused at a higher temperature. Glass now displayed greater clarity and brilliance than formerly as well as greater durability. The contemporary term used to distinguish table-ware made from this new metal was 'white flint'. Glass-houses operating the Perrott furnace used the term 'white flint' in their business addresses, such as the Cockpit White Flint Glass House, Southwark, and the White Flint Glass House, Bedminster. *Matthews' Bristol Directory*, 1793, lists several 'white or flint-glass houses', proving the term to have been in use until the end of the century.

White flint-glass must be distinguished clearly from the white opaque glass shortly to be made at Bristol and elsewhere, and from white glass. *Instructions to be observed by the Officers Concerned in Ascertaining the Duties on Glass* was published privately by the Government to assist its officers in administering the Excise Act of 1745. This publication defines white glass as follows: 'In Flint Glass Houses there is likewise made a Metal . . . White Glass, being made from the refuse or waste in flint Moils and in crown and plate Houses with Sand, Ashes, etc., which are generally near 30 hours melting before fit to work, save in small pots.' This white glass was used in the manufacture of chemistry ware and bottles.

Instead of being a trade in the hands of small men, glass-making became an important and prosperous industry. This prompted the Government in

1745 to impose a tax of 9s. 4d. per cwt. on the raw materials used in the manufacture of 'flint-glass and white glass'. Levied on a basis of weight the tax discouraged extravagance in the use of metal. The new flint-glass with its improved manipulative possibilities enabled more pieces to be made from each batch, weight for weight. One important consequence of the new metal was the abandonment of pure undecorated form and a rapid development of ornament. It is unlikely that tax imposition influenced this movement.

There seems to be no basis for the widespread theory that the Excise Act was responsible for an immediate increase in glass prices and a decrease in the size of individual pieces. A tax of one penny per pound on raw materials, less certain allowances for waste, would not appreciably affect the cost of flint-glass as, until 1777, cullet was not accounted a raw material, and Professor Turner has pointed out that this might constitute more than half of the mixture. The tax would amount to less than a halfpenny on table glass weighing less than one pound. On a dozen wineglasses weighing four ounces each the tax might be three-halfpence.

A further statute in 1777 repealed the duties of 1745, replacing them with a tax of 18s. 6d. a cwt., or 2d. a pound, upon 'materials or metal that shall be made use of in the making of all flint glass'. The duty on flint-glass continued for exactly one hundred years, reaching $10\frac{1}{2}$d. a pound by 1820. Three excisemen were permanently allotted to each glass-house.

Flint-glass table-ware was now usually priced by the dozen, cost depending upon the amount of decoration put into the piece. Undecorated ware increased in price per pound owing to the labour involved in producing a greater number of lighter pieces: until the mid-1740's these, generally speaking, were similar in form to the glasses made by the old methods. In 1746, the year that the first Excise Act became operative, best undecorated flint-glass was advertised by glass-sellers at 9d. a pound; by 1752 the price had risen to 10d. a pound.

Glass-selling was an important branch of the trade, and today the sellers' illustrated trade cards are valuable documentary evidence of their periods' styles (figs. 27 and 28). *The London Tradesman* in 1747 described glass-sellers as 'a set of shop keepers, and some of them very large dealers, whose only business is to sell all sorts of white flint glass. Here and there they are masters also of the art of scalloping glass which is now greatly in vogue. They take apprentices also and with one expect £20. A person as a shopman has £20 a year and his board and to stock a shop in a middling manner will require £200 to £500.'

During this period, the 1740's, porcelain teacups and saucers were

66

first manufactured in England: from 1743 at Chelsea, between 1744 and 1748 at Heylin's Glass House, Bow, from 1748 to 1750 at Bristol. Tea had been served mainly in drinking-glasses standing on glass plates, only the well-to-do being able to afford Oriental and Continental porcelains. English glass-makers were now faced with the competition of more delicate but colourful wares. The glass-makers replied with carefully fabricated and skilfully ornamented glass. Porcelain, however, won the contest, only the cordial-glass remaining part of the tea-table equipage for a further quarter-century.

Glass-houses by the middle of the century had become extensive premises accommodating five main departments to carry out the following processes:

1   Preparation of clay, and pot-making.
2   Washing and drying sand until it became a white glittering mass.
3   Cleansing and preparing potash.
4   Mixing and sifting dry sand, potash, and lead oxide to produce a fine, salmon-coloured powder.
5   The glass-house with its furnace and annealing leer.

The *Dictionarium Polygraphicum*, 1735, noted that 'nothing makes finer and clearer Glass than common flint, but the charge for preparing it hinders the Glass-men from using it. Maidstone in Kent furnishes the London glasshouses with fine white sand for flint-glass.' Barrow, writing in 1751, repeated this, adding 'perfect colour and transparency are obtained by adding a small proportion of Manganese from the Mendip-hills in Somersetshire'.

A formula for white flint-glass at this period consisted of sand, 1,000; red oxide of lead, 660; potash, 330; potassium nitrate, 40; borax, 30. To ensure smoothness in the molten glass a proportion of old flint-glass, known as cullet, was added. The majority of flint-glass formulae published between 1699 and the end of the eighteenth century require lead oxide to constitute one-third of the whole, a proportion used in present-day glass-of-lead. The mixture was shovelled into clay crucibles and heated by the furnace. The compositions used or recommended at different periods, and which vary considerably, are given in *Lardner's Cabinet Encyclopaedia*, 1839.

Five days were required to bring the contents of the crucible to a workable state. After the first day the glass appeared as a honeycombed mass, very white and opaque. Eventually this changed to a transparent body containing thousands of air bubbles. The white colour gradually changed to a light purple tint produced by the oxygen given off by the manganese. As the melting continued the purple gradually vanished, the air bubbles

67

became fewer and larger, and at length vanished. The glass was then fused and ready for use. The materials are not actually melted: chemical reactions occur between the ingredients when brought to a high temperature and glass results. When completely fused the mass was permitted to cool until it became a thick viscous substance, bright red in colour. Only then was it of correct working consistency.

During the second half of the eighteenth century flint-glass became even clearer with slightly enhanced brilliance, transitions being so gradual as to be almost imperceptible. From 1785 talc earth was mixed with Stourbridge clay to make melting-pots resistant to the effects of lead. Metal worked from such pots was distinctly clearer: records prove their immediate use by the Midland glassmen and at Waterford. The clays used in pot-making contained many impurities even when washed: at least one technical work of the period gives this as a reason why flint-glass could not then be cleared. Technical difficulties for long prevented entire removal of some impurities contained in the ingredients. These were liable to tint the finished metal: a trace of copper, for instance, would give a bluish tint, whilst metallic lead was responsible for a blackish tint.

Hodkin and Cousan, in their work *A Textbook of Glass Technology*, 1926, point out that 'until the beginning of the nineteenth century flint-glass was universally melted in pots set in a furnace and directly heated'. Concerning this direct heating they note that 'quite apart from heat losses, which render such a furnace most inefficient, the fact that the fire was so close to the furnace chamber resulted in a light ash being carried into the chamber with deleterious effects upon the walls, pots, and colour of the glass'.

Such furnaces were outmoded by the Donaldson furnace, patented in 1802 and first used by Ricketts, Evans & Co., of Bristol. This furnace used only one-third the amount of fuel formerly required, yet provided such intense heat that the materials fused in half the time, whilst producing a more crystal-clear glass. Further improvements to the furnace were made in 1824, when the Stourbridge firm of Wheeley endeavoured to 'secure purity and crystalline appearance in flint-glass'. In these furnaces, as in all others until the Bacchus patent of 1834, impurities rose at the sides of the pot and flowed towards the centre 'causing a quantity of scum commonly called stones or cordes on the surface of the metal, rendering it necessary to be skimmed from time to time'. When Henry Bessemer patented his glass-furnace in 1846 it was claimed that the resulting metal possessed 'a degree of cleanliness formerly unknown'. The clarity of metal was even further improved by the Henry Howard furnace patented in 1849 and 'having a more regular uniform heat than any previous furnace'.

That flint-glass had not been fully cleared by the middle of the nineteenth century is evident from the official catalogue of the Great Exhibition of 1851 which says: 'English manufacturers have lately been making important experiments with a view to discovering a method of producing glass free from tint and striae.' After inspecting the exhibits, the jury, which included distinguished experts in the glass-trade, noted that English flint-glass was 'charged with the defect of colour, of striae, of globules, and of undulations'.

Table-ware was made by a glass-blowing team known as a 'chair', and usually consisting of four men controlled by a gaffer directing operations and carrying out the most important processes. He was assisted by a servitor, a foot-maker, and a taker-in, each playing an essential part in the production of each single glass (fig. 26).

The tools used by the team were few and simple, including a blowpipe measuring 4 to 6 feet in length with a $\frac{1}{4}$-inch bore, shears for cutting the blown glass, small callipers, and a solid iron rod with a serrated tip used to hold the glass while it was being worked, known as the punty. The tool that played a principal part in the shaping of blown vessels, particularly in the opening out of rims, was a spring appliance resembling large sugar-tongs with hardwood tips: continual contact of these tips with hot glass necessitated frequent replacement.

The Universal Dictionary of Arts and Sciences, 1751, detailed the processes by which Georgian hollow-ware was made. With his blowing-iron one of the team picked up a 'gather' of viscous flint-glass from the pot in much the same way as treacle is picked up with a spoon. By rotating the blowpipe above a tank of cold water he caused the metal to adhere securely to the iron and consolidate more firmly with the next gather taken from the melting-pot. Four gathers in all were taken, great care being needed in lifting each or the finished glass might appear curdy or contain small air bubbles. After the fourth gather he placed his mouth to the lip of the blowpipe and blew gently through the iron tube until the glass expanded like a bladder about a foot in length. He then rolled it on a marble stone to polish the surface and blew a second time, producing a sphere. After each blowing he placed the mouthpiece quickly to his cheek.

The iron was then handed to the gaffer in his chair. He placed the blowing-rod across the chair's flat-topped, slightly inclined arms, and rolled it quickly backwards and forwards, causing the glass sphere to rotate. Simultaneously he used a small wooden paddle to shape the bowl, moulding

69

it approximately to the form of the finished article. Continual rotation preserved evenness on the face of the glass.

In its viscous state one mass of glass will adhere permanently to another without any sign of a weld: this makes it possible to build up a glass object from several units. Even the simplest stemmed drinking-glass was built of units produced in sequence and joined whilst red hot.

Meanwhile, another gather of glass was brought from the furnace by the servitor who allowed it to flow down on top of the bulb. Gauging the amount of glass required to form a goblet stem, he sheared away the remainder. The blowing-iron was then rolled briskly along the chair arms and while the glass rotated the stem was shaped to its final form. Then the foot-maker added another gather of glass from which the foot was shaped with a wooden paddle. The servitor, with a small blob of viscous glass on the end of the punty, applied this rod to the centre of the foot, to which it adhered. The glass was then cut away from the blowpipe, but remained firmly attached to the punty.

The excess glass was then sheared from the goblet rim, the bowl opened out and the rim smoothed and finished by heating at the furnace mouth. The rounded edge thus produced is one of the hallmarks of hand-made glass. Machine-made products of the 1830's and later were ground, leaving a sharp angular rim. The completed goblet was separated from the punty by a sharp blow with a knife-like tool dipped in water. The taker-in then carried the glass on a long forked stick to the annealing leer.

Figure 26

The final processes in the making of a glass goblet in an eighteenth-century glass-house. To protect his eyes from the glare and heat of the molten metal the gaffer wears a visor.

(1) The servitor applying hot metal for the gaffer to shape into a foot; (2) opening and shaping the foot; (3) the servitor applying the punty rod to the half-finished goblet, while the gaffer removes the blowing-iron; (4) reheating the partly finished goblet at the furnace mouth; (5) shearing surplus metal from the rim of the bowl; (6) opening and shaping the bowl. The finished goblet is then placed in the annealing oven. From Diderot, 1765, copied from *Dictionary of Arts and Sciences*, London, 1751.

Figure 27

William Parker's trade card issued from his glass warehouse, established in 1762 at 69 Fleet Street, London, two doors from Water Lane where the Whitefriars Glass-house operated. He became celebrated as a maker of finely designed and lavishly cut chandeliers, and by 1770 his trade card referred to him as glass manufacturer to the Prince of Wales. This card illustrates the highly fashionable facet cut glass ware of the 1760's. Of the thirty-two pieces it will be noted that fifteen are associated with illumination: ceiling and table chandeliers, candlesticks, wall branches, hall-lights, candle shades. Decanters are all-over facet-cut and it will be noted that the footed globular type was in vogue. The hollow pedestal foot is present on drinking-glasses and ewers. The elaborate sweetmeat epergne at the top with hanging-baskets illustrates flat fluting to advantage. The barrel-shaped wine fountain with silver harness and tap proves their quarter-century vogue.

In the British Museum

Figure 28

Maydwell and Windle's trade card: their glass warehouse and cutting workshops flourished in the Strand, London, until 1778. Illustrated is a glass-cutting machine powered by a wheel-boy and operated by a cutter, together with a selection of richly resplendent glass capable of spectacular scintillation by the light of wax candles. The two-tiered pyramid supporting an elaborately cut master-glass with a hollow pedestal foot, heavy enough to balance the expansive bowl above, displays glasses for wet and dry sweetmeats, and bottles for scented flowers. The chandeliers and lustres each incorporate two reflecting globes, their surfaces covered with large diamond-cutting capable of reflecting all possible brilliance. Their deeply curved branches are facet-cut and each socket is fitted with a scalloped sconce. Glass tankards at this time were fashionable for punch drinking: the covered example displays the newly fashionable barrel-form body.

In the collection of Sir Ambrose Heal

Figure 29

A trade card advertising red-streak cider, a popular brand of the eighteenth century. The cider is seen being drawn from the cask into a wide-lipped serving-bottle of pale green bottle-glass such as was used in taverns. The cider is being drunk from goblets with deep conical bowls and hollow pedestal feet; c. 1760.

In the British Museum

Figure 30

A bill detailing a consignment of flint-glass bought in 1773 by Edward Gibbon, the historian, from Colebron Hancock of Cockspur Street, London. Wineglasses at this time, according to household books of the period, contained one gill of liquor, and it was fashionable to fill them two-thirds: goblets were double their size. The bill prices goblets at 9d. each, and wineglasses at 5d. The champagne flutes at 8s. a dozen would resemble those shown in fig. 156. Water-cups at 1s. 3d. each were finger-bowls with vertical sides. The term 'hollowed' indicates that the punty scar has been ground smooth — use of the word suggests that it had not yet become standard practice to remove such scars.

In the collection of Sir Ambrose Heal

CHAPTER FOUR

STEMS: ANGLICIZED VENETIAN, BALUSTER, PLAIN

T HERE IS UNIQUE SATISFACTION in tracing, step by step, the changing fashions in drinking-glasses by collecting a chronological sequence from 1675, when Ravenscroft introduced lead oxide as a flux into his flint-glass, to the invention of machine-moulding in 1833. Such a collection will demonstrate the progressive refinements brought about by technical developments in fine-quality flint-glass. The coarser-quality glass, distinguished by its poor metal, clumsy design, indifferent finish, and lack of decoration, sold for everyday domestic use, and for the bars of taverns, punch houses, confectionery shops, and elsewhere, will produce few specimens of importance apart from occasional commemorative pieces.

The arrangement of drinking-glasses and other stemmed vessels into chronological sequence means recognition of six main and twenty-two subsidiary types of stem: these may be further divided according to bowl forms and types of feet.

The various stem groups, together with the approximate dates of their appearance and decline, are given in the following table:

1	*Anglicized Venetian*			*1676–1695*
	a	Hollow and solid buttons	. . .	1676–1695
	b	Quatrefoil		1676–1690
2	*Balusters*			*1685–1760*
	c	Heavy baluster		1685–1720
	d	Flat-faced silesian		1705–1720
	e	Reeded silesian		1720–1745
	f	Light baluster		1720–1760
	g	Heavy knopped		1720–1735
	h	Light knopped		1735–1760

3 *Plain*   *1700–1820*
   i   Drawn with tears 1700–1740
   j   Drawn without tears   1720–1820
   k   Plain straight 1725–1760
   l   Plain hollow 1760–1775

4 *Twists*   *1776–1780*
   m   Twisted rib   1676–1720
   n   Incised-twist 1735–1750
   o   Air-twist 1735–1760
   p   Mercury-twist   1740–1760
   q   Opaque white-twist   .   .   . 1750–1780
   r   Colour-twist 1760–1780
   s   Mixed-twist (air-twist and opaque-white) 1760–1775

5 *Faceted and Cut*   *1745–1820*
   t   Early facet   1745–1760
   u   Late facet   1780–1800
   v   Cut   1780–1820

The earliest flint-glass stems were simplified versions of Venetian designs, the immediate tendency being away from the fragile delicacy of Venice towards simple sturdiness dictated to English glassmen by the viscidity of the molten metal. John Greene, a prosperous glass-seller with a shop and warehouse in Poultry, London, imported from Morelli of Venice a wide range of soda-glass drinking-vessels which were sold here in competition with English-made crystal from 1660. More than 25,000 Venetian glasses passed through his hands between 1667 and 1672. Detailed drawings accompanied each of Greene's orders and it seems reasonable to assume that they reflected styles then being manufactured in England. Greene's drawings, preserved in the British Museum, show a great variety of stem forms, invariably short, and ornamented with perpendicular ribbings or curved mouldings. The majority of stems were merely knops, referred to in the orders as buttons, with collars joining bowl to stem and stem to foot: a few were very short plain balusters. The importation of Venetian glass eventually proved unprofitable in competition with English flint-glass, and had ceased by 1690.

Stem buttons made from flint-glass were at first blown hollow as if made from the light soda-glass to which the glassmen were accustomed (fig. 21).

74

32 Sir Godfrey Kneller's portrait of the Duke of Newcastle holding a wanded wine-flask and a Kit-Cat drinking-glass; c. 1718

These pear- or melon-shaped hollow buttons, which might be plain or ribbed, were too fragile to endure temperature changes and the joltings of road travel by pack-horse. Breakages were costly. Hollow stems were superseded, therefore, by solid stems of similar form, ribbed and collared. These in their turn were succeeded by squat bulbous knops without collars, which continued to be made until the 1690's.

A series of solid buttons was pinched into winged or quatrefoil form (Nomenclature varies: Thorpe, quatrefoil; Buckley, four-lobed; Francis, winged.) The squat, fat button was pinched into four projecting vertical or twisted lobes, the metal being drawn out with a tool resembling sugar-tongs. The surfaces of the lobes might be pressed with strawberry prunts. Taller stems were soon demanded to harmonize with large V-shaped bowls (fig. 34f). To accomplish this the quatrefoil for a short period surmounted a moulded knop or collar, disappearing entirely by about 1690.

The solid baluster knop meanwhile grew tall and sturdy, a shape known in furniture at the time as the Portuguese swell, but collectors prefer the term baluster, defined in the *Oxford Dictionary* as 'a short pillar, slender above, pear-shaped below', a form which made its appearance in Italian architecture in about 1470. The baluster, slenderly elegant, was used on many silver-gilt standing cups throughout the Elizabeth I–Charles I period. In the world of flint-glass the inverted baluster is more usually encountered (figs. 38, 39).

It has not been fully appreciated, perhaps, that the evolution of baluster stems in glass reflected a contemporary evolution in turned furniture. On chairs, for instance, the unimaginative reel or ball-turning of the mid-seventeenth century existed side by side with the knop and button stem found on some early drinking-glasses. The massive flint-glass stems in baluster form were but reflecting a silhouette favoured by many generations of furniture-makers, just as the earliest writhen stems followed the lines of the immensely popular twist-turning of post-Restoration chairs and tables.

Then, towards the end of the century, when expensive chairs were being graced with particularly rich leg design, swelling strongly at knee-height in the various well-known trumpet styles, the baluster stem rapidly followed suit with the introduction of the cushion knop. In furniture, as in glass, the baluster outline, true and inverted, persisted during the early decades of the eighteenth century, completely dominating the design of chair backs.

A collection of early baluster stems is likely to display evidence of the stem-building experiments carried out during the formative years of

75

flint-glass when design was endeavouring to overtake the technical improvements then being developed in the preparation of the metal. Technique is notably poor in provincial work but gradual improvement is to be discerned in a chronological series of glasses. In comparison with Continental standards of table-glass design, the English baluster stemmed flint-glass drinking-vessels, including the standing cups or tallboys, were decidedly heavy and clumsy. They did, however, possess the valuable quality of durability.

Stems incorporating the baluster, either true or inverted in their design, graced flint-glass drinking-glasses from about 1685 until 1760. At first such a stem would support either a conical (fig. 38) or a round funnel bowl (fig. 40), tapering gracefully to the base and perhaps occupying more than half the total height of the glass.

Collectors place balusters into two groups, the heavy and the light. Heavy baluster stems (fig. 36a) are those associated with solid-based bowls whose interior depth is seldom equal to their stem length. The bowl might be welded into the stem, so that as much as one-third of the bowl would consist of a solid glass base (fig. 35a). More often, however, the stem was drawn from the bowl and manipulated into shape (fig. 37b). Such baluster stems were entirely plain, avoiding trivial decoration, and depending instead upon crystalline solidity and simple proportions. Feet on baluster stems might be either folded (fig. 39), plain (fig. 37c), domed (fig. 37a) or domed and folded (fig. 40.)

The term 'heavy baluster' has more recently come to include not only sturdy true and inverted balusters unaccompanied by knops, but also the stem dominated by a single knop, such as the cushion or acorn knop (fig. 37c) with subsidiary knops above and below.

The introduction of a wide angular knop above the baluster was an early attempt at elaborating stem design. The next innovation was the addition of the drop knop and the cone knop in about 1700. Some five years later the annulated knop (fig. 42) and the inverted acorn (fig. 37c) were incorporated into stem designs, each supported by a short stumpy baluster but dominating the stem (fig. 45). The same decade saw the appearance of double baluster stems, that is, a pair of short balusters placed head to head between a pair of knops.

Stems in which balusters and knops are associated became numerous, and from 1710 the collector may note the cushion or mushroom, cylinder, egg, and rare dumb-bell knops. The knop most often found in heavy baluster stems is the cushion variety, however, generally containing air

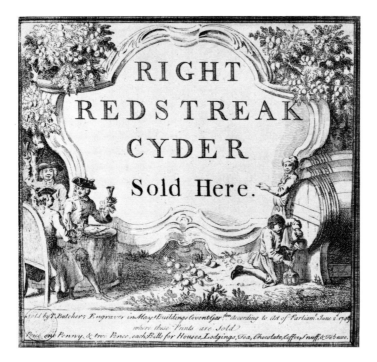

29　A cider trade card illustrating goblets with
hollow pedestal feet

30　A bill for table glass supplied to Edward Gibbon, the historian, by Colebron
Hancock, 1773; this refers to champagne flutes

31 'A Punch Party' by Joseph Highmore, c. 1740. Illustrating punch glasses

33   'A Dinner Party' by Marcellus Laroon, *c.* 1740. Illustrating a goblet-boy with glass salver and wineglasses

Reproduced by Gracious Permission of Her Majesty The Queen

34 Wineglasses and tapersticks of the late seventeenth century, all with folded feet

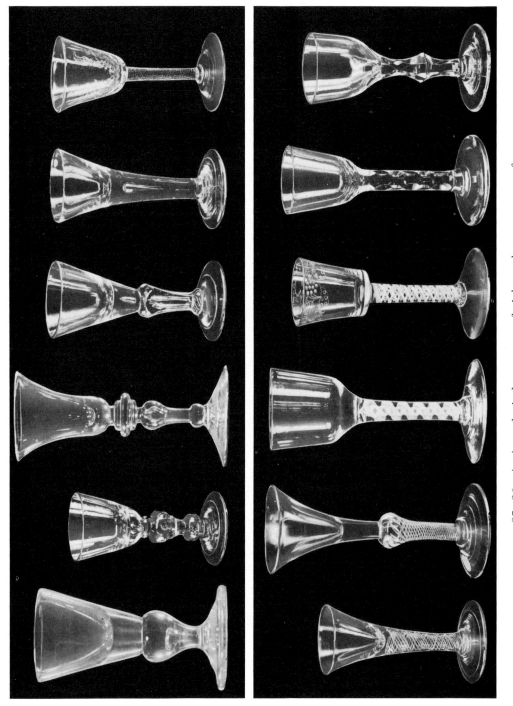

35, 36 A chronological sequence of eighteenth-century stem forms

37–40 Drinking-glasses with solid-based bowls

41–46 Drinking-glasses with solid-based bowls, knopped stems and folded feet

47–50 Drinking-glasses with silesian stems and folded feet

bubbles or tears and placed either centrally or above an inverted baluster or other knop formation. Most frequently it is found in company with a waisted bowl. The cylinder knop was generally placed below either a knop and collar or a single knop: it has also been noted in association with a short dumb-bell knop. This uncommon feature is itself usually found between a pair of twin knops.

To these, during the early years of George I, were added triple and multiple rings, angular and swelling knops, simple balls and ridged knops. Sometimes knops of two or three differing forms may be found in association with a true, inverted, or double baluster set upon a basal knop rising from the foot.

Baluster stems might enclose one or more tear-shaped bubbles of air (fig 40). This form of decoration is thought by some authorities to be a legacy from the days of hollow stems. Occasional tears are, in fact, so large that the stem appears to be practically hollow. During the early days of flint-glass when furnace heating was little more than primitive, the viscous metal was insufficiently molten for the air bubbles to rise through it and escape. It was soon realized that these disfiguring bubbles were a potential source of decoration in otherwise plain glass, and they began to be formed deliberately. The glassman gathered the metal from which the stem was to be drawn, made a dent in the surface, and picked up a second gather of metal. The heat expanded the entrapped air into a spherical bubble which the glassman elongated into tear-shape whilst drawing the stem. The silvery brilliance of such tears in bowl-bases and knops enriches the beauty of flint-glass. After about 1715, well-placed clusters of spherical air beads might be found either in the solid base of the bowl (fig. 153) or in a knop (fig. 197a). Clusters also embellished the finials of covers (fig. 152) and bottle stoppers.

Stems of more slender proportions, now termed 'light balusters', appeared on fashionable drinking-glasses from about 1720 (fig. 42). In these, the baluster outline was no larger than its surrounding knops. At the same time the bowl lost its thick solid base. The bowl of this graceful wineglass was at first more capacious, a merese or collar at the base of the bowl sometimes separating it from the stem. Collectors sometimes classify these as neck-and-collar balusters.

The knop additions, which tended to increase stem-length, were well proportioned, harmonizing with their accompanying baluster. As stems grew longer, bowls tended to shorten. Such glasses were manufactured in best flint-glass until 1740, then began to deteriorate in quality as filigree-

85

twist stems in flint-glass became fashionable. They were illustrated on trade cards as late as 1760. In domestic metal the light baluster continued until 1775.

A variant of the light baluster stem, associated with a similar thin-based bowl, was the heavy knopped stem. This, like the knopped variety of heavy baluster stem, consisted of several well-modelled knops built into a single harmonious and sometimes elaborate entity, with none sufficiently large to dominate its fellows. From about 1735 knops began to be placed with less care for their relation to each other, with the result that stems lacked artistic cohesion. Sometimes such stems consist merely of shapeless blobs in varying forms, suggesting them to be the products of small glass-houses.

A long series of light knopped stems appeared before 1740, spindly affairs enlivened by one or two simply moulded knops. Knopped stems are found in flint-glass drinking-vessels as late as 1760.

It has frequently been stated that the purpose of balusters and knops was to enable three-bottle fingers to grip the wineglass stem with safety. During that period, however, and even into the reign of Queen Victoria, it was customary for the drinking-glass to be lifted from the table with the left hand, and carried to the lips by grasping the foot between the first finger and thumb of the right hand. This is seen in Sir Godfrey Kneller's portraits of the Duke of Newcastle and Henry Clinton, Earl of Lincoln, members of the Kit-Cat Club (fig. 32). A fashionable drinking-glass with a true baluster stem on a thick-based round funnel bowl is clearly depicted in the hand of each nobleman, the duke holding his by the rim of the foot. This type of glass has been termed the Kit-Cat by collectors. The upper portion of the stem is knopped and merges into a true baluster below. Several types of light baluster are also pretenders to the term Kit-Cat, although with no apparent justification. These include a plain inverted baluster, a baluster with a knop at each end, and one with a single knop below it.

Contemporary with baluster and knopped stems of the eighteenth century were the moulded silesian stems, known also as pediment and shouldered stems (figs. 47 to 50). Various authorities have stated this style of stem to be of Hessian or West German origin. This seems unlikely, however, for the term 'silesian stem' is of comparatively recent usage. The design was adapted from silversmiths' candlesticks dating from the turn of the century, with stems of a tapered square in inverted baluster silhouette: examples have been noted bearing London hallmarks ranging from 1702 to 1725. Soon they were given the jewel brilliance of hexagonal or octagonal shaping.

In flint-glass these flat-faced inverted baluster stems varied in length (fig. 234). Quickly moulded with a single tool and welded to a short shank drawn from the bowl, this stem might even be called the square baluster. With the plain upper shank removed, it seems reasonable to consider it as the prototype of the silesian stem, referred to by Powell as an attempt to 'conceal irregular bubbles and other defects of workmanship and of material by actually shaping the stem in a mould'. Powell refers to this stem as the 'square-stemmed Windsor'.

The earliest of these stems to be attached directly to the bowl was a high-shouldered, four-sided inverted pyramid with plain flat sides and a domed top — a heavy inverted baluster cut square and tapering downward into the foot. By about 1710 the plain shoulders were being moulded in the form of four arches (fig. 48).

The flat stem-surfaces were sometimes diamond-inscribed with a toast or political slogan such as 'Sayer of Braintree' which appears on a specimen in the collection of H.M. the Queen. In about 1715 one glass-house moulded in relief on each shoulder-face the phrase 'God Save King GR' — a single word to each face.

Occasionally a flat-sided silesian stem might contain a long silvery tear: very rarely is this found in later types. Towards 1720 a triple merese or annulated knop might be placed above the wide conical folded foot (fig. 47c). One rare variety shows a cable-coil.

From 1720 the four surfaces of silesian stems were enriched with deep, vertical reeds or flutes, nail-head bosses in relief sometimes decorating the flute heads. The six-reeded stem (fig. 50) arrived before 1727, its shoulders sometimes embellished with clearly defined diamond-bosses, or, immediately following the accession of George II, well-modelled crowns in relief. Reedings now began to take on a slightly spiral twist, the stem body being made slimmer (fig. 47c), to accentuate the shoulders. These silesian stems, finely modelled and more highly finished than formerly, were used on high-quality drinking-glasses until 1730.

Throughout the 1720's silesian stems were footed and capped with a variety of knops such as ball, bullet, bobbin, single, double, and triple mereses. Clusters of spherical bubbles often enlivened ball, bullet, and bobbin knops, but not the stem itself. Sometimes the stem was inverted (fig. 253) and there was also the double silesian in which the upper section was inverted and the two separated by a knop (fig. 250). Feet might be domed (fig. 236), ribbed, and bossed to match moulded panels found pressed upon the bowls above.

After 1730 appeared the eight-sided silesian stem, usually made in the provinces. This lacked the precision and elegance of former types, reeding, shoulder outline, and bosses having lost their clear definition. The silesian stem now tended to become slighter and appreciably lighter in weight, and by the mid-century had degenerated into a thin, coarse, ribbed, and twisted caricature of its early forms. Towards the end of the century a well-designed silesian stem was popular, enhanced by clever use of the cutting-wheel.

The silesian stem had but a brief vogue on drinking-vessels, often being found in association with round funnel and waisted bowls. The finest are found on tapersticks and candlesticks (figs. 249 to 254); they were usual on sweetmeat glasses (fig. 231) and tazza-shaped champagne glasses until about 1745, and on salvers (fig. 241) for a century more.

The streamlined goblet with a trumpet-shaped bowl merging into a plain, solid stem was blown from four gatherings of glass, the stem being drawn from the bowl base. Such a stem formed from the same piece of metal as the bowl was termed a straw shank, to differentiate it from the more usual type of drinking-glass stem which was a separate piece of glass welded to the bowl and known as a stuck shank. Two-piece glasses with these straw shanks were made during the early days of flint-glass, but few specimens now remaining bear evidence of pre-1710 origin. During the next quarter-century the drawn trumpet was made in large, heavy forms. From about 1735 it became a standard pattern in drinking-glass design, varying in height from the 12-inch heavy goblets of fine flint-glass to the tiny public-house drammers of cloudy metal. The waisted thick-based bowl on a drawn stem (fig. 44) dates from about 1720 and there were other variants.

The tear was a decorative element in the drawn trumpet stem, and in the bowl base of the waisted variety, until the mid-1740's (fig. 59). Tears in such stems are longer and more slender than the fat, stumpy commas sometimes enclosed within the bowl bases. From about 1730 the tear in the drawn trumpet might follow the stem silhouette, tending to develop into a long, slender, irregular cavity, sometimes little more than a vertical thread of air extending from the bowl to within $\frac{1}{8}$-inch of the foot. The popularity of this decorative thread encouraged glass-blowers to experiment until the air-twist stem could be produced commercially.

The result was that early air-twists are found in drawn trumpet stems with some frequency, either as a single spiral (fig. 60), as two or four corkscrews (fig. 167), or as multiple-spiral twists (fig. 90). Opaque-twists are extremely rare in drawn trumpet stems. An occasional drawn trumpet may be found with a diamond- or hexagonally-faceted stem.

By 1760 the drawn trumpet glass was tending to degenerate into a short, funnel-shaped bowl supported by a thin stem. Of poor metal, such glasses were made in large quantities until after 1830, generally lacking tears, but sometimes with folded feet.

Plain straight stems had a forty-year vogue in fine flint-glass from about 1725, and the tavern variety continued until well into the nineteenth century. This type of stem has been consistently antedated: few examples are known that can be placed with accuracy earlier than the coronation of George II. Some collectors are inclined to date their first appearance as late as 1740. A print dated 1733 and titled 'Coffee-house Politicians', however, illustrates a tall, plain-stemmed drinking-glass with a straight-sided bowl. For such glasses to have become familiar objects in coffee-house and tavern indicates general use over a long period. The tavern ranked higher than the inn or ale-house, being patronized by a more prosperous class of customer. Ale-house glasses were at this time made from a cheap glass, pale bottle green in hue.

Plain straight stems first appeared on the more usual three-piece glasses, the bowl-stem weld usually being faintly visible. The stem itself might have a distinct central bulge. Sometimes the bowl was attached to the stem by means of a spherical knop, giving the stem a shouldered appearance. In general, most of the three-piece plain-stemmed glasses made previous to 1735 were built with thick, heavy cylindrical columns which might occasionally be enlivened with tears. When a slight protuberance can be felt within the bowl, at the base, the specimen is a three-piece glass. Early bowls were long in proportion to stem length. Feet might be folded or plain.

Few plain straight stems are found in a metal of quality equal to that used in contemporary baluster, knopped or air-twist stems. They were minor productions so far as the London glass-houses were concerned. Irregularity of construction is visible in early specimens and the bowl is generally clumsily welded to the stem. These might be termed tavern glasses.

Some plain straight stems were made of fine flint-glass, their bowls being cleverly engraved with flowered and other motifs, vine and grapes perhaps being the most obvious and popular design. These bowls might be straight-sided (fig. 51), waisted (fig. 56), or bell-shaped (fig. 52) until about 1748 when the waisted and bell-shaped varieties began to be replaced by small straight-sided or ogee bowls. The double ogee is rarely found on such a stem. Late bowl forms on straight stems may resemble those used half a century earlier on baluster stems.

Straight stems made later than 1748 tended to be thinner than formerly, metal at the bowl base also being used more economically. Later in the century there was a noticeable reduction of height in conformity with cut-stem design. A particularly brilliant metal was used at that time by several glass-houses, and bowls were usually ovoid.

As a group, straight-stemmed glasses cannot be associated with the continual development of form in the finer flint-glass drinking-vessels of the eighteenth century. Fashion changes first occurred in the quality glasses: those with plain straight stems were for the most part heavy glasses: at best aping their more expensive prototypes like much of the cheap, square-legged painted furniture of the mid-century. Plain straight stems were made in large numbers, and a comprehensive collection could illustrate very clearly every bowl type made during the period.

Hollow-stemmed drinking-glasses (fig. 95), a popular novelty from the early 1760's until the late 1770's, have been considered by some authorities to date no earlier than the mid-1780's, others classifying them as of early nineteenth-century manufacture. This theory was in line with the belief that the tunnel annealing leer was unknown in England until 1780. By passing hollow-stemmed glasses twice through the tunnel leer they were sufficiently strengthened to withstand the buffeting of everyday use; even so, few examples have survived. Tunnel leers are now known to have been operating in England during the 1740's (*see* Chapter 3).

Further confirmation is found in a bill, now in Sir Ambrose Heal's collection, issued in 1768 by the London glass-seller Colebron Hancock for '12 Hollow Shank Wines 6/-'. Furthermore 'hollow-stemmed wine-glasses' were advertised in 1765. Body and stem were drawn in a single piece somewhat resembling a tun-dish with a parallel-sided tube. The plain foot was made with a nipple on its upper surface to fit into the tube, and the two pieces were welded together. The stem and the lower part of the bowl were cut with plain vertical fluting and the punty mark ground smooth.

Figure 31

'A Punch Party', painted by Joseph Highmore, c. 1740. The punch glasses have round funnel bowls, slender baluster stems, and folded feet. The punch is necessarily cold as flint-glass at that period was unlikely to withstand continued fillings with hot liquor. The taperstick with its burning taper is for members of the party to light the tobacco in their clay churchwardens.

In the collection of Mr Leslie Hand

Figure 32

Sir Godfrey Kneller's painting of Thomas Pelham-Holles, first Duke of Newcastle, K.G. (1693–1768) with Henry Clinton, Earl of Lincoln (1684–1728). This picture was included among the forty-two portraits of members of the Kit-Cat Club, painted by Kneller to the commission of Jacob Tonson between the years 1700 and 1720. The sitters were invested with the Order of the Garter in 1718 and the picture painted shortly afterwards. It is reasonable to assume that these leaders of fashion would have the newest style in wineglasses associated with their portraits. The duke, in lifting his wineglass with the rim of the foot between the first finger and thumb of his right hand, follows the style fashionable between c. 1660 and c. 1760. This type of wineglass with heavy-based pointed funnel bowl and slender true baluster stem with round knop above, supported by a folded foot, has come to be known as the Kit-Cat glass.

In the National Portrait Gallery

Figure 33

'A Dinner Party', by Marcellus Laroon, c. 1740. The scene is actually a banquet, a service of fruit and wine taken after the main courses of a dinner, and usually in another room. The goblet-boy is carrying a glass salver supporting four wineglasses with conical bowls and knopped stems. The host, at the head of the table, wearing the Garter and its ribbon, is pouring wine from a wanded flask into a glass. On the side-table, among other goblets, is a large-bowled rummer.

By Gracious Permission of Her Majesty the Queen

Figure 34

WINEGLASSES AND TAPERSTICKS
OF THE LATE SEVENTEENTH CENTURY

Top left. Wineglass, its deep-pointed funnel bowl spirally moulded and encircled with

91

trailed work developing into ears; spirally fluted stem; folded foot. Late seventeenth century. Height 5¾ inches.

Top and lower centre: Tapersticks with characteristic nozzles; baluster and drop knop stems; domed and folded feet. Late seventeenth century. Height 5¼ inches.

Top right: Funnel bowl with applied moulding around lower half; quatrefoil knop; folded foot. Height 5 inches.

Lower left: Bell-shaped bowl with vertical moulding; plain stem; domed and folded foot. Early eighteenth century. Height 6½ inches.

Lower right: Conical bowl with alternating spiral and diamond moulding; quatrefoil winged stem with collar above and knop below; folded foot. Late seventeenth century. Height 6 inches.

All formerly in the Berney Collection

Figures 35, 36

A CHRONOLOGICAL SEQUENCE
OF EIGHTEENTH-CENTURY STEM FORMS

(*a*) Plain heavy baluster; conical bowl with solid base; folded foot. (*b*) Baluster with ball knop below and collar above; funnel bowl; folded foot. (*c*) Light baluster with annulated knop above and ball knop below; bell-shaped bowl; conical foot. (*d*) Square silesian; conical bowl with solid base containing a tear; folded foot. (*e*) Drawn with tear; trumpet bowl; folded foot. (*f*) Incised stem; honeycomb-moulded funnel bowl; low-domed foot. (*g*) Air-twist in drawn stem; trumpet bowl; folded foot. (*h*) Baluster air-twist; drawn trumpet bowl with short plain stem; plain foot. (*i*) Opaque-twist, double corkscrew within spiral band; ogee bowl; plain foot. (*j*) Opaque-twist with pair of spiral gauzes; bucket bowl; plain foot. (*k*) Hexagonally faceted; ogee bowl; plain foot. (*l*) Centrally knopped and diamond-faceted; ogee bowl; plain foot.

Figures 37–40

(37) Drinking-glasses with solid-based bowls.

Left: Funnel bowl on stem with cushioned knop and flattened knop, domed foot.

Centre: Cup-topped bowl, knopped stem, highly domed foot.

Right: Pointed funnel bowl with acorn knop stem and plain foot.

By courtesy of Messrs Cecil Davis Ltd

(38) Conical bowl with solid base on baluster stem; highly conical folded foot. *c.* 1700.

Formerly in the Bles Collection

(39) Conical bowl with solid base on baluster stem containing large tear, folded foot. Diamond-engraved in script: 'A Cherishing Bumper. In Vino Veritas'; *c.* 1700.

In the Corning Museum of Glass

92

(40) Round funnel bowl with baluster stem, annulated knop above, on domed and folded foot. George I period.

Formerly in the Berney and Bles Collections

Figures 41-6

DRINKING-GLASSES WITH SOLID-BASED BOWLS, KNOPPED STEMS AND FOLDED FEET

(41) Williamite goblet with round funnel bowl; stem with annulated knop and ending in a flattened knop; domed and folded foot. Bowl encircled with two wheel-engraved arabesque wreaths separated by a diamond-point engraved inscription: 'To the Glorious and Immortal Memory of King William.' Early eighteenth century. Height 13½ inches.

Formerly in the Bles Collection

(42) Conical bowl with solid base; baluster stem supporting an annulated knop; folded foot. Early George II period.

(43) Waisted bell bowl with solid base; three-knopped stem; folded foot. Early George II period.

(44) Drawn conical bowl with solid base drawn into a truncated cone on short plain section rising from domed and folded foot; *c.* 1700.

(45) Bell bowl with solid base containing a tear; baluster stem supporting annulated knop; on plain conical foot. Early eighteenth century.

In the Victoria and Albert Museum

(46) Waisted bell bowl with solid base, on composite stem consisting of an acorn knop containing a tear between two rounded knops; folded foot. George I period. Height 5¾ inches.

In the collection of Mr T. Scholes

Figures 47-50

DRINKING-GLASSES WITH SILESIAN STEMS AND FOLDED FEET

Fig. 49 has the four shoulders impressed with alternate crowns and diamonds in relief. The two left-hand examples have the bowls set directly on the stems without the usual collar.

Top row: Courtesy of Messrs Cecil Davis Ltd
Lower left: In the Brooklyn Museum

Figures 51–6

DRINKING-GLASSES WITH STRAIGHT, KNOPPED STEMS

(51) Williamite glass with conical bowl; straight stem encircled with two conjoined applied bands, and mereses at top; plain foot; bowl engraved with an equestrian portrait of William III. George II period.

In the Brooklyn Museum

(52) Bell bowl with solid base, knopped stem, domed foot; engraved with a fruiting orange-tree and the inscription 'For Ever Flourishing'. George II period.

In the Brooklyn Museum

(53) Bell bowl with solid base and composite stem consisting of a hollow knop between two mereses; annulated knop; straight section; round knop; folded foot. Early George II period.

In the Brooklyn Museum

(54) Bell bowl with solid base containing a tear; straight stem containing long tear rising from annulated knop on domed and folded foot. George II period.

(55) Waisted bucket bowl with solid base; straight stem rising from a drop knop and terminating in mereses; folded foot. Early George II period.

(56) Waisted bell bowl with solid base; stem with annulated knop rising from round knop; on folded foot. Early George II period.

Figures 57–9

DRINKING-GLASSES WITH DRAWN TRUMPET BOWLS

(57) With pear-shaped tear in stem; wide folded foot. Engraved with full-face portrait of Charles II with love-locks and laced collar: reverse, between a crowned lion and unicorn, an ornately designed monogram C II R above a conventional ornament. George II period, Height 8 inches.

Formerly in the Grant Francis Collection

(58) With tear in stem and folded foot. Engraved with portrait of Dean Swift, inscribed in ribboned oval 'The Rev. D^r. J. Swift, Dean St. P. Dublin', and on the reverse 'Memoria in Eterna Divine' and 'Author. Wt. Obit. 1745'. Height 8 inches.

Formerly in the collections of the Earl of Cork and Orrery, and Mr Joseph Bles

(59) With pear-shaped tear and conical foot. Engraved with equestrian portrait of William III.

In the Brooklyn Museum

Figures 60-2

DRINKING-GLASSES WITH AIR-TWIST STEMS OF THE 1740's

(60) Trumpet bowl with stuck air-twist stem and plain foot.

In the Author's collection

(61) Drawn trumpet bowl, multiple air-twist stem and folded foot.

(62) Drawn trumpet bowl, multiple air-twist stem, air-beaded knop and folded foot.

CHAPTER FIVE

STEMS: INCISED-TWIST, AIR-TWIST, ENAMEL-TWIST, AND CUT

Incised-twist stems (fig. 63) known to collectors also as writhen or rib-twist, supported the bowls of some of Ravenscroft's drinking-glasses. This was an inexpensive type of stem decoration consisting of a series of alternating narrow ridges and grooves spiralling around the stem surface. Their introduction into the world of flint-glass during the late 1670's may be taken as yet another link with the contemporary furniture styles in which twist turning was then in vogue.

The quick-setting quality of the earlier soda-glass had made possible the formation of delicately and accurately placed ribbings, a popular ornament of the Anglo-Venetian period. No example is known to remain intact, but fragments excavated in London and elsewhere show them to have been shaped in an earthenware mould. When applied to the more slowly cooling flint-glass, however, this simple ornament became graceless.

The earliest and rarest incised-twist stems in flint-glass bear little resemblance to the Venetian type. Until about 1700 such surface ribbings appear to have been inexpertly incised on some plain baluster stems. Occasionally the spiral grooves have obviously been hand-cut singly into the plastic metal. Incised balusters continued to be made until about 1720, but few have survived. The inadequate annealing of the period would cause stresses, making them more susceptible to atmospheric conditions and consequent 'flying' than smooth-surfaced glass. These early-eighteenth-century incised-twist baluster stems were more complete and regular in their spirals than were earlier productions in this medium.

A second period of incised-twists dates from the late 1740's until about 1770 (fig. 64). These might be straight or knopped stems incised with spirals more closely spaced than those found on balusters. Such uniform incisions were at first produced by tooling the plastic stem with vertical lines and then twisting it whilst hot. Such stems may be recognized by a gradual, almost imperceptible, reduction of the stem diameter towards the

97

centre. The corrugations on these vary from medium to coarse. Feet are nearly always plain, but occasional domed and folded feet have been recorded. Knopped stems were also made by this method and are now rare. There might be a half-knop at the top of the stem immediately below the round funnel bowl. Angular knops placed centrally in the stem have been noted.

From about 1760 straight incised-twist stems were made of unvarying diameter throughout their length and the corrugations were much finer than formerly (fig. 64). This technical improvement was brought about by a process which had been used by the Romans. The surface of a cylinder of solid glass measuring about 2 inches in diameter and 6 inches long was incised while plastic with a series of vertical ridges. The cylinder was then heated at the glory hole and drawn into a long rod, being simultaneously twisted. The result was a rod measuring about 4 feet in length and displaying well-defined spiral ridges. This was cut into suitable stem lengths for welding to drinking-glass bowls.

In most instances the incised-twist stem supported a round funnel bowl, the lower half of which might be either faintly hammered or moulded with shallow flutes (fig. 36 right). A wide unfolded foot was usual and this might be decorated to match the base of the bowl above. Francis Buckley was of the opinion that these incised-twists were a Stourbridge speciality as they were so abundant in that district early in the present century. In 1757 Thomas Betts of the Strand charged 6d. each for $1\frac{1}{2}$ dozen 'twd $\frac{1}{2}$ Rib'd Wines', The term 'half ribbed' suggests that the lower part of the bowl was moulded with shallow flutes.

The drawn stems of certain tavern glasses might be ornamented with incised spirals from about 1780 until the end of the century. These were made by the pre-1760 process.

The spirals of filigree thread-work which enriched the stems of fashionable table glass from about 1740 until the 1780's have long been celebrated for their exquisite delicacy. The craftsmen who made the finer specimens of both air-twist and enamel-twist stems were highly skilled: threads were of uniform diameter throughout and were spiralled with precise regularity.

The earliest of these filigree traceries in drinking-glass stems were the air-twists, known at the time as 'worm'd glasses' (fig. 71), a development of flint-glass by 1740 and rarely made after 1765. A chronological series displays the general trend towards refinement and an almost mechanized precision of spiralling. Some exquisite stems were being made when manufacture seems suddenly to have ceased.

98

Drinking-glasses with air-twist stems were about 25 per cent more costly than those with plain stems. Entries in the day-book of John Cookson, glass-maker, South Shields, at the date 12th May 1746 confirm this: '6 doz Worm'd Brittanick Wine, 32 lb' were invoiced at 10d. a pound; plain-stemmed Britannick were 8d. a pound; and 'worm'd ale glasses' 10d. a pound.

There is no evidence of earlier or even contemporary use of the air-twist by Continental glassmen working in soda-glass. The scintillating brilliance of an entrapped air bubble at the top of a stem had been a desirable feature in the eyes of glass-sellers from about 1682. Once that tear had been drawn into a slender vertical thread of air running the full length of a baluster or straight stem it was but a step to the air-twist in its simplest form. This consisted merely of two long, thin vertical tears loosely spiralled about each other within the clear metal of the stem (figs. 69d and e). These simple uneven spirals are not necessarily earlier than the more elaborate forms. Being comparatively easy to make they were used throughout the air-twist period.

The earliest air-twists appeared in two-piece glasses with drawn shanks and trumpet-shaped bowls, probably in the rare inverted baluster or shouldered knop variety, the last relics of the old baluster (fig. 70). A symmetrically arranged group of air bubbles was introduced into the thick base of a partly made bowl by pricking and covering. This was then drawn out and twisted, usually spiralling down a plain unknopped stem. Few two-piece air-twists are found with knopped stems, and all have multiple-spiral twists. The sides, seen in silhouette, are irregular.

Early air-twists in drawn stems are usually to be distinguished by constructional faults and imperfections (fig. 71). Inexperience might produce weak, thin filaments, too wide apart or spiralled only part of the way down the stem. Sometimes threads were but slightly spiralled, and in the rare examples with shoulders or central knops they frequently appear to have broken in the making. Irregular intervals between the inceptive tears in the bowl vase were the prime cause of unsymmetrical coiling. Air-twists drawn too closely in the stem appear cramped and graceless. One or two air beads might remain undrawn in the base of the bowl. For some years little attempt was made to deviate from the multiple spiral, the only variation being in their number and spacing. Two corkscrews and four corkscrews were made from about 1745. The later spirals in drawn stems have their air threads of uniform thickness and spaced with regularity, the spirals being carried from well into the solid base of the bowl (fig. 74). E. B.

99

Haynes is of the opinion that probably no more than one in three of air-twist stems now remaining is of the drawn variety although they were made throughout the period.

With drawn flint-glass stems it was uneconomical to produce splendidly intricate air-twists such as were achieved by treating the stem as a separate entity. Stuck shank or three-piece air-twist drinking-glasses date from about 1740. In these the bowl was blown separately, the air-twist welded to its base, and the foot attached last (fig. 73).

The stuck air-twist shanks were cut from long rods produced by a process less costly — type for type — than that required for the drawn shank. A new method had been devised for making air-twists by which the gleaming filaments could be finely drawn and coiled with remarkable precision. These date from about 1750 to 1765, the earliest being multiple spirals (fig. 75). Some thirty variations soon followed, such as the spiral gauze and the pair of spiral gauzes.

Single-twist multiple coils were simple to produce in straight stems. A thick, cylindrical pottery or brass mould some 5 or 6 inches long, with its interior surface corrugated longitudinally, was filled with plastic glass attached to the end of a gathering-iron. The ribbed glass cylinder thus formed was enclosed within a further gathering of metal, converting the vertical corrugations into air-filled tubes. This was again heated at the furnace mouth and a second gathering-iron attached to the free end. The plastic cylinder was then drawn and twisted until a long rod of stem thickness was formed. The diameter of the air threads diminished proportionately with the lessening diameter of the rod. Uniformity of diameter throughout stem length was obtained by drawing out in this way, an achievement seldom possible in the glasses with individually drawn stems. A slight depression following the line of each spiral may be traced with the finger-tip when it is near the stem surface.

Later such a spiral might coil around one or more independent air threads: this was the compound air-twist of which more than a dozen variations are known, including a pair of threads spiralling around a gauze column; a vertical column with four spirals; and a spiral gauze enclosed by a pair of corkscrews. Compound air-twists necessitated the use of a more complicated version of the ribbed cylinder process. Two or more ribbed cylinders were enclosed within a gathering of plastic glass which was moulded in or around them, and finally reshaped to cylinder form. This was then drawn and twisted in the same way as a single twist.

Early air-twists of this type have constructional faults such as coarse,

100

51–56 Drinking-glasses with straight, knopped stems. George II

57–62   Drinking-glasses with drawn trumpet bowls

63–68 Drinking-glasses with decorated straight stems: incised, air-twist, white opaque-twist, colour-twist, facet-cut

69   Drinking-glasses with engraved bowls, air-twist stems, plain feet

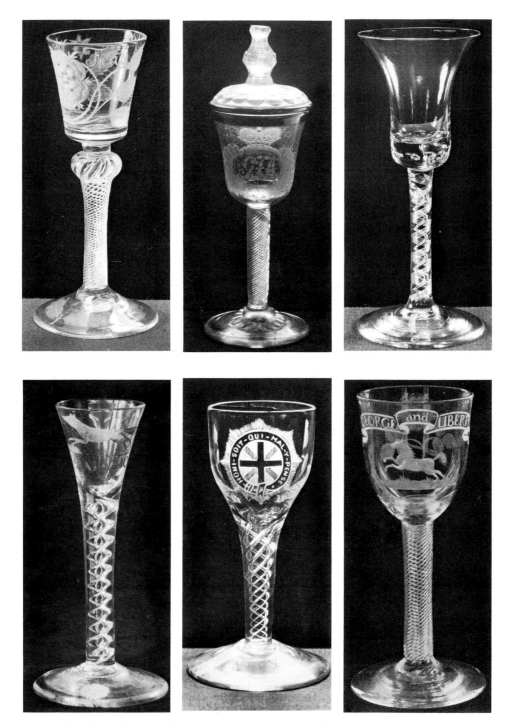

70–75 Drinking-glasses with air-twist stems and plain feet with unground punty scars

Figs. 71 and 74 are reproduced by Gracious Permission of Her Majesty The Queen

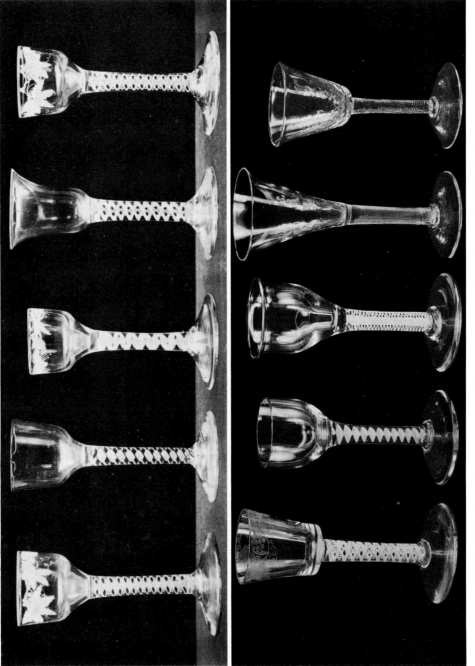

76, 77   Drinking-glasses, opaque white-twist stems, and two (*lower right*) incised-twist stems

78–80 With small bowls, tall stems, and folded feet

81–83 With drawn ovoid bowls

Fig. 81 is reproduced by Gracious Permission of Her Majesty The Queen

DRINKING-GLASSES

84–89 Drinking-glasses with white opaque-twist stems

heavy threads, poorly coiled and of irregular thickness. These defects were soon overcome and few may be dated later than 1750 in single twists (fig. 69b) and about 1760 in compound twists (fig. 72). Compound air-twists are found only in association with unrelieved straight stems.

Some exceptionally brilliant effects were achieved with the so-called mercury- or silver-twist (fig. 74). This consisted of air-twists of exceptionally wide cross-section spiralling down the centre of the stem in close coils, usually a pair of corkscrew threads.

Knops on air-twist stems magnify the spirals enclosed within them in a highly decorative manner (fig. 108). They are found in association with single multiple spirals to the virtual exclusion of any other type of air-twist, the air-threads running in a continuous line throughout the length of the stem. Either shoulder knops (fig. 70), or central knops, or a combination of the two were the main styles. The central knop, a bulge giving a cusp-like effect, appears in several shapes varying from a bulbous swelling to an angular knop. In the case of a combination of shoulder and central knop, the upper knop is always the larger. Sometimes as many as four or five knops are found in gradually diminishing sizes on a stuck air-twist stem without breaking the continuity of the spiral.

Occasionally an air-twist stem will be found sandwiched between top and bottom knops, each knop enclosing a group of sparkling air bubbles. A centrally applied triple ring or cable-moulded band of clear flint-glass sometimes breaks the line of a straight air-twist stem without interrupting the continuity of the air spiral (fig. 114c). Some of the closely spiralled air-twists have collars beneath the bowl and above the foot against which the ends of the stem fit flush.

When short lengths of air-twist have been utilized with plain baluster or knopped features to form a stem, this is likely to be an early example of its type. Francis Buckley was of the opinion that this device was used because one end of the air-spiral had been spoiled and afterwards shortened (fig. 111). Such composite stem formations are numerous, the most frequent being a multiple-spiral air-twist above a short inverted baluster, the shoulder of which may contain tears: tall inverted balusters are scarce. Other types consist of an air-twist section below a section of plain stem, and two short air-twist sections joined by a central knop.

Two-piece air-twists support either trumpet or waisted bowls, the spirals starting high in the heavy base of the bowl. Three-piece air-twists (fig. 69), are found with almost every shape of bowl, the round funnel, waisted, and double ogee being the most frequent. Early round funnel bowls on air-twists usually have the interior base unsymmetrically hollowed, the inner sides of the bowl being drawn together sharply at the base and away from the centre of the glass. The base of the bowl is finished with a short plain neck, about $\frac{1}{4}$ inch long, to which the stem is welded (fig. 198). Little moulded decoration is associated with air-twist glasses, but the lower half of the bowl may be moulded with shallow flutes, honeycombing, or dimpling. Some elaborate compound spiral stems support wheel-engraved bowls.

The upper surface of the foot supporting an air-twist stem is usually given a delightful silvery sheen by light reflected from the spirals. Feet are usually plain, but a few of the early drawn air-twists rise from folded feet (fig. 61) or, more rarely still, domed feet.

Drinking-glasses with stems displaying spirals of white (fig. 76) or coloured enamel (fig. 67), varying from mere hairs to broad solid tapes, date from the mid-1740's. They resemble air-twists in character but are opaque instead of transparent and are often of more complicated design. Three types of these filigree opaque-twists were made: white, coloured, and a combination of the two, the majority being in pure white enamel.

The interlacing and twisting of fine threads of opaque white enamel in a body of clear glass had for long been an exclusively Venetian craft, but Bohemia, the Low Countries, and France were making them in soda-glass long before English glassmen copied the idea in flint-glass. The colour quality of the enamel is an important point to the collector. English white opaque-twist is recognized by its dense texture and intense whiteness: a faintly bluish tinge is usually, but not invariably, apparent when looking downward into the spiral through the base of the bowl. Such twists in Continental glass were of a watery milk-white. English colour-twists are of richly brilliant hues: Continental productions are less opaque and of subdued brilliance. Continental opaque-twists in light-weight soda-glass contrast unfavourably with the clear brilliance of English flint-glass which entirely outsold them abroad. Collectors will easily avoid modern reproductions in which the spirals are made from thin-textured enamels, but virtually identical copies have been made.

The enamel used was specially prepared to avoid distortion when it came into contact with viscous flint-glass. Enamel making was a specialist craft, the manufacturers preparing it in brick-shaped blocks. These were converted into short cylinders known as canes. Hughes and Brettell of Southwark announced in the *Daily Advertiser* during 1748 that they could supply 'all sorts of coloured cane at 10^d per pound . . . likewise all sorts of composition and enamels'. This suggests that both white and coloured opaque-twist stems were already in production.

Opaque-twist stems quickly captured the imagination of the Georgians, and as glass-makers became more skilled in their production air-twists became almost unsaleable although about 40 per cent less costly. Stems have been noted displaying early opaque-twists in close imitation of early air-spirals, suggesting that originally the white opaque-twist endeavoured to copy its predecessor.

The theory is widely held that enamel filigree vanished from drinking-glass stems in 1777, following the doubling of the Excise duty, cullet and enamel then being taxed for the first time. This is untenable, however, as the instructions issued to excisemen under the Glass Excise Act of 1745 laid down that 'there is likewise made Enamelled, and Stained or Coloured glass of various Colours, as Black, Green, Blue, etc. which are chargeable with the like Duty as Flint Glass'. As enamelled glass is shown to have been liable already to taxation, the new tax — an additional penny per pound — would not have caused glassmen immediately to abandon its manufacture. Decorative art at this period laid emphasis on clear-cut classical designs, thus creating a vogue for drinking-glasses with faceted and cut stems. This naturally affected the demand for opaque twists which, however, continued to be made and advertised in ever-lessening numbers until the close of the collector's period.

Opaque-twists were of two types: single (fig. 130c) and compound (fig. 83). Treble twists are so rare as to be virtually unobtainable. The single twist consists of either one formation of cotton-white enamel threads spiralling around a clear glass centre (fig. 130c), or a pair of reciprocal spirals (fig. 137). Single opaque-twists preceded the compound, at first being a multiple spiral of coarse threads. Fine elaborate threads resulted only from the practical experience of experimental years. Single twists usually ornament straight stems: single and double knops are rare.

More often, however, there are two spiral formations, one within the other (fig. 133). These are the compound twists in which a central spiral or a closely knit central cable has another twist spiralling around it. They are found only in straight stems and appeared early in the period. The varieties of opaque-twists recorded by Haynes exceed one hundred, of which more than two-thirds are compound twists. A collection of ninety-three straight-stemmed opaque-twist drinking-glasses, each displaying a different type of twist, was sold at Christie's in 1947 for £280. No attempt can be made here to list the various stem formations as difficulties

111

of terminology would necessitate a close-up photograph of each: reference to E. Barrington Haynes's Pelican book *Glass* is valuable in this connection.

Drinking-glasses with opaque stems were manufactured on the three-piece system because it was costly to draw single stems containing such filigree work with neatness and accuracy. The simple opaque-twist was formed by placing two, four, or eight white enamel canes in grooves cut vertically into the inside surface of a tubular mould of pottery or brass about 6 inches deep, its lower end closed with soft clay.

Molten glass was poured into the mould which was later removed, disclosing a glass cylinder with enamel canes embedded in its surface. This was reheated at the furnace, covered with a thin layer of clear flint-glass, and manipulated into a compact cylinder form drawn out, as described for the air-twist, by two men holding it horizontally between a pair of punties which they twisted while moving backward in opposite directions, lengthening the soft mass of the cylinder whilst reducing its diameter. The proportions of its interior structure were in no way altered, the ornamental enamel canes always remaining the same relative distance from the axis of the stem, no matter where placed or how long the rod was drawn. They were usually stretched into hair-like filaments with a covering of transparent glass varying from a mere film to $\frac{1}{16}$ inch in thickness. When the cylinder was reduced to stem diameter the men brought it into a straight line. Stem lengths were later cut off with a cold iron.

It is astonishing how few enamel canes were required to produce the most intricate effects. Spiral beads of close fine threads alternating with transparent spaces were made by omitting enamel canes on half the circumference of an abnormally large mould. The gauze-twist (fig. 84), common in compound formations, was produced by the same method as the single twist, with enamel canes placed towards the centre of the cylinder. The resulting twist resembled a tube of fine network. The less frequent lace-twist (fig. 137) required two parallel rows of enamel canes. A thicker enamel cane placed at either end of the rows produced a lace-twist outlined by a thicker spiral.

Corkscrew twists (fig. 133) were made by placing a flat ribbon of enamel across the diameter of the mould. This solid-looking twist generally forms the outer spiral of a compound twist. Spiral bands were produced by arranging groups of fine enamel canes on the circumference of the mould. A tape with coloured edges was made by attaching a fine cane of coloured enamel to either side of the white enamel before it was flattened.

112

Combinations of air- and opaque-twists in a single stem decorated wine-glasses with handsome effect from the late 1740's and continuing in production until the late 1760's (fig. 72). In some of these mixed-twist stems the air-twist was entwined around a single opaque-twist: in others air threads spiralled down the centre of a multiple opaque-twist. Thread-like tubes of flint-glass produced air threads in association with enamel canes, the tubes being drawn from a metal capable of melting only at a temperature higher than that of the basic flint-glass used. Rarely a colour-twist might be combined with an air-twist: rarer still are stems containing air-, colour-, and opaque-twists.

Colour-twists in association with opaque-twists might enrich filigree stems from the late 1740's to the late 1770's. They were but brilliant variants of white opaque-twist processes. Blue, green, and ruby are the colours most commonly found allied with white: sapphire, red, yellow, gold, black, and a greyish blue are less frequent. The coloured canes were of glass which might be opaque or transparent, and used in combination, with a melting-temperature higher than that of the metal within which they were enclosed. A single colour might be used with the white, but loveliest of all are those stems displaying threads in two or three colours.

Funnel- and bell-shaped bowls with thick bases and thin walls are found on drinking-glasses with early opaque-twist stems. The ogee bowl is far more common in this association throughout the period, and might be engraved, but bowls in every contemporary shape are to be found, sometimes flute-moulded at the base. Plain feet are usual; folded feet are rare, but often found on reproductions; domed feet are also scarce.

Facet-cut stems (fig. 90), displaying all the prismatic colours in flint-glass, were made concurrently with the later air-twists and the opaque-twists, continuing until the end of the century.

Drinking-glasses with facet-cut stems are usually of two-piece manufacture, the straw shank being drawn from the base of the bowl. Clear metal, produced by the Perrott furnace and double annealed in the tunnel leer, was found an ideal medium for facet-cutting, being tough enough to take the strain of the cutting-wheel. It is doubtful if facet-cutting could have been a profitable proposition before the introduction of double annealing in the tunnel during the late 1740's. Some authorities date a group of facet-cut glasses made from corded and striated metal to the period 1735–50.

Stem faceting required a high standard of skill for the craftsman to place the cuts with geometrical exactitude. They were never made very small for by reducing their area a great deal of their beauty would have been lost. The facets were cut across the stems and not along them. At first they were lightly cut with an almost flat-edged wheel. Stems were encircled with staggered rows of simple and elongated diamonds measuring two or three times more in length than in width, and with angles of 120 and 60 degrees (fig. 90b). Elongated hexagonal facets soon followed (fig. 90d). Until about 1760 faceted stems were straight; then they might have a central knop, the facets from above and below meeting at the extreme width of the knop in triangles (fig. 90a). From the 1770's facets were cut deeper and appear with greater emphasis. During the last decade of the eighteenth century facet-cut stems were shorter than formerly.

Closely spaced scale facets, shallow depressions resembling in shape the fashionable fish-scale motif on porcelain of the period, were cut with a rounded wheel. They were laborious to produce and were a rich man's luxury.

Wineglass bowls on facet-cut stems bear a close resemblance to each other, and might be described as a cross between the round funnel and ovoid shapes. This design displayed to fine advantage the six shallow flutes known as cresting or bridge-fluting (fig. 82). To begin with the cresting was short, merely ornamenting the junction of the stem and bowl: from the late 1750's it might extend over the bowl base in simple designs. Then cresting began to be supplemented by six shallow flutes rising from the vertical columns of stem facets, and from the late 1770's these might extend almost half-way up the bowl. In some instances cresting received a circuit of double or treble sprigs incised with a sharp mitre-edged cutting-wheel: these might be repeated on the surface of the foot. Scale-cutting is also found, rarely more than two circuits.

The body of the bowl might be wheel-engraved and polished to resemble shallow-cutting. A circuit of engraved stars alternating with polished ovals or circles was a popular rim decoration.

Facet-cut stems are seldom found in association with folded feet although this is frequent in reproductions. Usually the foot was plain, but surface decoration is sometimes noted in the form of sliced cutting, a sprig circuit, or fine radial cutting extending from the stem junction to the foot-rim or half-way. The rim of the foot was usually circular, but scalloped and petal-cut outlines are to be found and, rarely, the arch-and-point. The solid conical foot was sometimes used and occasional examples are found with a thick heavy disc foot.

Facet-cutting ran concurrently with vertical fluting during the last two

114

decades of the eighteenth century. At first the stem was centrally knopped with fluting above and below and the knop itself facet-cut. The fluting might be staggered at the knop with horizontal grooving above and below. Flutes were then cut on straight stems and these are usually accompanied by notching on alternate angles or horizontal grooves. Feet were usually plain, although some pre-1790 examples might be scale-cut, and afterwards radially fluted.

Figures 63–8

DRINKING-GLASSES WITH DECORATED STRAIGHT STEMS

(63) Waisted bell bowl with solid base; incised stem, folded foot, c. 1740. Height 6½ inches.

In the Brooklyn Museum

(64) Cider glass with flute bowl; stem with multiple-spiral air-twist; conical foot. Engraved with growing apple-tree; c. 1760. Height 8 inches.

Formerly in the Bles Collection

(65) Round funnel bowl; multiple-spiral air-twist stem; conical foot; engraved with two carnation flowers.

In the Brooklyn Museum

(66) Ogee bowl; white opaque-twist stem, gauze, and a pair of corkscrews; folded foot. Enamelled in brilliant yellow with crest and cypher of the Horsey family. Late 1760's. Height 7¼ inches.

In the Corning Museum of Glass

(67) Cordial glass with round funnel bowl ribbed around base; colour-twist stem, with two white corkscrews encircling a blue pillar; plain foot. Bowl painted with grapes and vine-leaf border in white enamel; c. 1760.

In the Corning Museum of Glass

(68) Ogee bowl cut around base; facet-cut stem; plain foot. Engraved with Chinese scene; 1770's.

In the Corning Museum of Glass

Figure 69

Drinking-glasses with engraved bowls, air-twist stems, and plain feet, 1740's. (*a*) Pointed funnel bowl with hops and barley. (*b* and *d*) Pan-topped bowls, flowered. (*c*) Bucket bowl engraved with apple-trees. (*e*) Flute with flowers.

By courtesy of Messrs Delomosne & Son Ltd

Figures 70–5

DRINKING-GLASSES WITH AIR-TWIST STEMS

Drinking-glasses with air-twist stems and plain feet with unground punty scars; late George II period.

(70) Fiat glass with bucket bowl and shoulder knop stem with multiple-spiral twist; engraved Jacobite rose and two buds, and Star of Hope.

In the Brooklyn Museum

(71) Covered goblet with early air-twist stem; rims of bowl and cover heavily gilded; cover and foot encircled with shallow-cut ovals; bowl engraved with the cypher of Prince George Frederick Augustus in a cartouche with a royal crown above. 1750's.

In the collection of Her Majesty the Queen

(72) Waisted bell bowl with solid base containing air beads; air-twist stem with spiral column.

In the Brooklyn Museum

(73) Drawn bowl and stem with pair of brilliant corkscrew air-twists, engraved with running fox and 'Tally Ho'. Height 6¾ inches.

In the collection of Mr T. Scholes

(74) Drawn ogee bowl and stem with pair of corkscrew twists; engraved with the Star of the Order of the Garter enclosing the crosses of St. George and St. Andrew, the eight points of the star being hatched; reverse, thistle and rose.

In the collection of Her Majesty the Queen

(75) Round funnel bowl with multiple-spiral air-twist; engraved with the horse from the arms of Hanover and inscribed 'George and Liberty' in ribbon; heraldic rose on reverse; *c.* 1745. Height 6¾ inches.

Formerly in the Bles Collection

Figures 76, 77

Drinking-glasses, eight with opaque white-twist stems, and two (*lower right*) with incised-twist stems.

Figures 78–83

DRINKING-GLASSES

(78–80) Drinking-glasses with small bowls, tall stems, and folded feet.

(78) Opaque-twist stem with pair of spiral threads within ten-thread spiral gauze.

(79) Opaque white-twist stem with pair of spiral tapes within seven-thread spiral gauze.

(80) Plain shouldered stem.

In the Author's collection

(81) Goblet with drawn ovoid bowl; short vertically fluted stem; plain foot with domed instep. The bowl has a gilded rim and is engraved with Queen Charlotte's cypher below a royal crown. 1780's.

Reproduced by Gracious Permission of Her Majesty the Queen

(82) Wineglass with drawn ovoid bowl cut in facets at base; faceted stem and plain domed foot. Late eighteenth century.

(83) Goblet with drawn ovoid bowl moulded into eight panels; opaque-twist stem with pair of spiral tapes within six-thread spiral gauze; plain foot. Alternate panels engraved with grape and vine-leaf motifs. 1770's

In the Brooklyn Museum

Figures 84–9

DRINKING-GLASSES WITH WHITE OPAQUE-TWIST STEMS

(84) Funnel bowl; stem containing multiple-spiral pillar within double corkscrew.

In the Brooklyn Museum

(85) Pan-topped bowl; stem with spiral cable and corkscrew.

In the Victoria and Albert Museum

(86) Bucket bowl engraved with running fox and inscribed 'Tally Ho'; stem with double corkscrew and lace spiral; folded foot. Height $7\frac{1}{2}$ inches.

In the Author's collection

(87) Ogee bowl with gilded rim, engraved with flower motifs, also gilded; stem with pair of corkscrews. Height 6 inches.

In the collection of Mr T. Scholes

(88) Bucket bowl with three spiral gauzes; engraved with a two-masted ship in full sail, and inscribed in reverse 'Success to Irish Navigation and Trade' with scrolls and shamrock leaves. c. 1775. Height $7\frac{1}{8}$ inches.

By courtesy of Messrs Arthur Churchill Ltd

(89) Funnel bowl; stem with double corkscrew and lace spiral; engraved with grape and vine-leaf border.

Figure 90

DRINKING-GLASSES WITH FACET-CUT STEMS

Drinking-glasses with facet-cut stems, the cutting extending into the base of the bowl.

Top left and right: Ogee bowls engraved with flowered borders; knopped stems, folded feet.

Top centre: Ale flute engraved with hop and barley.

All in the Victoria and Albert Museum

Lower left: Ogee bowl; long hexagonal facets; plain foot; *c.* 1770. Height 6 inches.

In the Author's collection

Lower centre: Similar, but with conical foot; engraved with a bird freed from its cage and the inscription 'Liberty and Wilkes'. Probably made when the Wilkes's campaign was at its height in 1768. Height 5½ inches.

Formerly in the Bles Collection

Lower right: Similar, with plain foot; engraved 'Magna Charta' with reference to the Wilks movement. *c.* 1768. Height 5½ inches.

In the collection of Mr T. Scholes

Figure 91

'William Fullerton of Carstairs and Captain Lowis', painted by J. T. Seton, 1773. The wineglasses which are probably of Scottish manufacture have deep ovoid bowls, plain stems, and expansive feet: the wine-bottle has a silver label hanging from its neck.

In the Scottish National Gallery

119

CHAPTER SIX

WINEGLASSES: BOWLS AND FEET

WINEGLASS BOWLS were made in several more or less standard shapes, fashionable for perhaps a quarter of a century and then either falling out of favour or continuing in company with newer forms. They may be divided into clearly defined groups, however: the heavy, thick-walled types, general until about 1745, and the light, thin-walled types, which only came to be produced economically after the introduction of the Perrott furnace and the tunnel leer.

Bowls are usually only of subsidiary assistance in dating stemmed ware for precise chronological sequence appears to be a matter for controversy. Shape of bowl, stem, foot, decoration, and metal must all be taken into consideration by the collector wishing to date a piece of flint-glass.

The walls of early bowls were thick, the metal wavy and irregular, the stems lumpy and uneven — defects due to insufficient furnace heat. The lip and foot might be imperfect circles, the bowls were liable to be set slightly off vertical. It is important to note the junction of bowl and stem. Judging from the curious features found at this point in early stemmed ware it appears that some flint-glass workers experienced difficulty in welding the stem to the bowl without leaving some trace of the join.

No attempt was made at first to give the bowl a neck, its base being attached roughly to the top moulding of the stem (fig. 34d). The result was an undulating crease in the metal. One device used to overcome this difficulty was to draw the bowl base into a short neck or stalk and weld this to the top of the stem (fig. 41). Another method was to conceal the join with an irregular moulding which was developed later into an ornamental ribbed collar. Even with a well-defined neck, traces remained of imperfect welding, a flaw not entirely absent even when Savory's bellows were in general use after 1710. This difficulty did not, of course, occur in drawn stems.

The earliest wineglass bowls drawn by John Greene to illustrate his orders to Morelli of Venice were short, wide-mouthed, straight-sided funnels; the later illustrations of the early 1670's showed them narrower across the

121

rims with a less pronounced taper. This obviously indicates a changing taste in fashionable English table glass.

This later shape was the forerunner of the straight-sided funnel (fig. 37c) and round funnel (fig. 40) bowls in flint-glass. The former, with straight sides and a horizontal bowl base inset directly into a wide-topped stem, is found with short simple balusters, usually inverted, and gradually lengthening, until 1700; then with short heavy knops until 1710, and with silesian stems 1710 to 1730 (fig. 50). This bowl form was seldom made after 1740.

Contemporary was the round funnel, the characteristic bowl of the seventeenth century, rarely introducing a collar at the stem and bowl junction. Until 1690 the round funnel bowl was long in proportion to its stem: the bowl might even be set directly upon the foot. As the heavy baluster stem increased in length, so the bowl lost depth and became wider at the rim, a corresponding increase occurring at the foot. Round funnel bowls became less massive from 1710 and soon it was found that the shape did not harmonize with the lighter stem formations which were becoming fashionable. The final vestige of the round funnel bowls was seen in the shorter straight-sided bowls, found at first on plain straight and air-twist stems (fig. 65), but from 1755 popular on all types of stem. Such bowls might be wheel engraved with borders or all-over designs, gilded, or enamelled in white or colours.

In about 1715 the lip on the round funnel bowl might be expanded and its straight sides were gracefully incurved, forming the bell bowl (fig. 97). Bowl curvature did not harmonize with the baluster stem and the two are seldom found together. The tremendous success of the bell bowl was the main reason why the baluster disintegrated into a series of knops. Bell bowls were fashionable until about 1760 on filigree stems, but quantities were made for household use as late as 1780. Between 1725 and 1750 bell bowls were usually capacious, their profile flowing smoothly into that of the stem. From about 1745 there was a reduction in wall thickness and five years later a series of small thick bell bowls appeared. Bell bowls were seldom engraved.

Waisted bowls (fig. 43), in several profiles such as the thistle bowl ran contemporaneously with the bell bowl, and as the capacity of the bowl was reduced, so the stem grew taller. The drawn or trumpet bowl may be included in this group.

The waisted-ogee bowl, a descendant of the roemer, consisted of a waisted bowl, swelling in convex profile both above and below the waist. Large shallow examples were made as early as 1700 and continued for twenty years. In about 1750 appeared a smaller waisted-ogee bowl with thin walls. This form, engraved with a border, was a great favourite at Bristol, but was also made in London and elsewhere. Waisted-ogee bowls are found in association with silesian stems.

The simplest ogee bowl, its outlines following a smooth double curve from lip to stem, convex above, concave below, came into its own shortly after 1745, although made in heavier metal as early as 1730. Normally it may be considered later than the waisted types of bowl. The walls became thin a little way above the stem and the upper part might be engraved, enamelled or gilt. After about 1760 some ogee bowls were again made with thicker walls to allow of cutting. The profile of the bowl merged easily into the line of the stem. A variant of this was a bowl which curved inwards slightly near the rim and then expanded in a lip.

Sharing popularity with the ogee bowl was the square bucket bowl (fig. 114), known to many collectors as 'straight-sided rectangular'. Sides were almost vertical and depth less in proportion to width than in other bowls of the period. The bucket bowl was never associated with curves and in its pre-1745 heavy form it appeared on a short plain stem, from about 1730. The bucket bowl formed an excellent field for decoration and continued fashionable until about 1770.

These bowl forms were followed, on fashionable table glass, by such other shapes as the ovoid (fig. 81) and round and various moulded designs. By the 1790's many of these were being enriched with the deep relief cutting then beginning to dominate glass decoration.

Until the Georgian era a stemmed drinking-glass might be capped with a cover terminating in a knop (fig. 100). In 1709 the *London Gazette* referred to wineglasses with covers. During the next half-century it was customary for covered goblets to be used on ceremonial occasions: trade cards illustrated them until the end of the century (fig. 27).

The feet of drinking-glasses and other stemmed ware are quite as important as the stems in the chronological classification of old English table glass. Indeed, they exhibit almost as much variation of form.

The drinking-glass foot was usually made from a separate gathering of metal taken by the gaffer's second assistant and attached to the stem (fig. 26). The iron punty, manipulated by the gaffer, held the glass beneath the centre of the foot while he completed its shaping; it was then snapped off, leaving a sharp-edged scar. The larger and rougher this punty mark, the older the glass is likely to be. The fold on the foot served to lift the punty mark above the table surface and thus avoid scratching.

123

From about 1750, punty marks might be removed by grinding the scar against a stone wheel of somewhat curved profile, producing a saucer-shaped depression which was afterwards polished. This type of finish was known as 'hollowed'.

In the earliest stemmed vessels of flint-glass the rim of the foot, while still plastic, was turned or folded back on itself. At first the fold was hollow (fig. 18). But within a few years this had developed into a flat welt varying from $\frac{1}{4}$ inch to $\frac{1}{2}$ inch wide (fig. 22). The folds on early flint-glass, both hollow and welted, were invariably narrow (fig. 16). These may be dated pre-1690. During the next quarter of a century welts were wide and thick containing plenty of metal — a typically English feature (fig. 47). They gradually became slighter on fashionable ware and between 1720 and 1740 were more or less uniform in size (figs. 41 to 46).

John Greene's working drawings fail to show the folded foot, but as the sketches are mere outlines this is hardly surprising. It is noticeable, however, that with few exceptions the bowl diameter considerably exceeds that of the small frail foot, a feature continued by the early flint-glass makers. By the 1690's, however, the typical foot, whether folded or plain, was slightly larger in diameter than the bowl rim, ensuring stability and facilitating the fashionable custom of holding a drinking-glass by the foot (fig. 31). This expansive foot continued until about the mid-eighteenth century.

Folded feet are associated with baluster, knopped, and plain stems. They may be present on some early two-piece air-twist stems, but are uncommon on the later air-twists and absent on fashionable glass from about 1735. A folded foot in association with an opaque-twist or facet-cut stem is rare. The folded foot is indicative of the rather better class of vessel, more highly finished, as compared with a contemporary plain foot. The fold continued as a provincial relic of an outmoded fashion until the mid-nineteenth century: in a price list dated 1829 welted feet are quoted.

Some of the earliest feet, however, were of the plain variety. These were almost flat underneath, showing marks and scratches of wear over an extensive area (fig. 35a). The rising central portion became a high, firm, well-formed conical instep at the stem-joint (fig. 35e). By 1735 this typically English foot, concave beneath, to avoid scratching the table with the punty mark, was resting upon its extreme rim, well defined and often sharp to the touch (fig. 57). The diameter of the plain foot, until about 1750, exceeded that of the bowl rim to avoid top-heaviness (fig. 34). The punty mark now tended to be smaller and less jagged than formerly. The plain foot

90 Drinking-glasses with facet-cut stems, cutting extending into base of bowl

91 'William Fullerton of Carstairs, and Captain Lowis', by J. T. Seton, 1773.
Illustrating Scottish wineglasses

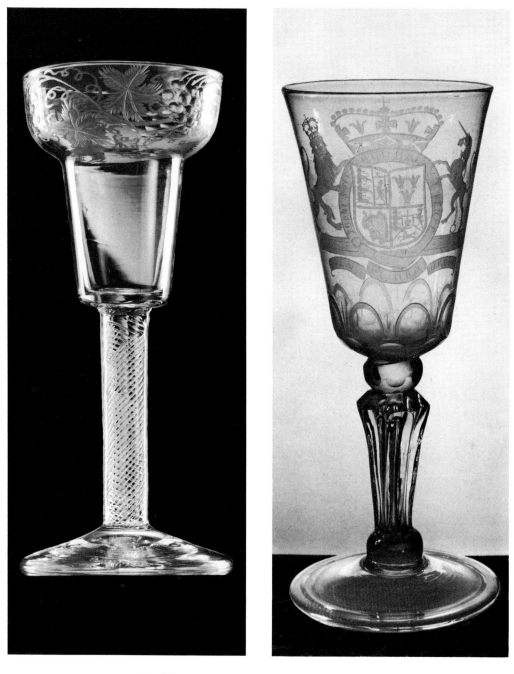

92   The vine-and-grape motif parcel polished

93   Engraved with the arms of George II

EARLY WHEEL-ENGRAVING

94, 96   Toast-master's glasses
95   Wineglass with hollow stem

97   Drinking-glasses with flowered borders

98–103 Georgian drinking-goblets

Reproduced by Gracious Permission of Her Majesty The Queen

104–109   Early-eighteenth-century drinking-glasses with all-over engraved bowls

110–113   Drinking-glasses with engraved bowls dating between *c.* 1750 and *c.* 1760

114, 115 Drinking-glasses engraved with Williamite motifs

continued throughout the century, its diameter and instep-height gradually diminishing until about 1780, and always tapering gracefully up towards the stem junction (fig. 90). During the last fifteen years of the century it became almost flat beneath, with the punty mark ground away. Badly made, ill-cooled feet were liable to sag while in a plastic condition — hence the large number of tavern glasses found with poorly shaped feet.

Domed feet, with hemispherical, sloping, or square insteps (fig. 190), were a feature of the days of heavy metal from 1690, giving strength and stability, but as a general rule domed feet were discontinued after 1730. A spreading dome with reticulated or diamond decoration was made by impressing the mould upon a lump of plastic glass which was then blown into a spherical bubble. This was afterwards tooled into a foot which was seldom symmetrical and on which the rim might be either plain or folded.

Until about 1705 the surfaces of domed feet, used on many drinking-glasses, were plainly smooth (fig. 38a). Then they began to be moulded in various decorative motifs matching ornament on the bowl surface above (fig. 115a), their numbers simultaneously decreasing in comparison with the ordinary plain or folded foot. Radial ribs were the earliest of such moulded forms, and from about 1720 these were drawn into high bosses around the dome, matching similar bosses on the head of the silesian stem above. The sturdy, highly domed foot belonged rather to the tazza-shaped bowl than to any specific date. It continued on candlesticks and sweetmeat glasses during the second half of the eighteenth century.

Small domed feet without folded rims (fig. 190e) appeared in small numbers associated with opaque- or coloured-twist stems after 1745, when domes might again be used on highly expensive glasses, but seldom on ordinary domestic table-ware. A domed type of the mid-eighteenth century was the terraced foot, consisting of a series of two to four smooth, circular steps rising in the form of a bold dome. These are thought by some authorities to have been made at Newcastle.

The thick, square foot with a solid dome supporting a four-sided pedestal stem was a purely English innovation (fig. 151a). The dome was usually plainly smooth, but might sometimes be moulded in terraced form (fig. 138 below). These appeared first about 1785, but were little used until about 1790. Beneath, they were either ground flat or moulded in hollow-dome form. After 1810 the square foot was enlivened with a star, either cut or impressed beneath (fig. 149).

The glass-cutter soon found the foot gave scope for the use of his wheel. Edge-cutting, such as simple scalloping and the effective arch-and-point outline, was a fashionable finish between 1760 and 1780. Feet supporting facet-cut stems hardly repaid cutting; facet-cut feet are only associated with metal of the highest quality. Plain, heavy feet, almost discs, might be similarly decorated. Various types of polygonal, oval, and scale cutting also decorated wineglass feet. Circular, tool-shaped feet appeared about 1800 and continued until after 1820.

The hollow pedestal foot (fig. 18) blown in the form of a trumpet, with its end opened out to form a flat rim and folded for strengthening purposes, was introduced by the Venetians and included among the types of wine-glass feet made at Verzelini's glass-house in Crutched Friars. In flint-glass the pedestal foot appears to have been in use during the 1680's, existing examples being mainly associated with salvers and jugs.

This foot was not again in production until the late 1740's. It is displayed on most illustrated glass-sellers' trade cards (fig. 27) from the 1750's until the end of the century: some excellent examples are shown in the 1792 trade card of John Harwood, Norwich. Sheraton's *Cabinet-Makers' Dictionary*, 1803, illustrated hollow pedestal-footed wineglasses thus proving their fashionable use in the early nineteenth century.

Figures 92, 93

EARLY WHEEL-ENGRAVING

(92) Wineglass with saucer-topped bucket bowl, the saucer wheel-engraved with a scrolling vine-and-grape motif parcel polished. The metal displays distinct striae. The air-twist in the stem has been excellently manipulated, suggesting long experience on the part of the craftsman. The conical foot has a punty scar beneath. Height 7 inches.

This is one of a set of ten in the Corning Museum of Glass

(93) Heraldic wineglass with base of the deep funnel bowl encircled with facet-cutting, engraved with the arms of George II. Moulded silesian stem with a ball knop at each end, the upper knop cut. Folded foot with punty scar. Height $6\frac{1}{2}$ inches.

In the Lecky Collection of English Glass, Brooklyn Museum

135

CHAPTER SEVEN

DECORATION: ENGRAVING

GLASS GOBLETS AND DECANTERS ornamented with landscapes, flowers, figures, animals, trees, heraldic devices, were regarded by beauty-loving Georgians as the supreme elegance in table appointments. Surface decoration included the rare use of diamond-point engraving; the long era of wheel-engraving and cut ornament; gilding; and enamelling.

Diamond-engraving on glass was a luxury decoration early in the fifteenth century, but by 1562 Martin Luther's friend, the Saxon pastor Johann Mathesius, in his *Sermons to Glassmakers* could remark: 'Nowadays all sorts of festooning and handsome lines are drawn with the diamond on the beautiful bright Venetian glasses.'

The earliest specimens of English table-glass to be engraved were goblets of delicate soda-glass from Verzelini's glass-house in Broad Street. These were decorated by Anthony de Lisley, a free-lance engraver of pewter and glass practising his craft in St. Martin-le-Grand (*see* Chapter I and figs. 5 to 7). It was possibly he who decorated in 1588 'eight dishes of glass graven about the rims' for Robert Dudley, Earl of Leicester. It is improbable that such plates were of Venetian origin for it was customary for private houses to hire them when entertaining on a large scale: there is evidence that the Duchess of Rutland, for example, hired them later in the century. The Worksop accounts for 1593 show that four glass plates then cost 2d. The diamond was eminently suited to engraving fine lines on hard, thin soda-glass, the technique resembling that of fine engraving on silver and pewter, with results that were interesting rather than handsome. Exceptionally clear effects were produced by avoiding intersecting lines although details in pictorial work might be emphasized by their use.

Diamond-point engraving on glass was a favourite pastime in Holland during the early seventeenth century, but there is no record of similar dilettantism in England. Table glass was engraved professionally thoughout the monopoly period, cross-hatching being brought into use during the 1660's, thus making possible greater contrasts in light and shade (fig. 13).

Stippling on glass with diamond-needle and hammer was a technique introduced to English glass-sellers during the early 1690's. Little of this appears to have been carried out, for to be appreciated on glass such work requires close inspection, often in a certain light.

The diamond-point was employed in early eighteenth-century England to inscribe epigrams, toasts, names, upon drinking-glass bowls. These were often the spontaneous efforts of amateurs using the stones in their finger rings, although some pewter engravers undertook this work which they advertized as 'scratching'. Clearly executed armorial designs and single floral devices were fashionable in this medium during the 1720's. From about 1725 these were contemporary with diamond-etched arabesques and scroll patterns which decorated drinking-glass rims. At about this time engraving with the wheel superseded the diamond for commercial work. Traces of the diamond-point appear from time to time during the following hundred years, Francis Buckley noting an advertisement in 1756. Occasionally, indeed, an individual artist would decorate a series of glasses with elaborate pictorial designs: most of these were signed. An owner's initials might be diamond-engraved upon the bowls of domestic glass, the device being arranged in the form of a triangle, with the single letter at the apex indicating the surname, the lower-left letter the man's Christian name, and that to the right his wife's.

As early as 1680 another process for decorating glass had been evolved by Heinrich Schwanhardt. This was the etching technique, which enabled decorators to produce more delicate effects than were possible with the diamond. The design was traced with a needle point through a thin, resinous coating — the resist. The glass was then subjected to hydrofluoric acid fumes which bit into the lines exposed by the needle. The etched lines are exquisitely fine yet remarkably clear. There is no evidence, however, that acid etching on glass was practised in England until early in the nineteenth century.

A somewhat similar technique was patented in 1806 by John Davenport, the celebrated potter of Longport. This method required cut-out paper patterns to be pasted upon clear glass, the entire surface then being waxed. When the patterns with their coating of wax were removed they left the design exposed upon the glass. Frosted effects were obtained by adding ammonia to the acid. Warm water washed away the surplus acid before the resist was removed with benzine. Glass etched by this method is marked beneath with the word 'Patent'. Silhouettists were employed to make the paper patterns which were cut with scissors and penknife. The designs were cut with such skill that hair-line details appeared finer than was usual in a pen-and-ink drawing.

It was wheel-engraving, however, that supplanted the diamond-point for decorating flint-glass table-ware. The sketchy type of decoration resulting from the diamond-point lines was unable to withstand competition from the more vigorous designs ground into the glass by the rapidly revolving copper wheel. This was a method used by the craftsmen of Roman Britain but the art is not known to have been practised on glass for at least a thousand years previous to about 1590 when it was redeveloped by Casper Lehmann at Prague. A protective patent, the appointment of 'Privy Engraver and Glass-Cutter to the Emperor Rudolf', and 'twenty marks in gold, fine alloy', were his reward. There is no evidence that soda-glass decorated in this way reached England until 1665 when the Glass-sellers' Company began importing wheel-engraved glass.

The process itself is believed to have been introduced into England by George Franz Kreybich, a 26-year-old itinerant wheel-engraver and enameller of glass who arrived in London late in 1688. Early Victorian writers on English glass were of the opinion, however, that wheel-engraving on soda-glass was being executed at Stourbridge in 1661 by one Schinner.

Kreybich discovered the newly invented flint-glass to be an ideal medium for the wheel, but until patronized by members of the Court of St. James's his fine craftsmanship was ignored. Drinking-goblets engraved in the Kreybich manner at once became fashionable and other wheel-engravers soon arrived from Germany. Several examples of armorial wheel-engraving on flint-glass goblets of this period still remain: one in the British Museum bears the arms of William III.

No direct evidence has yet come to light to prove that wheel-engraving was practised by Englishmen in the seventeenth century. The registers of St. James's Church, Duke's Place, record in 1699 the marriage of Alexander Nichols, an 'engraver in glass and living near the Star in Nightingale Lane, Wapping'. Whether he worked with diamond or wheel is unknown, but the probability is that he was a decorator of glass mirror-frames. Mirror-plates at this period were enclosed in frames of blue or plain glass elaborately ornamented with wheel-engraved designs: the mirror-plates themselves might also be engraved. The number of authentic frames still existing is proof enough that wheel-engraving was a well-developed craft in England long before it was applied commercially to table glass. A mirror at Heydon Hall, Norfolk, made and wheel-engraved at the Bear Garden Glass-house, Southwark, in 1700 is ornamented with the arms of the Dashwoods, festooned with graceful arabesques and knots of flowers. The Earl of Nottingham has a mirror of the same date magnificent with wheel-engraved borders composed of crests, cyphers, and knots of flowers. A mirror sent by Queen Anne as a gift to the Emperor of Morocco was 'scoloped, diamond cut, and engraved with flowers' by Philip Arbuthnot of Hungerford Market. Mirror-frames 'wrought with flourishes' were engraved by Richard Robinson and Thomas Howcroft, both of London, throughout the reign of Queen Anne. Wheel-engraving on mirrors of this period displays craftsmanship of remarkably high quality and masterly skill in the layout of design.

Anton Wilhelm Mauerl (1672–1737), an engraver of glass and a maker of fine parchment cut-outs for ornamental purposes, set up in London during 1699. Within two years he had established a considerable household and was celebrated for the splendour of his engraved emblems and chinoiseries, figures and landscapes. He returned to Germany in 1710. It seems reasonable to suggest that he was responsible for some of the magnificent wheel-engraving which ornamented mirror-frames and plates of that period. The Victoria and Albert Museum stores a flat-sided flask superbly wheel-engraved with an all-over design of leaves, flowers, birds, animals, and scrolls, bearing Mauerl's signature in diamond-point.

The decline of the glass mirror-frame from about 1720 coincided with the commercial development of wheel-engraving on flint-glass table-ware, the softer metal and the curved surface necessitating adjustment of the craftsman's technique. A goblet bearing the arms of Queen Anne before the union with Scotland in 1707 (fig. 105) and another with the Chatfield arms and the date 1718, remain as early experiments by mirror-engravers seeking to widen the scope of the craft.

The early Georgian glass-engraver worked on his own account, the front room of his dwelling forming the workshop. The craftsman, steady handed, accurate of touch, and with keen sight, worked a small treadle-operated lathe, regulating the speed according to the requirements of the work in hand. Into his lathe were fitted, one at a time, interchangeable copper discs, some as thin as a hair, others measuring $\frac{1}{4}$ inch across the cutting edge, their diameters varying from $\frac{1}{8}$ inch to 4 inches. A complete set consisted of about one hundred discs, and in some of the later intricate work all might be brought into use.

Designs were commissioned from pattern books containing sketches of the engraver's own invention or copied from published works, artists being called upon only for important work. Such patterns were outlined on

140

the glass with quill-applied white paint, but in commercial copying, however, the engraver worked from a design hanging before him, starting directly with the wheel and developing the pattern as the rotating disc played on the glass surface, changing when required to a finer or coarser wheel.

The engraver, gripping the glass with both hands, held it against the cutting edge of the rapidly rotating copper disc, moving and twisting it to secure the desired lines. The disc was fed with an abrasive mixture of linseed oil and fine emery powder applied from the pointed tip of a leather strap hanging above the work. The result was a shallow intaglio, apparently raised in low relief, an optical illusion causing the most deeply hollow parts to appear the most prominent while the plain surface acted as a background.

Good wheel-engraving is recognized by firmness of line, sharpness of edge, and delicately flowing curves. Early wheel-engraving was left matt, but from 1740 it might be partly polished with wheels of willow wood. The tendency to polish increased as the century progressed, particularly in glass-engraving manufactories.

There was little standardization of engraved design on table-glass until the late 1750's when some of the leading glass-sellers employed a full-time engraver on the premises. Employment advertisements such as that in the *Weekly Mercury*, July 1771, for a 'glass-cutter and flowerer' suggest that a single worker might be employed in both crafts. Thomas Billinge of Liverpool (flor. 1767–1800) advertised himself in the *Liverpool Advertiser* during 1777 as 'a glass flowerer cutting patterns representing flowers on vases and other domestic glassware'. William Horton and Joseph Fogill, both of Liverpool, advertised themselves as glass-flowerers from time to time during the 1780's.

The improved glass of the 1740's was well-suited to wheel-engraving, the cut incisions showing as clear sharp lines: formerly the engraved lines had been deep furrows. Engravers operating on their own account continued throughout the century and beyond, producing individual work of high artistic merit in which no line irregularities occur.

Wheel-engraved decoration until the late 1730's was limited almost entirely to crests and cyphers (fig. 101) and inscriptions: few examples are known that may be dated earlier than 1727. The accuracy demanded in armorial engraving made this one of the most difficult tasks in glass decoration. It was fashionable for complete sets to be ornamented in this way. Armorial engraving ran parallel with other forms of decoration throughout the eighteenth century, and was usually the work of specialists

141

whose advertisements were frequent. Typical was the *Morning Post* announcement 17th January 1781: 'Coats of Arms and Devices engraved, enamelled, and painted by the advertiser at Collet's Glass Manufactory, by the King's Arms, Cockspur Street.' Armorial glasses are now rare.

The formal, symmetrically engraved borders which encircled the rims of drinking-glasses from the late 1730's were chiefly simple patterns of intertwined scrollwork and leaf arabesques (fig. 41). Occasional pre-1750 examples might also have the surface of the foot rim engraved to match. In the 1740's appeared rather wider floral borders in which daisies predominated, and vine-leaf edging became fashionable. By 1750 individual motifs might be larger, extending the full depth of the border (fig. 76). Rim borders of these types were produced by provincial engravers throughout the eighteenth century: such borders must therefore be considered in association with the type of metal and its form.

'Flowered glasses' was the trade name for table-ware engraved with naturalistic flowers on the body of the bowl. These are in a style much resembling flowers on porcelain and date from about 1740 to the 1780's (fig. 97). At first a single flower such as a rose, carnation, daisy, or other wild flower might ornament one side of a drinking-glass bowl. During the 1750's other flowers such as sunflower, tulip, or passion-flower might also be used while the reverse of the bowl was engraved with a bird, butterfly, moth, bee, or other insect. Simple motifs were usual and some have been noted in printed pattern books of the period such as *The Ladies Amusement* by Jean Pillement. Vine sprays with grapes formed another popular motif. The growing vine is rarely found, although the bowls of a few drawn drinking-glasses have been noted with deeply cut and polished vine-leaves and grapes, starting half-way up the stem and covering the entire bowl. At this time there was a minor fashion for engraving drinking-glass bowls with emblems suggesting a specialized use such as hop and barley (fig. 161) for strong ales, sprays of apples for cider (fig. 69 centre), pears for perry.

Engraving manufactories appear to have been established from the 1760's. Here engravers were employed to decorate table-ware bought by the proprietor from the glass-houses and sold by him to the glass-sellers after decoration. Earlier formalistic styles were again brought into use chiefly because they could be engraved quickly. Under poorly illuminated factory conditions an open-flame lamp burning train oil was the only light available during the darker hours of a working day that extended from 6 a.m. to 8 p.m. Single patterns were copied by the gross for dispersal to the glass-sellers. Festoons, trellis-work, dentil-edges, and geometrical borders could

142

encircle bowls inexpensively. Large formalistic roses with disc-like petals and cross-hatched centres were tremendously popular. Polishing became a feature, and for a period after 1770 the entire design might be polished. The classical influence also brought formal designs such as festooning to the body of the drinking-glass bowl, although flower motifs continued. 'The pheasant in flight', a strange-looking bird with a long tail and always shown rocketing, is a lively motif found on a series of late-eighteenth-century wineglasses.

Some of the most ornamental wheel-engraving enriched commemorative and scenic glasses. This was a development of the independent craftsman too costly to be carried out to any great extent in the manufactories. Subject engravings earlier than about 1750 were usually of political significance such as those associated with the Jacobite movement (see Chapter 15). Masonic emblems decorated a wide variety of drinking-glasses intended for lodge use.

Pictorial engraving, fashionable between about 1760 and the 1780's, included quaint pastorals in the current Chinese taste, landscapes (fig. 150), and classical, allegorical, historic, and social scenes. Naval subjects (fig. 138), were highly popular, particularly, from 1780, on rummers whose capacious bowls provided extensive grounds for crowded scenes. Sea engagements, apart from Camperdown and Trafalgar, were seldom commemorated on glass. Naval engraving requires close inspection to ensure authenticity.

Sporting scenes were obviously special favourites and might be inscribed with names, places, and dates. Examples belonging to the eighteenth century are rare, fox- and stag-hunting (fig. 155), fishing (fig. 154), steeple-chasing, shooting, and cockfighting being found. Goblets commemorative of horse-racing successes were engraved with the picture and name of the winning horse and were usually presentation pieces from the owner.

More ambitious engraving came early in the nineteenth century, many scenic and pastoral pieces of this period being deservedly classed as works of art. In 1800, on the occasion of the union of Great Britain and Ireland, commemorative glasses were issued engraved with handsome designs including the rose, thistle, and shamrock (fig. 173). After about 1825, however, design tended to become stiff and pretentious. Elaborate engravings are sometimes added to the bowls of plain eighteenth-century glasses, the deception often being difficult to detect after suitable treatment.

143

Figures 94–7

(94) Toast-master's glass with wide-mouthed conical bowl; spool stem with central ball knop; folded foot; *c.* 1730.

In the Victoria and Albert Museum

(95) Wineglass with hollow stem cut with flutes continuing into the bowl base. Height 7½ inches. 1760's.

In the collection of Lady Kathleen Ward

(96) Toast-master's glass with trumpet bowl; collared annular knops at top and base of short plain stem; folded foot. Height 6 inches.

(97) Flowered wineglasses with wheel-engraved borders of scrollwork and formal flowers; all with plain feet. 1740's.
    Left and right: Waisted bowls with solid bases.
    Centre: Drawn trumpet bowl.

Figures 98–103

DRINKING GOBLETS IN THE COLLECTION OF HER MAJESTY THE QUEEN AT BUCKINGHAM PALACE

(98) Covered goblet with slightly everted round funnel bowl and smooth stem cut hexagonally; rims of bowl and cover heavily gilded; cover and folded foot encircled with sliced oval facets; bowl engraved with the cypher of George III in an elaborate crowned cartouche. Probably made at the time of the coronation and marriage of George III in 1761.

(99) Covered goblet with slightly everted round funnel bowl on straight air-twist stem of the early type lacking regularity of spiral; bowl and cover rims encircled with bands of heavy gilding; cover and foot encircled with sliced oval facets. Bowl engraved with the cypher of Prince George Augustus Frederick, later George IV (1762–1830), surmounted by a coronet. This was probably made for the christening of Prince George and obviously was made at the same glass-house as that on the left.

(100) Covered goblet with pointed funnel bowl, its base encircled with fluting, slightly notched; cut stem composed of baluster between two facet-cut knops, on plain foot; the spire finial has been cut in a style found on decanter stoppers from 1765. The bowl is engraved with a scene showing a youthful St. Vitus, haloed and carrying a palm branch, and is accompanied by a small sword-bearing winged attendant; set in scrollwork in the vitruvian style. Early George III.

144

(101) Wineglass with heavy-base pointed funnel bowl on a reeded silesian stem with expansive folded foot bearing a rough punty scar beneath; traces of gilding visible around bowl rim. Bowl engraved with cypher and crown of Augustus III, King of Saxony and Poland. This glass, with others still preserved at Buckingham Palace, was engraved for use at a state banquet given to Augustus in 1720. They are among the few early pieces of inscribed flint-glass to have a flawless pedigree. One glass of similar size and shape bears the arms of Augustus, cypher and crown on the reverse. Shorter glasses in the series in the collection have solid-based bell bowls, plain baluster stems, and folded feet, and the gilding on the bowl rims is worn.

(102) Covered goblet with drawn trumpet bowl and plain stem containing a tear; rims of bowl and cover are heavily gilded. Bowl engraved with cartouche and crown resembling those on the example immediately above, and enclosing the cypher F B.

(103) One of a pair of unusual wineglasses, the thick-based bowl drawn into baluster stem, on highly domed and folded foot; air-ball in the bowl base, and well-formed tear in the stem; gilded bowl rim. Queen Mary recollected that in about 1920 the crizzling on these glasses was less pronounced.

Reproduced by Gracious Permission of Her Majesty the Queen

Figures 104–9

ENGRAVED DRINKING-GLASSES

(104) Goblet with conical bowl, short knopped stem containing a William III sixpence dated 1697; flat folded foot. Bowl diamond-point engraved with two peacocks and peacock's feathers; *c.* 1700. Height 7 inches.

Formerly in the Bles Collection

(105) Armorial glass with round funnel bowl, baluster stem above knop, on domed and folded foot. Bowl engraved, partly by diamond and partly by wheel, with the royal coat of arms as used by Queen Anne and before the union with Scotland in 1705. Probably a coronation souvenir, 1702.

Formerly in the Grant Francis Collection

(106) Armorial goblet with round funnel bowl, short baluster stem, and folded foot; bowl encircled with short wide fluting enriched with a band of line engraving; stem cut to match. The foot bears a very close resemblance to that on the King Augustus III glass (fig. 101), and its diameter similarly exceeds that of the bowl rim, a feature rarely found after 1750. Gilding encircles bowl and foot rims but is considerably worn. The bowl is engraved with the royal arms as borne by the House of Hanover until 1801. This glass might belong to the service bought in honour of Augustus III in 1720, or perhaps for the coronation of George II.

Reproduced by Gracious Permission of Her Majesty the Queen

(107) Jacobite goblet with round funnel bowl, plain stem containing a heart-shaped tear, and domed and folded foot. Bowl engraved with full-face portrait of Charles I in ruff and embroidered mantle, and inscribed on the reverse 'Memoria in Eterna' within a double branch of oak leaves and acorns. Mr Grant Francis has recorded that this glass was mentioned in the will of Robert Martin, 'a leader of Stuart supporters in Southern Ireland' Height 8⅝ inches.

Formerly in the collection of Mrs E. H. Thomas

(108) Jacobite goblet with funnel bowl, double-knop, air-twist stem, and plain foot. Bowl engraved with a stricken oak, a sapling growing from the ground, and the word *Revirescit* in script; *c.* 1750. Height 9½ inches.

Formerly in the Bles Collection

(109) *Audentior Ibo* glass with round funnel bowl, double-knopped air-twist stem, and plain foot. Engraved with a full-face portrait of Prince Charles Edward in tartans and wearing the Order of the Garter; flanked with rose and buds and thistle; *c.* 1750.

In the Brooklyn Museum

Figures 110–13

ENGRAVED DRINKING-GLASSES

(110) *Left and right:* Two sides of a goblet with cup-shaped bowl on opaque white-twist stem and plain foot. Bowl engraved with a scene depicting a parade of Lord Claremont's Irish Volunteers in Dublin, outside the west front of Trinity College Dublin, with the statue of King William III, and inscribed 'Success to the Irish Volunteers'; *c.* 1760.
   Centre: Goblet with round funnel bowl on double air-twist stem and plain foot. Bowl engraved with Britannia bearing the olive branch, four ships in full sail, and the inscription 'O Fair Britania Hail'; *c.* 1760.

(111) With drawn ogee bowl; composite stem consisting of air-twist on inverted cone kno p, on domed foot. Bowl engraved with a profile portrait of the Duke of Cumberland, the victor of Culloden in 1746, with mantlings of military trophies and inscribed 'Prosperity to the Duke of Cumberland'; *c.* 1750. Height 7⅜ inches.

Formerly in the Bles Collection

(112) Ogee bowl on fine air-twist stem and plain foot. Bowl engraved with the arms of the Turners' Company of London, with the motto 'By Faith I Obtain'; *c.* 1760. Height 9½ inches.

By courtesy of Messrs Arthur Churchill Ltd

(113) A political and commemorative glass, with bucket bowl, opaque-twist stem, and plain foot. One side of the bowl is engraved to record the victory of the British fleet under Admiral Hawke at Quiberon Bay in 1760, displays a warship flying the broad pennant and is inscribed 'Success to the British Fleet'. On the reverse are the royal arms commemorating the accession of George III in 1760.

Formerly in the Grant Francis Collection

Figures 114, 115

WILLIAMITE GLASSES

(114) *Left:* Goblet with drawn trumpet bowl and plain stem containing large pear-shaped tear, on folded foot. Engraved with equestrian portrait of William III wearing a triple-plumed hat and wig, pointing a drawn sword in his right hand and with a pistol in his holster bearing a crown. Inscribed 'The Glorious Memory of King William III Boyne July 1st 1690'; *c.* 1720. Height 7½ inches.

Centre: Goblet with bucket bowl, plain stem, and folded foot. Bowl engraved on one side with wreathed portrait of William III with palm leaves beneath and above the inscription: 'The Glorious and Immortal Memory 1690'; on the reverse, *au pair*, a portrait of a soldier in breastplate, cloak, and wig, with the inscription: 'George Walker Defender of Derby 1688'; *c.* 1740. Height 7 inches.

Right: Bell bowl on an air-twist stem with a cable coil around the centre. Bowl engraved with portrait of William III on a walking horse beneath the inscription: 'The Glorious Memory of King William III', and, on the reverse, 'Boyne 1st July 1690'. Height 7¾ inches.

(115) *Left:* Ogee bowl, composite stem — air-twist rising from an inverted drop knop — on domed and folded foot. Bowl engraved with equestrian portrait of William III holding a baton; *c.* 1750. Height 7⅞ inches.

Centre: Round funnel bowl, plain stem, domed and folded foot. Bowl engraved with grapes and vine-leaves and rim inscribed: 'To the Glorious Memory of King William'; *c.* 1750. Height 8½ inches.

Right: Bucket bowl, plain stem and plain foot. Bowl engraved with equestrian portrait of King William and inscribed with a full version of the Orange toast: 'To the glorious pious and immortal memory of the great and good King William, who freed us from pope and popery, knavery and slavery, brass money and wooden shoes, and he who refuses this toast may be damned crammed and rammed down the great gun of Athlone.' Height 8 inches.

By courtesy of Messrs Christie, Manson & Woods Ltd

116 Six types of cutting: (*top row*) fine diamonds, large shallow diamonds, cross-cut diamonds; (*bottom row*) chequered diamonds, strawberry diamonds, printies

117, 118   Punch glasses: (*left*) with Apsley Pellatt crystal cameo of George III
Reproduced by Gracious Permission of Her Majesty The Queen

119, 120   Water-jugs: (*left*) cut with large relief diamonds, 1820's; (*right*) on square pedestal
base, inscribed 'A Trip to the Fort'

121, 122 Cut-glass casters and salt-cellars. *Below:* a pair of covered bowls and
a three-footed tea-caddy bowl

151

123   A collection of late-Georgian cut-glass, including a pair of pickle-jars, three covered urns, sugar-bowl, butter-dish and piggin

DECORATION: CUTTING

CUT-GLASS FASCINATES CONNOISSEUR and tyro alike. In Georgian homes flickering candlelight displayed its formal devices to their finest advantage. The decoration of glass by cutting into its surface to enhance refractive power is at least 1,800 years old in England. Remains of a glass-furnace operating during the Roman occupation of Britain were excavated at Warrington in 1899 revealing a 10-inch diameter stone cutting-wheel made of hard, fine-grained sandstone, accompanied by fragments of glass cut with circular concave hollows —the same 'printie' so successfully used by the Irish glass-cutters early in the nineteenth century.

The century-long revival and development of cut-glass in Georgian England can be chronologically traced through the hundred newspaper references collected by Francis Buckley. In 1678 John Roberts, London, pa⋅ented a machine worked 'by the motion of water and wheels for grinding, polishing and diamonding glass plates for looking glasses'. *London Gazette* advertisements of the same year describe this decoration: 'Borders cut most curiously Hollow and with a better Lustre than any heretofore done.' This was not flint-glass, however. Glass-grinding had long been a branch of the optician's craft in England: the Howard Accounts of 1618 refer to spectacle lenses being made at Keswick.

The scope of the grinder's work increased as the years progressed and by 1714 he was grinding lustres for 'schandelers'. Two years later Lady Mary Wortley Montagu noticed the new fashion, observing that 'almost every room was made gay with large lustres of rock crystal'. That rock crystal from the hills of Bristol and from Cornwall and Derbyshire should be used for lustres is significant confirmation that its refractive properties were greater than those of flint-glass at that period. Only by about 1740 were its brilliance and lustre exceeded by flint-glass.

Not until a depression is ground into glass can it be termed 'cut'. Cutting, a technique entirely different from grinding and requiring the skill of experience for its successful accomplishment, was widely used to decorate Continental glasses before its establishment in England as an independent craft. A possible record of cut flint-glass was found by Buckley in the *Whitehall Evening Post* of 1719 in which it was announced that 'John Akerman, at the Rose & Crown, Cornhill, continues to sell plain and diamond-cut flint glasses'. This phrasing in no way suggests that diamond-cutting was an innovation to the world of table glass. The small diamond-shaped German facet, produced by cutting with a flat or slightly curved edge, was probably first copied commercially by the London glass-grinding fraternity after the Glass-sellers' Company had endeavoured to protect its own interests by breaking up an auction sale of imported glass to be held at Stationers' Hall in 1709. The advertisements announced 'a great parcel of very fine Cut and Carved glasses' described as 'Jellies, Wine and Water Tumblers, Beer and Wine Glasses with Covers, and divers other sorts'.

Glass-cutting in England gradually developed into a specialized craft, glass-sellers buying plain ware from the glass-houses and themselves employing the cutters, usually as out-workers. Table-ware at this period was sturdily made and metal used lavishly. In 1710 the Whitefriars Glasshouse was selling undecorated table-ware at one shilling a pound. E. Gerspach in *L'art de la verrerie*, Paris, 1885, commenting on English flint-glass of this period declared that it 'dealt a heavy blow to the Bohemian trade in colourless glass. The English material lent itself to facet-cutting infinitely better than the Bohemian, eclipsing that glass just as the Bohemian had eclipsed Venetian glass.'

As had already been proved with engraved flint-glass the large lead content of the metal made it remarkably soft in comparison with Continental glass. The latter, although now being made brighter and more transparent by the use of potash instead of soda, was still exceedingly hard and difficult to cut.

There were, and still are, three fundamental types of cutting: hollow-cut, produced by a wheel-rim rounded in contour; mitre-cut, formed by a wheel having a pointed or V-shaped rim of about sixty degrees; panel-cut formed by a flat-edged wheel. All cut forms were produced by about fifty variants of these three elements until the late 1790's when John Dovey of Brettle Lane, the first to use wrought-iron cutting-wheels, introduced the double-mitre wheel. Curvilinear cutting is rare because the operator necessarily had to cut the curved outline upon a curved surface along the rotating edge of his cutting-wheel.

English cutting may be grouped into three distinct phases dependent upon manufacturing processes:

1 Pre-1740. Edge-cutting and scalloping (fig. 231); almost flat cutting disposed in simple geometric patterns; giant diamonds and triangles in low relief (fig. 236); shallow slices (fig. 238).

2 1740–1805. Similar types of cutting on a clearer and more refractive metal of thinner section.

3 1790–1830. (More especially 1805–30.) Elaborate cutting in deep relief on thick metal (fig. 122).

Pre-1740 flint-glass was not yet of a quality to disperse any great amount of prismatic light owing to its lead-tinged greyness and the presence of specks, seeds, cords, and striations. This early cutting was of a type that would not impair translucency; rather did it bestow a liquid beauty unknown in the days of deep complicated cutting which might reduce transparency. The object of cutting at this time was to beautify glass by the addition of small, sparse decoration rather than to make a display of the quality and quantity of intricate ornament. Cutting was, therefore, simple and unostentatious (fig. 236).

Scalloping or edge-cutting of bowl rims (fig. 231) was possibly the earliest form of cutting to appear regularly on English table-glass, as this work could be carried out by the long-established glass-grinders with little difficulty. First came the zigzag edge-cutting (fig. 238) with uniform undulating curves, followed by arch-and-point rims (fig. 231), a combination of the two earlier types. These were displayed on sweetmeat glasses by the early 1720's (Chapter 17). This early scalloping was sharply ground, the edges being pared off at the sides. There were also several types of foot-rim scalloping, the most frequent being shallow arcs (fig. 238).

What collectors usually term flat-cutting really consists of depressions ground lightly into the metal. Even though the metal was usually thick in section, it is doubtful whether flint-glass table-ware, considered as a commercial proposition, was strong enough to accept any but the most shallow cutting until the introduction of the tunnel leer for annealing. The earliest flat-cutting was applied in the form of small facets to the stems of two-piece drinking-glasses (fig. 82) in which the stem was drawn from the bowl. Such faceting, found only in association with round funnel, ogee, and ovoid bowls, in which the diamond was two or three times greater in length than in width, was produced by grinding into the glass a series of closely spaced concavities, their overlapping edges being arranged in the form of a diamond. Long hexagons were also cut. Occasionally a knopped stem is found decorated with small flat-surfaced facets in a style copied from Germany (fig. 100). Shouldered stems were sometimes cut with flat vertical flutes and the knop between stem and bowl might be faceted (fig. 93). The upper surface of the foot was then ornamented with a circle of facets, either hexagonal or diamond-shaped. From about 1730 the lower rounded part of the bowl might also be cut with a circuit of flat vertical flutes (fig. 106). Drinking-glasses and other hollow-ware of this period might be ornamented with large triangular facets or large diamonds in very low relief.

The simple edge-flute or slice was an early type of flat-cutting which continued in use until the end of the century. It was executed holding the glass at an incline against the edge of a rotating mitred wheel. The basic operation was not difficult, but considerable skill was required to produce ornamental motifs solely by means of shapely scoops in varying outlines and depths. Its earliest appearance was during the early 1730's, and few examples will be found on glass which may be associated with this period. When found the slices are invariably cut into the metal at a slight angle and display rounded edges. Sharp points at intersections were removed by cutting heart-shaped notches. The more frequently used motifs in this medium decorated bowl forms and included circuits of zigzags, the angles of which might be cusped; lunar slices of various types; arches; festoons with leaves formed by removing no more than a film of glass.

1740–1805. The flint-glass available by 1740, improved in quality and given greater toughness and refractive power by passing through a tunnel leer, brought a wider variety of cutting motifs. Facets ground into the surface of such glass dispersed transmitted light so as to display all the colours of the spectrum. Fashion soon required table glass to be of thinner section: deep incisions were not possible in such ware. After about 1745 increased brilliance and strength were secured by passing the glass twice through the tunnel leer.

Flat motifs, shallow and economical of line, were used almost exclusively: the thin sides of drinking-glass bowls seldom permitted deep slicing and incising, but these were common on sweetmeat glasses. Seven main types of cutting were usual during this period. These include:

1   Large flat diamonds found on hollow-ware.

2   The frequently advertised sprig motif often found encircling drinking-glass bowls, triple sprigs being most frequent.

3   Fluting, more frequent towards the end of the period when the edges might be notched and including (*a*) comb-fluting, the hollow flutes encircling the base of a decanter (fig. 222), wineglass cooler (fig. 246), or other hollow-ware; (*b*) neck fluting (fig. 227c), (*c*) stem fluting (fig. 81).

4   Stem diamonds of various flat or concave facet forms such as parallelo-

grams with angles approximating 120 degrees and 60 degrees, long diamonds which might be crested, various polygonal facets such as long hexagons, and scale patterns intended to suggest fish scales such as ornamented porcelain of the period, shallow depressions cut with a slightly rounded wheel and costly in time, found mainly on stems, decanter necks and sometimes on the base of an ogee bowl.

5   Incised zigzags and lunar slices.

6   Sliced motifs in various forms found chiefly on candlestick and sweetmeat glasses.

7   Plain diamonds in large sizes in shallow relief which, from about 1750, might be double-cut. These were usually cut in a single row touching each other and encircling a bowl form.

Scalloping (figs. 240 and 266) was carried out more artistically than formerly, with edges ground less sharply. In various designs it encircled candlestick feet and nozzles (fig. 265) and the rims and feet of sweetmeat glasses and ornamented epergnes and table chandeliers (fig. 235). Castellated rims (fig. 293) in various forms date from about 1770.

1790–1830. As the classical mood in industrial art reached its peak of popularity, luxury ware demanded that economy of material and ornament should be abandoned. By 1790 luxury table glass, notable for the weight of metal incorporated in its form, was being manufactured and decorated with cutting in deep-relief, V-shaped grooves crossing each other at right angles to produce pyramidal projections or convex diamonds. Diamonds in relief have not been noted on the numerous glass accessories illustrated in pattern books of the 1790's, thus emphasizing the restriction of their use to luxury ware. This deeply incised diamond-cutting eventually consisted of fields of such decoration finished in a variety of points.

The earliest deeply incised diamond decoration was a narrow encircling band of plain diamonds in relief (fig. 116): after about 1810 plain relief diamonds, were mainly used a border decoration. There size gradually lessened and, with the introduction of steam-power into glass-cutting mills, the tendency was to reduce cross-cut diamonds to the size of small plain diamonds, and the latter to still smaller dimensions cut in metal of thinner section (fig. 116). Cross-cut diamonds, sometimes referred to as 'hob-nail cutting' (fig. 116), consisted of large relief diamonds, each with a flat point, and this flat surface incised with a simple cross. Cross-cut diamonds appear to have been used during the 1790's, but their heyday was between 1800 and 1810. English table-glass of Regency years might be ornamented with large areas of small plain diamonds in relief.

157

The chequered diamond (fig. 116) is an elaboration of the cross-cut, the flat surface of the basic diamond being cut with four small diamonds. Even more elaborate was the strawberry diamond (fig. 116) of Regency days. In this, the flattened point of each large relief diamond was cut with numerous, very fine relief diamonds. This style appeared between 1805 and 1810 cut in very uneven lines: steam-driven cutting-wheels cut the parent diamond much deeper and the fine diamonds sharper than the hand-operated wheels. Various combinations of diamond-cutting were used to enhance the prismatic fire of the flint-glass: all-over cutting (fig. 276), however, impaired translucency.

Prismatic-cutting or step-cutting (fig. 125) — those deep, simply cut, sharp, horizontal prisms so easily adaptable to curved surfaces and used with scintillating effect from about 1800 to 1820 — required fine-quality metal for its perfect display. During the reign of William IV it enjoyed a second vogue, on the period's lavishly cut luxury glass.

Plain vertical fluting (fig. 126), slightly concave, was a popular decorative motif throughout this period, both alone and associated with various diamond patterns. Reeding, those convex half-sections of cylindrical columns requiring metal of thick section for effective display and known to many collectors as pillared flutes (fig. 126), was used in broad bands between about 1790 and 1805.

Printies (fig. 116) constituted another favourite theme for the Georgian glass-cutter. These circular concavities may dot the entire surface of a bowl, encircle its rim, or glistern in two or three rows on jug or decanter. Major-General H. T. MacMullen of Waterford says that the term 'should really be "punties" which is used in the Waterford pattern sheets and is so called from its resemblance to the ground-off mark left by the punty-iron'.

Another well-used aid to refraction was the herring-bone fringe (fig. 227b), known to some collectors as blazes. These upright or slanting lines cut in an alternation of crest and trough are often found associated with strawberry cutting (fig. 227d). The formally arranged upright grooves known as splits are found associated with other motifs such as stars.

In addition many other motifs ornamented the surface of flint-glass table-ware, some of the better known being arched pillars (fig. 227a): swag and line cutting; rows of semi-circles; basket-weavings; geometric patterns composed of eight-, twelve-, sixteen- or twenty-four-pointed stars; fans and festoons. Great quantities of flint-glass were enriched with numerous combinations of cut motifs to produce a scintillating prismatic display beneath the newly instituted gas chandeliers.

Edge-cutting continued in the form of scalloping (fig. 280) as before, but by 1790 more ornate trefoil scalloping had become a characteristic rim ornament, continuing until about 1805. Scalloping then became outmoded by the celebrated escallop rim known also as the platen shell or fan-cut edge (fig. 287). The turned-over rim cut with flutes and facets also belongs to this period (fig. 123 top).

The cutting-wheel was operated by a wheel-boy or woman turning a large driving-wheel connected by a leather belt to a pulley fixed on the cutting-wheel spindle (fig. 28). An experienced turner operated the wheel at unvarying speeds. The introduction of steam power and cone-pulleys into glass-cutting mills dates from about 1807. The first steam-engine designed specially for operating machine tools developed six horse-power and was built by the firm of Dixon, Maid Lane, Southwark. There is no evidence that such an engine was associated with glass-cutting earlier than 1807 when William Wilson, 40 Blackfriars Road, London, issued a trade card advertising his 'Steam Mills for Cut Glass' and illustrating all-over diamond-cutting. The London Post Office Directory for 1811, compiled in the previous year, lists thirty-nine glass-cutters operating by hand-power, but Wilson appears to be the only one using steam power. Francis Buckley refers to a firm in Bristol operating a steam-driven glass-cutting mill in 1810.

The power-driven cutting-wheel, rotating at greater speed, enabled glass-cutters to produce deep, symmetrical sharp-angled cutting in much less time. The use of the cone-pulley gave variations of speed with consequent greater flexibility. Removal of the entire original surface of this annealed glass was found immensely to enhance its prismatic effect.

The cutter worked from a drawing: in addition, the pattern was drawn in hair-lines upon the clear, smooth-surfaced blank with black japan well thinned with turpentine, or a mixture of resin, red lead, and turpentine. Excess colour resulting from applying the medium too thickly was liable to cause the whirling wheel to drag and blur the outlines being cut.

The cutter sat at a cutting-frame (fig. 28) pressing the curved surface of the glass along the edge of a soft-iron wheel rotating upon a horizontal spindle, spinning away from him and fed with a fine stream of wet sand from a conical overhead hopper. The abrasive edge of the sanded cutting-wheel was visible to the operator through the transparent glass. Until the introduction of steam power much glass was cut underhand: advertisements for glass-cutters might specify 'overhand' or 'underhand' operators. Skilful craftsmanship was essential to prevent sand from cutting so deeply into the glass that the resulting scratches could not be removed. The presence of this flaw in a specimen suggests its having been cut at Stourbridge, Birmingham or Sheffield early in the nineteenth century. After the pattern had been cut to the required shape and depth, the rough surface produced by the abrasive was smoothed with a blue-stone wheel moistened with water and dressed when required with either powdered pumice stone or rotten stone.

The action of these wheels left the glass smooth but dully white: transparency was restored by polishing on a wheel of willow wood fed with putty powder and water. Uniformity of brilliance was accomplished by finishing on a rouge-fed wheel lined with cork or felt.

Little cutting was carried out in glass-houses before the introduction of steam cutting-mills. The cut-glass manufactories bought glass blanks from the glass-houses, decorated them to their own design, and sold them to glass-sellers and export merchants. Such factories might employ as many as fifty men and women. The wheel-operated glass-cutters, in a smaller way of business and sometimes working in their own homes assisted by the family, received small consignments of blanks from glass-sellers, decorating these to commission. By the 1830's nearly the whole of this work was being carried out in the flint-glass houses.

Difficulty is often experienced in distinguishing antique cut-glass from modern hand-cut productions displaying the same motifs. At least one firm has copied the greyish hue of early glass, but decorated it with relief cutting in the early-nineteenth-century style. The old cut-glass takes to itself the reflected colour of surrounding objects. Modern cut-glass lacks the richness and fullness of the old, although prismatic colour may be even more brilliant than in late-Georgian flint-glass.

Figure 116

ILLUSTRATIONS OF SIX KINDS OF CUTTING

Top row: (*a*) Fine diamonds; (*b*) large shallow diamonds; (*c*) cross-cut diamonds.

Bottom row: (*a*) Chequered diamonds; (*b*) strawberry diamonds; (*c*) printies.

Figures 117–20

PUNCH GLASSES AND WATER-JUGS

(117)   Handled cup containing Apsley Pellatt crystal cameos of George III and the Prince Regent, between panels of finely cut diamonds; 1819–20. Height 4 inches.
Reproduced by Gracious Permission of Her Majesty the Queen

(118)   Handled punch glass, from a set of flint-glass table-ware made for Queen Charlotte, whose crowned cypher it bears; base encircled with shallow fluting and rim with deep border of gold; 1770's.
Reproduced by Gracious Permission of Her Majesty the Queen

(119)   Water-jug, its lower half cut with large relief diamonds; rim and handle notched; 1820's.
By courtesy of Messrs Delomosne & Son Ltd

(120)   Jug on square pedestal base, decorated with wheel-engraving and inscribed 'A Trifle from Yarmouth' and 'A Trip to the Fort'. An earthenware mug exists with the same design and inscription signed by Absolon, a ceramic decorator of Yarmouth; *c*. 1800.
By courtesy of Mr Howard Phillips

Figures 121, 122

CUT-GLASS OF THE EARLY NINETEENTH CENTURY

(121)   Pairs of castors and boat-shaped salt-cellars.
In the Corning Museum of Glass

(122)   Pair of covered, footed bowls lavishly cut with diamonds; and a cylindrical three-footed tea-caddy bowl cut with strawberry diamonds.

161

Figure 123

A COLLECTION OF LATE GEORGIAN CUT-GLASS

Top left and right: Pair of pickle-jars, the turned-over rim cut with alternating prisms; body cut with circuits of shallow facets; domed cover cut to match; square foot with spool stem. Early nineteenth century. Height 11½ inches.

Top centre: Covered urn, on square foot with hexagonal-cut dome. About 1800. Height 18 inches.

All in the Author's collection

Centre: Pair of covered urns with square stepped feet. Height 18 inches.

By courtesy of Messrs Delomosne & Son Ltd

Lower left: Sugar-bowl moulded and cut, with horizontal lip encircled with fan escallop border motif; circular foot and with radial flutes beneath.

Lower centre: Butter-dish with lid.

Lower right: Glass piggin used for butter, sugar, and so on, with cut edges notched and encircled with short vertical prismatic cutting; body cut with bands of relief diamonds and vertical prismatic cutting.

All in the Cecil Higgins Museum, Bedford

Figure 124

A collection of early-nineteenth-century cut-glass: water-jugs, cream jugs, celery vase, toilet bottles, honey jars, and butter-dish with cover.

By courtesy of Messrs Delomosne & Son Ltd

Figures 125, 126

WATER-JUGS OF TYPES MADE BY ENGLISH AND IRISH GLASS-HOUSES FROM ABOUT 1820

(125) *Top left:* Base encircled with pillar flutes; body with strawberry diamonds, neck with horizontal prismatic cutting; helmet spout with notched rim.

Top centre: With hollow pedestal; banded with relief diamonds and horizontal prismatic cutting; extended helmet spout with scalloped rim.

Top right: Cut with large relief diamonds; plain neck above two rows of prismatic cutting; plain rim.

(126) *Lower left:* Sunk rings separating bands of hollowed flutes; vertical prismatic cutting at each end of the handle; helmet-shaped spout with scalloped rim.

Lower centre: With fluted base; large diamonds in relief with sunk rings above and below; straight rim, scallop-cut.

Lower right: Body hollow-fluted with horizontal prism cutting above; helmet spout with notched rim.

By courtesy of Messrs Delomosne & Son Ltd

Figures 127–9

(127) Firing-glass, its heavy straight-sided drawn bowl engraved with Masonic emblems and the Garter ribbon enclosing the letter s cut against a matted ground, and surmounted by a ducal coronet; heavy disc foot. Originally made for Augustus Frederick, Duke of Sussex (1773–1843). Early nineteenth century.

In the Victoria and Albert Museum

(128) Water-glass and saucer with fan escallop borders. Early nineteenth century.

In the Corning Museum of Glass

(129) Toddy lifter, body cut with strawberry diamonds surrounding a medallion engraved as on adjacent glass; neck and stem cut with shallow flutes; three stem rings cut with plain diamonds. Early nineteenth century.

In the Victoria and Albert Museum

CHAPTER NINE

DECORATION: GILDING

ENRY VIII was an enthusiastic collector of Venetian glass, taking
special pleasure in ornamental table-ware enriched with gold leaf.
The cost of such an assemblage was immense, but by the 1580's
London-made drinking-glasses enriched with gilding could be sold at a
price that brought them within the reach of prosperous countrymen and
merchants. Richard Belassis, a yeoman of Houghton-in-the-Spring,
Durham, in his will dated 1596 made reference to his 'studie where all the
gilt glass do stand'. Late-Elizabethan wills and inventories suggest that
gilded glass was customarily displayed in glass cases.

Elizabethan drinking-glasses in the Venetian style were made by Jacob
Verzelini in his glass-house at Crutched Friars, London. This gracefully
designed and fragile glass was enhanced by diamond-engraving and gilding
with gold leaf. Traces of gilding are visible on at least three of the dozen
specimens known to remain. The earliest of these, dated 1586 and in the
British Museum (fig. 7), has a short bell-shaped bowl with signs of gilding
on the bowl rim and stem. A drinking-goblet in the collection of the Duke of
Northumberland was originally covered with gilded decoration. Although
this is much worn the arms of the Vintners' Company remain, together with
the name 'Wenyfrid Geares' and the date 1590. The diamond-engraved
'Barbara Potter' drinking-glass in the Victoria and Albert Museum is dated
1602; this has signs of gilding on the bowl rim and lower stem.

It must be assumed that little, if any, English-made table glass was gilded
during the period between the deaths of Elizabeth I in 1603 and Mary II in
1695 for no authentic examples appear to have been recorded. English
table glass from the 1680's was made chiefly from the newly introduced
flint-glass, thicker, heavier, and more resonant than any earlier glass.
Gilding ornamented such glass throughout the eighteenth century and was
at the height of its glory between about 1760 and 1790. Collectors, by
carefully noting the changes in the industrial processes, will be able to
distinguish the methods of gilding employed and class their specimens
accordingly.

It is probable that some flint-glass was gold illumined at the turn of the century, following the publication of *Art of Glass* by H. Blancourt, first in French, then in English during 1699. Here was outlined a method of permanent gilding by a process requiring more than usual skill, and consequently very costly. Enamellers often carried out this work.

The glass surface to be gilded was thinly coated with a weak solution of fine gum arabic and allowed to dry. By breathing upon this the gilder rendered the gum slightly sticky, so that the gold leaf could be blown upon it and then pressed down with cotton wool. This was dampened with borax water and then dusted with an impalpable powder of a glass which fused at a lower temperature than the fusing point of the object being decorated. The gilder necessarily required to know the fusing temperature of the basic flint-glass which at that period was subject to a wide variation in quality. The glass was now placed on an iron plate, covered with an inverted glass bowl, placed at the entrance to an enamelling furnace, and heated gently. When hot it was moved into the furnace, remaining there until red hot. The powdered glass thereupon fused, covering the gold with a protective film of transparent glass. Gradually the iron plate was drawn from the furnace and allowed to cool slowly at the entrance. Blancourt described such gilding as 'so fine that nothing in Nature can spoil it, unless it be broken'.

It was, of course, impossible to burnish gilding applied in this way. Such decoration usually appeared in the form of gold bands encircling bowl rim and foot rim. An early George I gilt-rimmed wineglass with a heavy baluster stem rising from a highly domed and folded foot (fig. 103) is in the collection of Her Majesty the Queen.

The much less costly and more lustrous japanned gilding illumined flint-glass throughout the reigns of the first two Georges. Unfortunately this gilding was very impermanent and little remains in mint condition. Such gilding on London-made glass was advertised in the Boston *News Letter* as early as 1723 and 1725 as 'japanning in gold'. But, contrary to the opinion of various authorities, it was subjected to a firing process.

The gold was cut from the leaf and applied to the glass by means of an adhesive such as japanner's size. This was fired in the same way as japanning on metal. Before burnishing the gold was scoured with a stipple dipped in fine wet sand as a test for permanency. If under-fired or insufficiently hardened the burnished gold would quickly lose its brilliance and regilding was essential: if over-fired the gold would not adhere to the glass.

Burnishing was a highly important process in this and all later gilding

166

as customers were only attracted by a highly lustrous gold. It was achieved by means of brisk rubbing with a bloodstone, agate, dog's tooth, or steel burnisher set in a wooden handle. So impermanent was japanned gilding, however, that direct burnishing tended to wear the gold from the varnish. The burnisher was therefore applied over a piece of smooth paper laid upon the gold.

Golden rims encircled bowls and feet of drinking-glasses, narrow until about 1750 (fig. 106), then wider (fig. 99). Wheel-engraving of the 1730's and later might be gilded to add radiance to the arabesques, vine borders, flowers, and foliage which might encircle the upper part of drinking-glass bowls (fig. 41). Coats of arms and cyphers might also be gilded. Traces of gold are sometimes to be detected by careful inspection of such engraving. During the late 1740's the demand for English gilding declined and little was produced during the next ten years.

The establishment of porcelain factories in England around the mid-century encouraged specialist enamellers and gilders to set up workshops for decorating china and glass to the commission of retailers. These workers gradually improved the permanence of gilding on glass. By 1755 gold leaf was being ground with one-third its weight in honey or other flux and tempered with oil of lavender. This was painted upon the glass with a pencil brush and fixed by gentle firing. The presence of the flux, however, destroyed the rich brilliance of the gold, imparting to it a slight dullness which burnishing did little to improve. A further disadvantage was that the presence of the flux raised the gold appreciably above the surface of the glass, a defect not found with gold-leaf gilding. Gold containing as little alloy as possible was essential for this work: the standard of purity was guaranteed by the use of golden guineas reduced to thin leaves by beating. Honey gilding was much harder than japanned gilding, even to the extent of withstanding scraping. But, being considerably less lustrous than japanned gilding, it achieved little popularity on glass, competing as it did with the permanent and highly brilliant German gilding.

Robert Dossie in 1758 recorded that 'drinking-glasses with gilt edges and other ornaments are now coming again extremely into fashion', and Doctor Lewis, the eminent early-Georgian scientist, noted three years later that English gilt glass was then 'as durable and with as fine a lustre as gilding imported from Bohemia and Thuringia'. This new gilding was basically an improved japanned gilding of German origin, the fixing medium being amber varnish which did not require firing.

Amber of fine quality was crushed to a powder and placed in a wide-mouthed glass jar with twice its bulk in olive oil. Jar and contents were then placed in a copper digester partly filled with water. The cover, which contained a valve, was screwed down tightly and the digester placed over a moderate fire for five or six hours. By then the amber was completely dissolved and when cold became a transparent, gelatinous mass. This was vigorously stirred with four or five times its bulk in oil of turpentine and then put aside for several days during which any undissolved grains of amber sank to the bottom. The varnish was then decanted for use.

To make the amber varnish adhere firmly upon the glass surface, the gilder ground with it a little white lead immediately before use. A thin film of this was brush-applied to the glass and left to dry for about a day. The glass was then placed in a stove until almost hot enough to burn the fingers when handled. The varnish had by then become glutinous: the gold leaf was applied in the usual way. The gilded glass was stored in a warm room until the varnish was hard, a matter of six to nine months. *The Tradesman* for 1809 states that this method of gilding glass was still the best, providing good-quality varnish was used, as the gold was fixed more evenly than in any other way.

The gold was then burnished by direct application of the burnishing tool rubbed in one direction only and immediately producing a lustre which continued as burnishing increased. A cloth dipped into a solution of whiting was used occasionally to clean the golden surface. To ensure extra brilliance for their gold some gilders polished the glass surfaces immediately beneath the rim bands before applying the leaf. Gilding applied in this way was consistently advertised until the late 1780's as London-gilt flint-glass.

In addition to golden bands encircling rim and foot, drinking-glasses were also illuminated with coats of arms and pictures such as oriental subjects, pastorals, landscapes, classical, allegorical, social, sporting, and historic scenes. Gilding might be the sole decorative form on glass table-ware, but more frequently it is found in association with wheel-engraving, faceting, cutting, or enamelling. A rich man's luxury was the vogue for handsome armorial glasses, their gold-rimmed bowls displaying coats of arms in colourful enamels enclosed within showy engraved and gilded cartouches. Gilding is found on decorative rims encircling cut-glass bowls, on the bodies of decanters, and the shoulders and stoppers of square toilet bottles. The blue glass of Bristol and elsewhere was frequently enriched with gilding (fig. 285). Engraved inscriptions were gilded on christening and other commemorative goblets. On covered drinking-glasses gold rim bands were matched by similar decoration on the closely fitting cover rims, thus

124   A collection of early-nineteenth-century cut-glass, including water-jugs, cream jugs, celery vase, toilet bottles, honey jars, and covered butter-dish

125, 126 Water-jugs of types made by English and Irish glass-houses from about 1820

170

127–129 Firing-glass, toddy lifter, and water-glass with saucer

171

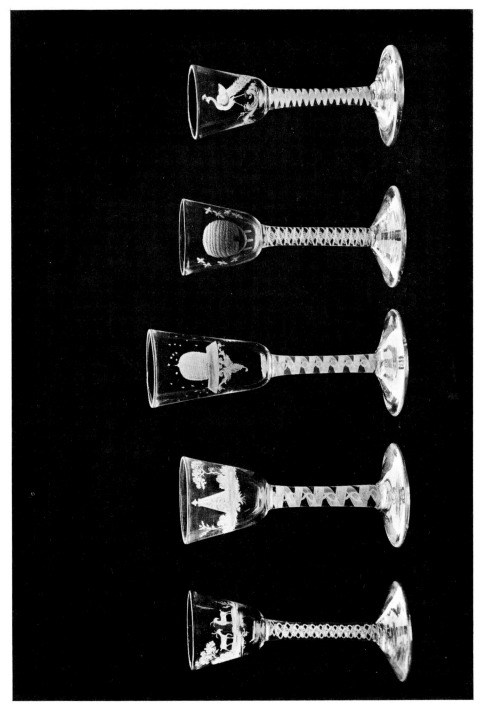

130   Drinking-glasses painted with scenes in white enamel

enriching each complete vessel with a wide encircling band of burnished gold (fig. 98). Several such drinking-glasses are in the collection of Her Majesty the Queen at Buckingham Palace. When gilt-rimmed drinking-glasses of this period have had but little use the gold remaining intact displays almost its original brilliance.

A less expensive method of gilding glass came into use from about 1780, although the *Dictionarium Polygraphicum,* published in 1735, contains incomplete instructions regarding the process. William Parker, the Fleet Street glass-seller, advertised glass gilded in this way as 'ornamented with an entire new Golden Lustre'. This was the now universally practised method of mercury gilding which, for more than a century, was a dangerous health hazard to all employed in the work.

The gilder prepared an amalgam of fine gold and mercuric oxide in equal weights. These were well rubbed together with some alcohol and a little bismuth subnitrate, and dried at a temperature no greater than 100 degrees Centigrade. The amalgam was then rubbed to a smooth soft paste with fat oil and applied to the glass with a pencil brush and fired. Firing drove off the mercury in vapour form, leaving a film of 'dead gold' on the glass surface. This, when cold, was given a high lustre by burnishing. Mercury gilding may be distinguished from others by its brassy appearance. Laid on heavily, such gilding could be chased. This was the only Georgian gilding which could withstand normal wear and decades of washing.

Genuine old flint-glass is sometimes given a fictitious value by the addition of gilding. Examples noted have been gilded with liquid gold requiring no burnishing. This gold, first used in about 1850, has a sparkling brilliance easy to recognize.

Figure 130

Drinking-glasses painted with scenes in white enamel: (*a*) Ogee bowl enamelled with a fishing scene, on white opaque-twist stem and plain foot; *c*. 1760. Height 5¾ inches. (*b*) Ogee bowl, enamelled with skating scene, on white opaque-twist stem and plain foot; *c*. 1760. Height 5¼ inches. (*c*) Goblet with bucket bowl enamelled with hunting scene, on opaque lace-twist outlined, and plain foot; *c*. 1770. Height 7⅜ inches. (*d*) Ogee bowl enamelled with a shooting scene, on white opaque-twist stem, and plain foot; *c*. 1760. Height 5¾ inches. (*e*) Round funnel bowl enamelled with sheep and landscape, on opaque and air-twist stem; *c*. 1770. Height 6¾ inches.

By courtesy of Messrs Christie, Manson & Woods Ltd

Figures 131, 132

ENAMELLED DRINKING-GLASSES OF THE 1760's–1770's

(131) (*a*) Tumbler enamelled in white, with a butterfly in flight, and a pheasant perched on a tree; height 6 inches. (*b*) Ogee bowl enamelled in white with a border of scroll acanthus leaves; opaque-twist stem with lace spiral within six-thread spiral; plain foot; height 6 inches. (*c*) Small tumbler enamelled with foliage and flowers suspending Masonic emblems in red, yellow, and white; height 3 inches. (*d*) Drawn trumpet bowl white enamelled with border of grapes and vine-leaves; opaque-twist multi-spiral stem; plain foot; height 6¾ inches.

Formerly in the Berney Collection

(132) (*a*) Ogee bowl enamelled in white with scene; opaque-twist stem, open lace-spiral within a double corkscrew; plain foot. (*b*) Ogee bowl enamelled in white with scene; opaque-twist stem, close lace-twist within double spiral. (*c*) Round funnel bowl, enamelled in white with sheep; opaque-twist stem, open lace-spiral within double corkscrew; domed and folded foot.

By courtesy of Messrs Christie, Manson & Woods Ltd

Figure 133

Heraldic goblets enamelled in colours: bucket bowls, opaque white-twist stems and plain feet.
Left: Arms of Buckmaster.
Centre: Inscribed Thos. Vauhan and Plymouth Dock.
Right: Arms of Turner of Kirkleatham.

In the Cecil Higgins Museum, Bedford

CHAPTER TEN

DECORATION: ENAMELLING

WINE CONNOISSEURS seem united in their opinion that decoration detracts from the beauty of the liquor seen through the bowl of a drinking-glass. Yet for twenty-five years enamelling in white and in colours enlivened the bowls of English drinking-glasses, in addition to gilding and wheel-engraving. At a glance white-enamelled decoration might resemble deep wheel-engraving, for which at first it was a cheap alternative, but with coloured enamels some fine illuminated effects were possible.

No evidence exists that the art of enamelling glass was practised in England earlier than the 1720's. The earliest references to English enamelling are to be found in the *New England Journal* in 1731 and subsequent years where 'fine glass white japann'd' is advertised among consignments of London-made flint-glass arriving in Boston. Japanning was at that time a fashionable art in England; the famous Pontypool japan works had been recently established, japanners were working in Bilston and Wolverhampton, and numerous small japanners were established in London and elsewhere, all decorating sheet iron and copper. But, in view of the wide use of the term 'japanning' to various types of painting on wood in the eighteenth century, it seems more probable that the word was even more loosely applied to what was in fact white enamel decoration.

The earliest reference to enamelled glass in England so far noted is to a pair of enamelled rummers which in 1758 cost 2s. In the same year, Robert Dossie was advising on the art of enamelling on flint-glass, insisting that the glass 'should be of the first degree of hardness, but at the same time colourless and without specks and wavings'. It was obviously essential that the vitrification of the applied enamel should take place at a temperature lower than would be required to melt the glass vessel which it decorated.

The medium used in white enamel decoration at this time was obtained by melting down white Venetian glass imported in the form of goblets, vases, and so on. This glass, according to Dossie, melted at a temperature considerably lower than that required to melt ordinary flint-glass, and also possessed a 'milky turgidness . . . coming nearer to translucency than any of the opake kinds made at present'. Coarser enamels were advertised at this period by such firms as Hughes & Brettel, Gravel Lane Glass-house, Southwark.

English enamel decoration was of two styles: a thinly applied wash enamel made from Venetian opaque glass, and a dense full-white enamel thickly applied (fig. 130). The wash decoration, because of its rarity, is considered by some authorities to be the earlier: more likely it was a passing vogue. Such details as the veining of leaves were accomplished by removing enamel with a fine needle.

Decorations appear to have followed contemporary tastes, the style of their work in white enamel suggesting that it was regarded as a cheap and speedy alternative to wheel-engraving. Books of designs intended for japanners, porcelain-enamellers, and the like proved invaluable to glass-enamellers.

The Ladies Amusement or Whole Art of Japanning (Pillement), published in 1760, was a source for many of the rococo scrolls, birds and animals, pastoral scenes (figs. 131, 132), classic ruins (fig. 132), hunting (fig. 130), skating, and similar pastimes that were adapted for enamelling upon flint-glass. Designs more specifically suited to drinking-glasses followed the vine-leaves and grapes (fig. 131 left), the hop and barley, and the like noted in wheel-engraving. On a shouldered decanter enamel might be used to depict a wine-label, enclosed within an elaborate cartouche and balanced on the other side of the vessel by a floral spray (fig. 221 lower centre).

Decorations in white enamel are mainly found on plain-footed ogee drinking-glasses often with white (fig. 130) or colour-twist stems. Occasional air-twists have been noted. The earliest japanned decoration probably copied the naturalistic flower and vine motifs encircling the rims of engraved glasses. Similar decoration is found in early white enamelling: motifs fashionable between 1750 and 1780 include a wide variety of sporting subjects and conventional scenes. Cordial glasses for the tea equipage were enamelled with Chinese figures and scenes, presumably intended to harmonize with contemporary porcelain decoration and other chinoiseries.

In the most magnificent specimens, coats of arms in vivid colours (fig. 133) decorated both the decanters and the bowls of wineglasses *en suite*. Such work was executed by enamellers whose advertisements may be found in newspapers and journals of the period. The number of announcements to be found between 1765 and 1780 proves a great demand for coloured armorial work as an alternative to engraving. Porcelain enamellers

176

also advertised their ability to enamel armorial and other devices on flint-glass table-ware.

The most celebrated enameller on flint-glass was William Beilby, junior (1740–1819), of Newcastle upon Tyne. To Beilby falls the credit for first decorating flint-glass in colour as an advance on the simple white designs. Before 1762 he was decorating tall goblets on plain stems with the royal arms, using intense white and vivid colours: these were possibly George III coronation pieces. Then he began to enamel armorial glasses in colours with mantlings of 'pulled thread work'. With his sister Mary he was decorating Newcastle glass until 1778. Some of his work is signed by name, and a life-like butterfly — again a typical motif of the period, largely featured in Pillement's *Ladies Amusement* — is generally regarded as a mark of a product from the Beilby *ménage*.

Following contemporary popular tastes, many of these designs on wineglass bowls closely resemble those decorating enamelled ware such as snuff-boxes, etuis, and the like, then being produced in abundance in South Staffordshire and Birmingham. W. A. Thorpe, writing on 'The Beilby Glasses' in *The Connoisseur* dated January 1928, notes that 'William Beilby had learned enamelling and painting at Birmingham . . . and he subsequently taught these arts to his younger brother Thomas and his sister Mary'. Albrathar Hawkes of Dudley, well known as an enameller and gilder of flint-glass from 1766, worked but three miles from the enamellers of Bilston. It is not unlikely that experienced Bilston enamel decorators were called upon to ornament Hawkes' flint-glass. The processes were identical.

Glass decorated with coloured enamels needed to be of a harder metal than was usual. Containing as it did more than 30 per cent of lead oxide, ordinary flint-glass was liable to distortion in firing. Vessels for enamelling were blown from a special flint-glass prepared in one of the piling-pots. They were probably the productions of three or at most four glass-houses, thus accounting for similarity in shapes of drinking-glass bowls used for this purpose; ogee or bucket shape appears to have been usual.

Glass-enamellers prepared their own colours at this period, using as a base dense optical glass, softer than ordinary flint-glass and giving greater brilliancy to the finished colours. This transparent glass was coloured by fusing it with metallic oxides. After being crushed to a fine powder these enamels were washed not fewer than eight times, the lighter portions, so microscopic that they would pass through the finest of hair filters, being removed in the form of mud. Their presence in the enamel would produce

177

minute air bubbles and give the fired enamel a cloudy appearance. The dried enamel was then mixed with a fluid, such as oil of lavender, which would enable the powder to be worked with a pencil brush and bind it to the ground, and yet be sufficiently volatile to evaporate without leaving a trace.

After each application of an enamel colour the glass was placed in a mufflle or reverberatory furnace, and the enamel fused into a thin film of colour. During firing the colour was carefully matched. As the glass became hot the enamel darkened and gradually appeared to be sweating. It then changed to a smooth shining colour. The metallic oxides varied in the temperature at which the various hues were induced. The technical skill of the enameller lay in familiarity with the exact melting-point of each vitrifiable colour in a day when precision instruments for this purpose were unknown. Each successively applied colour was fired at a lower temperature than those already applied, to ensure that the latter remained unaffected by the heat. Over-firing caused previously applied colours to blend into each other, and beauty and brilliancy of finish were also destroyed.

The original colours underwent a great change in firing so that the enameller painted in colours very different from those displayed in the finished decoration. Rose and crimson, for instance, when applied were a drab violet: firing converted these enamels through brown to a dull reddish hue until the correct tint was reached. Enamellers applied their colours as thinly as possible for thick coatings were liable to split during cooling.

Enamel decoration on flint-glass continued into the nineteenth century. Samuel Anness, Red Lion Place, London, advertised in 1805 that he enamelled glass 'by using a degree of heat not so considerable as to injure the vessels themselves'. This seems to suggest that 'burning' the enamel on flint-glass adversely affected its strength, thus accounting for its otherwise inexplicable rarity. The colours used by Anness included green, black, yellow, blue, olive, white, purple, rose, and brown. In 1806 Isaac Jacobs of Bristol, 'Glass Manufacturer to His Majesty', advertised 'Coats of Arms, Crests and Cyphers done (upon glass) in the greatest style, by some of the first Artists in the Kingdom'.

CHAPTER ELEVEN

ROMERS AND RUMMERS

THREE ENTIRELY DIFFERENT GLASSES — different in style, in purpose, and in age — have come down to us under the name of rummer. These are the English adaptation of the German *roemer*, for hock (fig. 134); the Georgian all-purpose drinking-rummer (fig. 141); and the toddy rummer (fig. 138).

The English version of the German *roemer*, although seventeenth-century writers spelled it 'rummer', had no association with the spirit, rum. It was intended to contain straw-coloured Rhenish wine and was probably introduced to the court of Charles I by that connoisseur of German wines, Sir Anthony Vandyke. Gayton in his *Pleasure Notes*, 1654, ordered 'a lusty rummer of Rhenish'; Davenant in *Man's the Master*, 1668, exclaimed 'then give him but a rummer . . . and he will drink so kindly, as if he had the heart of a whale'; Dryden in 1673 wrote 'then Rhenish rummers walk the round'; E. Ward in *Wooden World Dissertations*, 1706, recorded that he drank 'a large rummer of Rhenish and sugar'. Several London taverns devoted to the sale of Rhenish wines were known under the sign of 'The Rummer' in the late seventeenth century. Matthew Prior the poet (1664–1721) lived for several years before 1685 with his uncle Samuel Prior, landlord of the Rummer, Old Fish Street, near Charing Cross, and there is record of a tavern of this name in Bow Lane, Cheapside, in 1709. Bristol boasted four Rummer taverns, and Liverpool two.

The German *roemer* was made from pale green glass in varying soft tones, the vessel consisting of a bowl more or less spherical in shape with a slice removed from the top, so that the circle of the rim was smaller than the greatest swell of the bowl. This opened into a hollow cylindrical stem studded with strawberry prunts and supported by a hollow conical foot. A crimped thread of glass usually concealed the bowl-stem junction, and the foot was shaped by coiling plain threads of glass round a core of wood. This basic form was adapted by various European countries to suit their own national requirements.

The *roemer* had no great popularity in England, although recognized

179

as a type by the Company of Glass-sellers. In John Greene's working drawings (see Chapter 1), *roemers* are illustrated and referred to in the production list as *Rnish* (Rhenish) wineglasses. There is no record of such *roemers* being made in England at that period, but it is not improbable that some London glass-houses of Charles II's period made such ware in green-tinted soda-glass. When flint-glass was evolved and marketed during the late 1670's the design was adapted to suit the new metal. It has been found convenient to call this by its contemporaneous name romer.

The first truly English design in flint-glass appeared as a capacious goblet, its almost spherical bowl incurved at the rim and supported by a thick, hollow stem, vertically ribbed, and ornamented with six strawberry prunts. This stem rose from a ribbed pedestal foot with a narrow fold, and opened into the bowl, the junction being concealed beneath a narrow wavy collar. The bowl, which had a depth about equal to the height of stem and foot, might be vertically ribbed (fig. 14), 'nipt diamond wais' (fig. 15), or entirely plain. This pattern was approved by the Company of Glass-sellers, and those made at the Savoy Glass-house by George Ravenscroft between 1678 and 1681 display an applied raven seal on the stem (figs. 14 and 15).

Early in the 1680's the bowl was partitioned from the stem, which, however, still remained thick and hollow. By the mid-1680's this hollow design was replaced by a solid stem, thinner but still ornamented with strawberry prunts and rising from a flat folded foot, which had a diameter equal to that of the incurved bowl rim. The base of the bowl was now ornamented with applied gadrooning in the style of contemporary silver (fig. 134).

By 1690 the basal gadrooning of the bowl was moulded into its metal and the stem might be of baluster form such as appeared on contemporary wineglasses (fig. 135). The folded foot might now be conical. During the early years of the eighteenth century the incurved gadrooned bowls tended to become shallower. Plain stems were usual between 1720 and 1740.

The Hanoverian influence brought colour to these flint-glass vessels, imitating the sea-green tinge of the imported German *roemers* which again had a brief vogue: English tints varied from a popular pale hue to the occasional deep green. The formula for colouring glass a sea-green shade was given by Blancourt in his *Art of Glass*, 1699. Tovey in his manual *Wines*, 1856, quotes the early-Georgian saying: 'fill a rummer with old hock: let other wines have daylight through the glass'.

Opaque-twist stems carrying gadrooned bowls with incurved rims appeared by 1750 (fig. 137). In some of these the bowl was tinted sea-green

180

with a conical foot of the same colour. Gadrooning gradually disappeared from the sea-green bowl leaving it entirely plain on a stem which might be double-knop air-twist or one of the many types of opaque-twists. These very un-English glasses continued to be made until the 1770's, being listed as hock glasses.

During the Regency period the Edinburgh and Leith Glass Company, Leith, issued pattern books, printed upon paper watermarked with the date 1811, illustrating prunted hollow-stemmed vessels resembling the English adaptations of the *roemer* produced by the early makers of flint-glass (fig. 138). All were catalogued as *romers* in current production. Rummers were listed separately and were priced at 2s. a pound; with square feet 2s. 2d. a pound.

Festive, convivial occasions of Georgian days calling for such long drinks as rumbo, rum shrub, rumfustion, and the like, were celebrated with English rummers. These vessels had capacious ovoid bowls on short stems and were soon taken into general use for mulled wines, cider, and so on, where large drinking-glasses were required. A writer in 1782 tells of a visitor to a wayside inn who 'ordered in a bottle of the best port the beggarly place could produce and tossed it off in an ecstasy of two rummers'. Such a rummer, then, was of half-bottle capacity. Engravings of the period illustrate these rummers equally in connection with comfortable social occasions around the domestic fireside, with tavern scenes, and with rowdy hunting feasts.

Rum, under its original name of rumbullion, had been a common drink in England from about 1640. The Domestic State Papers of the Cromwellian regime refer several times to its importation, and soon a drink composed of one part rum and two parts water was highly favoured. The Commissioner of Revenue in 1666 recorded the success of the rum tax and the fact that two qualities were being imported, 'clean' and 'german'. The best-quality rum was noted by Hughes in *Physitian*, 1672, as being 'stronger than Spirits of Wine'. The existence of rum-punch houses was first noted in the Domestic State Papers of 1678.

Admiral Vernon in 1740 ordered that all sailors under his command should dilute their daily ration of rum with six parts of water. Because the admiral ostentatiously wore a cloak of grogram he had long been nicknamed 'Old Grog'. What more natural than to give the diluted naval rum the name of grog? In civilian life it became known as 'seven-water grog' to distinguish it from the two-to-one rum drunk by the general public, usually from tumblers. In 1777 the Treasury paid John Blackburn £9,062. 18s. 6d. for '68,000 gallons of Rum from the Islands of Antigua, St. Kitts, Montserrat, and Nevis'. This approximated half a crown a gallon.

Georgian rummers follow a design which probably originated in Roman goblets of similar shape, and was copied by the glassmen of Elizabethan England. Fragments of domestic glass-ware were revealed by excavations at Woodchester Glass-house, Gloucestershire, of which records exist proving its operation early in the seventeenth century. When reconstructed by Mr H. J. Powell, these fragments formed goblets of the rummer type with ovoid bowls supported by trumpet-shaped blown pedestals, their foot rims strengthened by up-turned folds. Woodcuts of the early seventeenth century occasionally illustrate similar goblets: by the mid-century short straight stems and circular feet were depicted in association with ovoid bowls.

This form is not noted in flint-glass until the 1740's when Marcellus Laroon recorded such a glass in his painting 'The Dinner Party' (fig. 33), now in the collection of Her Majesty the Queen. The earliest newspaper reference found by Buckley appeared in the *General Advertiser*, 1769, and differentiated between rummers and punch glasses. Their production in large numbers was made commercially profitable only by the discovery that flint-glass twice annealed was tougher and stronger than any transparent glass previously made.

The thinly blown bowls of early rummers were of generous proportions, ovoid with strongly curved sides, and supported by short drawn stems rising from plain round feet. They were satisfying to the eye and friendly to the hand (fig. 150). The short stem in such a two-piece rummer carried the centre of gravity near to the table, permitting the use of a relatively small foot at a time when glassmen were making long-stemmed drinking-glasses with bowl and foot diameters approximately equal.

The two-piece rummer shown in fig. 141 is typical of a style made throughout the collector's period. This specimen, with several others, came from the Cross Keys tavern, Wednesfield Heath, Wolverhampton, where it is known to have been in use during the year 1800. Edward Giles, an ironmaster who owned the Cross Keys and its adjoining pawnshop in the 1840's, found the survivors, engraved his name on their bowls with a diamond ring, and carried them to his new house opposite, where they remained until 1940. The Cross Keys, in common with other contemporary taverns, also possessed a set of rummers bearing signatures of regular customers diamond-engraved an inch below the rim, with the name of the tavern wheel-engraved in large capitals beneath.

Rummers with drawn stems in which the lower part of the ovoid bowl is hollow-fluted are perhaps the most numerous. Early examples were hand-cut and polished on the wheel; later specimens were blown-moulded and fire-polished to give clean-cut edges to the flutes which almost invariably numbered twelve. In some instances the fluting was continued from the ovoid bowl to the short stem and both might be slightly spiralled. Occasional examples are stemless, the ovoid bowl rising directly from a low cyst on the surface of the foot. The entire surface of the bowl was sometimes fluted, but examples are now infrequent. Viewed from above the lower part of the bowl displays a petalled-flower effect, the plain circle of the stem top forming the stamens. The upper part of the bowl might be encircled with wheel-engraving in a wide range of simple motifs extending from one-quarter to one-half its depth.

The stem of the drawn rummer ended in an expanded, dome-shaped cyst. To this was welded the round foot, its diameter approximately two-thirds that of the bowl. The majority of feet were flat, others slightly conical, but beneath a high proportion of the fluted rummers is a rough punty mark, despite the fact that it was usual throughout the period for these disfigurements to be ground from drinking-vessels.

The quality of the metal varied considerably in rummers. Those blown from the finer metal gathered from the top of the melting-pot were almost unflawed and in 1811 cost 2s. a pound at the glass-house; with square feet, 2s. 2d. a pound. Those blown from tale metal taken from the bottom of the pot displayed considerable numbers of striae, cords, and bubbles in the texture of the metal. These cost 2d. a pound less and were often ill-proportioned with thick, clumsy feet.

The most costly rummer design was that with a trumpet-shaped pedestal stem and a foot measuring no more than half the diameter of the bowl rim, the edge of the foot rim being folded under for greater strength. Such vessels were blown from fine metal gathered from the piling-pots. But these stems appear to have been unable to withstand the rough and tumble of frequent use for few such fashionable rummers remain. They were illustrated on at least two glass-sellers' trade cards of the late eighteenth century.

One further style of two-piece vessel may be mentioned, a smaller version of the rummer, of a gill or less capacity. Such drinking-glasses, entered in glass-house catalogues and dobbins, were intended for gin and other spirits.

Three-piece drinking-rummers, those in which bowl, stem, and foot were shaped separately and welded into a single entity, date from the early

1780's (fig. 143). The ovoid bowl and round foot were connected by a short spool-shaped stem collared at the top for attachment to the bowl, and expanded into a spreading dome at the lower end by which it was welded to a foot that was thick, plain, and flat-surfaced. From about 1805 the underside might be star-cut, a feature more frequent after 1820.

Greater stability was given to ovoid bowl rummers from about 1790 by fitting heavy square feet, at first completely solid, then hollow beneath (fig. 151 top). The hollow reduced weight at a time when excise tax was at its highest. It was usually impressed with gadrooning, thus enriching the foot's appearance by refractive effects. The stem might consist of a cut and polished four-sided pedestal (fig. 151a) or a moulded dome which might be terraced (fig. 151b) resting on a square plinth, sometimes stepped (fig. 138). From about 1805 the underside of the solid square foot might be ornamented with a cut star.

Square feet were made in a piece with their pedestal or domed stems by a group of glass-workers known as pinchers. These men might be employed within the glass-house precincts, but more frequently they operated their own small furnaces of the old-fashioned type, measuring no more than 6 feet in height. Pinchers often worked clandestinely to avoid the excise duty levied on flint-glass. They supplied units consisting of feet and stems to the established glass-houses at cut prices, in metal inferior to that of the blown bowls: the contrast between the two metals on a single rummer is often conspicuous. A square foot required trimming where the molten metal had escaped over the edge of the pincher's tool. This necessitated finishing on the grinding and polishing wheels. Round feet complete with short knopped stems were sometimes made by the pinchers.

Ovoid bowls began to be replaced during the 1790's by bowls in which the base tended to be flattened, such as the bucket-shaped bowl which usurped the ovoid bowl's popularity in best-quality glass, and continued in production until the close of the rummer period; the cylindrical or straight-sided bucket (fig. 149), the nearly hemispherical barrel shape and ogee forms. A bowl in any of these designs was almost invariably reinforced beneath by a strengthening disc with rounded or bladed edge (fig. 139), extending to more than half the diameter of the bowl base, and attached to the stem. These bowl shapes with round feet are all found on rummers issued in memory of Nelson and dated either 21st October 1805 or 6th January 1806, the date of his funeral at St. Paul's Cathedral.

The sides of bucket bowls tended to take on a more pronounced slope from about 1815, and the lower part might be encircled with flat-cut

184

or hollow flutes. Ovoid and ogee bowls, decorated with twelve flutes as on drawn rummers, appear also on three-piece rummers.

The short thick stem, seldom measuring as much as 2 inches in length, allowed little scope for variation in design: it might be plainly cylindrical, spool-shaped, knopped, or knopped and cut. The earliest knops were in the form of centrally placed flattened balls, a type which continued throughout the period: from about 1805 such knops might be all-over facet-cut with small diamonds. Early in the nineteenth century came the annular knop, followed by the bladed knop, and still later by the triple knop.

The boldly curved bowl-surface of the finer rummers formed an excellent field for wheel-engraved ornament, often of exceptionally skilful craftsmanship. Pictorial decoration was particularly favoured. The scenes depicted might have personal significance, or might commemorate some royal, historical, political, or social event. Portraits of naval and military heroes were frequent, whilst nautical, coaching, and sporting scenes were highly popular, including fox-hunting, racing, hare-coursing, cockfighting, and the like. Other rummers were engraved with elaborate cartouches enclosing coats of arms, crests, cyphers, or initials.

The toddy rummer, a giant version of the drinking-rummer and often mistakenly catalogued as a punch-bowl, dated from the late 1780's (fig. 151 below). A few years earlier hot toddy had been introduced, being then defined as 'hot grog with the addition of sugar, lemon juice, and grated nutmeg'. When toddy became a favourite drink in social circles during the Regency period, the rum might be replaced by whisky, brandy, or gin.

These rummers, with a capacity of a pint and a half or more, too heavy and unwieldy for drinking purposes, were the characteristic vessels in which hot toddy was prepared at home. They were constructed by the glass-maker in such a way that there would be no weak point susceptible to heat. They were, therefore, among the most sturdily built vessels made in flint-glass and possessed no counterpart elsewhere.

Toddy-making equipment included a small kettle for boiling water, one or two toddy rummers, toddy glasses, glass toddy-sticks or sugar crushers (fig. 141), and a glass toddy lifter (fig. 129) or ladle. The hot toddy was prepared in the rummer, or perhaps in a bowl of earthenware or bone china. It was then served into the drinking-glasses by means of the toddy lifter or ladle. Sugar was added to the individual glasses, which were two-thirds filled, and stirred with toddy-sticks. In hot weather the toddy was prepared cold or 'luke'.

In 1845 S. Judd recorded that grog-shop counters were covered with tumblers and glass toddy-sticks. The latter cost 1s. 6d. a gross and might be plain or ridged with spirals, the sugar-crushing end shaped like a pestle. Domestic toddy-sticks might be cut, and they were also made in silver and Sheffield plate.

Toddy rummers followed the same general form as the finer Georgian drinking-rummers, and displayed similar chronological changes, with engraved decoration carried out on similar lines. For a quarter of a century toddy rummers, suitably inscribed, were valued prizes in connection with many sports; enthusiasts, too, would commission toddy rummers to be engraved with scenes from their favourite sport. As christening cups and anniversary gifts they were in continual demand, and many a master craftsman ordered a toddy rummer engraved with the tools of his trade. Masonic emblems are also to be noted.

One uncommon series of toddy rummers was ornamented with all-over cutting in deep relief (fig. 148), the designs containing the various types of diamond-cutting, stars, flutings, and shells. These date from 1805. A few years later the Edinburgh and Leith Glass Company, Leith, was producing costly, square-footed toddy rummers with bowls ornamented with all-over cutting (fig. 308).

Figures 134–7

ROMERS WITH INCURVED BOWLS
ENCIRCLED WITH APPLIED MOULDED GADROONING

In all but the example *lower right* the depth of the bowl approximately equals the combined height of foot and stem, and the diameters of the folded feet equal those of the rims.

(134) Cylindrical stem ornamented with strawberry prunts and a wavy collar concealing the bowl-junction; *c.* 1685.

In the Victoria and Albert Museum

(135) Stem consisting of a baluster between a pair of ball knops, all hollow. A graduated triple-ring collar joins bowl to stem. Height 12¼ inches; *c.* 1690.

From the Bles Collection

(136) Baluster stem joined to the bowl by a thin disc. The stem, containing a long tear, merges gracefully into the folded foot. Height 5¾ inches; *c.* 1700.

From the Bles Collection

(137) White spiral-gauze opaque-twist stem. Conical folded foot. Height 5½ inches; *c.* 1750. Similar glasses have been noted with pale green-tinted bowls and feet.

In the Victoria and Albert Museum

Figure 138

Top left: Toddy rummer with bucket bowl with flat flutes cut around the base and reinforced beneath. Knopped stem rising from a flat foot star-cut beneath. The bowl is wheel-engraved with the two-masted schooner *Endeavour* flying top sails, yards, mainsails, and jibs. The reverse is inscribed 'To Mr and Mrs Richardson from their friend E Kay', crested by a basket of fruit and festoons of flowers and foliage, flanked by rose sprays; *c.* 1820. Height 9⅞ inches.

By courtesy of Messrs Arthur Churchill Ltd

Top right: Rummer of a type made in English, Irish, and Scottish glass-houses. The bucket bowl is cut with hollow flutes beneath an encircling band of fine diamond-cutting ringed top and bottom. Stem with bladed knop rising from plain foot; *c.* 1820. Height 5¼ inches.

In the Corning Museum of Glass

Bottom left: Rummer with ovoid bowl supported by a terrace-domed and stepped square foot, hollow beneath and impressed with gadrooning. Engraved on the obverse with an oval

187

medallion containing a portrait of Diana with a deer, and on the reverse with monograms contained in an oval, crested with bowls of fruit and festooned with flowers and foliage; *c.* 1800. Height 8 inches.

In the Cecil Higgins Museum

Bottom right: A page from a pattern book issued by the Edinburgh and Leith Glass Company: the paper is watermarked 1811. Above are two hollow-stemmed romers. The example on the left is illustrated in section, showing the bowl and hollow stem to be blown as a single entity, with four applied strawberry prunts. This is welded to a hollow-blown pedestal foot. The neck is encircled with a wavy collar. The right-hand example, painted pale green in the catalogue, illustrates a three-piece romer. The bowl is blown with a collar beneath into which is welded the hollow stem, sealed beneath by the attachment of a hollow, step-surfaced conical foot. Below are tavern rummers in their four standard sizes, 6 inches, 5 inches, $4\frac{1}{2}$ inches, and 4 inches in height. The specimen on the left is a three-piece rummer with a spool-shaped stem: the others have drawn stems.

Figures 139–42

(139) Rummer commemorating the union of Great Britain and Ireland in 1801, and the opening of Sunderland Bridge in 1796. The bucket bowl, reinforced beneath, is supported by a stem with an annular knop, rising from a plain foot. The reverse is wheel-engraved with a monogram enclosed in a rectangular panel, crested and flanked by sprays of rose, thistle, and shamrock. The obverse shows the west view of the bridge — its name inscribed around the lower part of the bowl — adapted from the etching by J. Roffield, published 1798. Sunderland Bridge was a celebrated engineering feat, being the longest single-span cast-iron bridge in the world. About 1801, and probably made in a Sunderland glass-house. Height 6 inches.

In the Victoria and Albert Museum

(140) George IV coronation rummer. The stem, with an annulated knop, rises from a plain foot. The bucket bowl, reinforced beneath, is engraved with an equestrian portrait of the King's Champion, armoured and plumed, with glove raised ready to fling to the ground. On the reverse is engraved the royal crown, the king's cypher G IV R, and the coronation date, July 19 1821. About 1821. Height 5 inches.

In the Victoria and Albert Museum

(141) Typical tavern rummer with ovoid bowl, drawn stem, and plain foot. The thinly blown metal displays numerous striations and seeds. Its origin is detailed on page 190; *c.* 1800. Height $5\frac{3}{4}$ inches, diameter at rim $4\frac{1}{2}$ inches; capacity to brim 1 pint. Below is a glass sugar-crusher with hemispherical pestle and ridged finial: these cost 1s. 6d. a gross.

In the collection of Mrs William Hopley

131, 132   Drinking-glasses painted with scenes or borders in white enamel

133 Heraldic goblets with bucket bowls enamelled in colours

190

134–137   Romers with incurved bowls encircled with applied moulded gadrooning

138 *Top left:* Toddy rummer; *below and top right:* drinking-rummers. The sketches show romers and rummers from an early-nineteenth-century pattern book

139–142   Masonic toddy rummer (*lower right*), *reproduced by Gracious Permission of Her Majesty The Queen,* and three drinking-rummers

143–146 Engraved drinking-rummers

194

147, 148   Toddy rummers decorated with diamond-cutting

149, 150   Engraved drinking-rummers

151 A collection of rummers and decanters engraved with Masonic emblems. The rummers illustrate the comparative sizes of toddy rummers (*below*) and drinking-rummers

(142) Rummer for serving toddy. The short stem with a central flattened knop and widely expanded ends was tooled as a single unit. The bowl is engraved with a long series of Masonic emblems, considerable use being made of engraved lines, an unusual feature. Early 1820's. Height 8½ inches.

Reproduced by Gracious Permission of Her Majesty the Queen

Figures 143–6

ENGRAVED DRINKING-RUMMERS

(143) Rummer with ovoid bowl joined to unknopped stem by a merese; plain foot. Wheel-engraved with a three-masted schooner, the inscription 'Success to the Owners', and a monogram. *c.* 1810. Height 6¼ inches.

By courtesy of Messrs Christie, Manson & Woods Ltd

(144) Rummer with bucket-shaped bowl reinforced beneath; stem with annulated knop rising from a flat foot. Bowl wheel-engraved with two men boxing and the monogram J E H encircled with a cartouche of foliage. This rummer was originally the property of the celebrated boxer, J. E. Heenan, who in 1860 was a contestant in the last bare-fist fight to take place in England. Mid-nineteenth century. Height 6¼ inches.

By courtesy of Messrs Christie, Manson & Woods Ltd

(145) Souvenir rummer with bucket-shaped bowl reinforced beneath; stem with bladed knop rising from a flat foot. Bowl wheel-engraved with the royal crown between the script initials Q C and inscribed 'God and my Rights'. Issued in 1820 when George IV instituted divorce proceedings against his consort to whom he had been married since 1795. Height 5 inches.

By courtesy of Messrs Arthur Churchill Ltd

(146) Rummer commemorating the union of Great Britain with Ireland. The bowl is encircled with a wheel-engraved scene suggesting prosperity: a farmhouse with cottages, horse, sheep, birds, and trees. Below, between two encircling bands of line trellis work, is a repeat motif composed of rose, thistle, and shamrock. *c.* 1801. Height 6⅝ inches.

By courtesy of Messrs Arthur Churchill Ltd

Figures 147–50

(147) Toddy rummer with hemispherical bowl about 8 inches deep, and solid square foot with dome. Bowl cut with diamonds containing eight-pointed stars, edge-fluted rim, and its base cut with short hollow flutes. Early nineteenth century. Height 10 inches.

(148) Toddy rummer with hemispherical bowl and strengthened stem junction. The short stem and knop are facet-cut, rising from a round foot star-cut beneath. The elaborately cut bowl is encircled with six circular panels crested with blaze-cutting and with oval facets beneath. The panels contain, alternately, the Brunswick star (*left*) and a field of cross-cut diamonds (*right*) encircled by rings of finely cut diamonds bordered on both sides with ring cutting. Rummers of this design were made by the Edinburgh and Leith Glass Company, Leith. *c.* 1820.

By courtesy of Mr John Bell

(149) Rummer with cylindrical bowl reinforced beneath and supported by a short plain stem rising from a terraced dome on a square foot hollowed and gadrooned. Bowl wheel-engraved with the London, York, and Newcastle royal mail coach, No. 175, drawn by four horses, and, on the reverse, a monogram within a Garter star. The lower part of the bowl is encircled with the toast 'Here's Health to the Sick, Honor to the Brave, Success to the Lover, & Freedom to the Slave'; *c.* 1820. Height 6½ inches.

In the Author's collection

(150) Rummer with hemispherical bowl and drawn stem cut with long hollow flutes carried up into the base of the bowl. Wheel-engraved with a landscape in which Alnwick Castle, seat of the Duke of Northumberland, is seen on the hill, with the ducal banner flying. The hill slopes down to the River Aln, spanned by a three-arch bridge; *c.* 1820. Height 6⅞ inches.

By courtesy of Arthur Churchill Ltd

Figure 151

A collection of rummers and decanters engraved with Masonic emblems. The rummers illustrate the comparative sizes of drinking-rummers (*top*) and toddy rummers (*bottom*).

(*a* and *c*) A pair of drinking-rummers with ovoid bowls, collared beneath, on solid four-sided pedestal stems with square plinths. Height 6 inches. (*b*) Ovoid bowl with stepped dome on square base, hollow beneath and gadroon moulded. (*d*) Prussian-shaped decanter with moulded flutes, two feathered neck rings, widely everted mouth, and moulded target stopper. (*e*) Toddy rummer with bucket bowl, spherical knopped stem, with plain foot. Height about 9 inches. (*f*) Toddy rummer with ovoid bowl collared beneath, plain stem with round foot. Height about 8 inches. (*g*) Prussian-shaped decanter with three plain neck rings and faceted disc stopper. Late eighteenth century.

By courtesy of Messrs Delomosne & Son Ltd

Figures 152–5

(152) Sweetmeat glass with cover; body and cover lobed to match; domed and ribbed foot; finial knob contains air bubbles and rises from a triple collar. Early George I period.

In the Victoria and Albert Museum

(153) Punch-bowl and cover decorated with moulding and trailed work; on pedestal foot with folded rim. The cover surmounted by a crown in pinched work, with a cross above. 1685–1700. Height 15½ inches.

Formerly in the Bles Collection

(154) Punch-bowl with incurved bowl on plain stem foot. Engraved with 'The Kill', a hunting scene set in a landscape with trees and a church in the distance; one rider is up and another arriving at a gallop; the huntsman holds the fox in his left hand with the pack around. Mid-nineteenth-century engraving, but the bowl probably earlier. Height 12⅜ inches.

By courtesy of Messrs Arthur Churchill Ltd

(155) Punch-bowl on knopped and hollow baluster stem. Engraved with a stag-hunting scene showing three stags at full speed with six hounds in chase; all on a grassy foreground with hills in the distance. Mid-nineteenth century. Height 12¾ inches.

By courtesy of Messrs Arthur Churchill Ltd

CHAPTER TWELVE

CHAMPAGNE GLASSES

CHAMPAGNE HAS BEEN ACCLAIMED in English literature for almost three centuries as the prince of sparkling wines. Little, if any, had been imported into England earlier than 1662 when Charles Marquatel de St. Denis, Lord of St. Evremond, introduced it to the courtiers at St. James's and to the wits of London. St. Evremond, a general of the French army, celebrated as a gourmet and epicure, had been imprisoned in the Bastille by Cardinal Mazarin. Within a few weeks he had made his escape to England where he was welcomed by Charles II, who invested him with the sinecure post of 'Governor of the Duck Islands'. The refinement in English table manners dating from this period was directly influenced by St. Evremond.

This epicure's favourite wine was champagne and soon small supplies were reaching London, dispatched to England each year shortly after the vintage. Here it was decanted from the barrel, bottled, and consumed within a few months in a semi-sparkling state. The Bedford household accounts of 1665 refer to '2 dozen glass [quart] bottles 10/-; two dozen corks 4d.; six gallons [two dozen quarts] of champagne 36/-'. It is important to distinguish between the two kinds of champagnes then available. André Simon has described the early semi-sparkling champagne as 'a greyish or yellowish effervescent wine creaming, if not actually sparkling'. This was the 'brisk champagne' of the period. On the other hand Doctor Plot in his *History of Staffordshire*, 1679, noted that 'champagne has a faint reddish colour', referring to the still red champagne imported into England until about 1850.

There has been considerable disagreement among collectors regarding the style of glasses used for the early champagne, so that it is particularly interesting to note contemporary evidence. St. Evremond himself decreed that the fashionable drinker of champagne should take it only from the flute, a form of vessel which displayed the rising bubbles of carbonic acid gas to best advantage. The *Oxford Dictionary* defines the flute as 'a tall, slender wine-glass, used especially for sparkling wines'. The earliest English reference given dates to 1650 when the poet Lovelace eulogized 'flutes of Canary'. The custom of drinking Canary and Spanish wines from flutes continued until the end of the seventeenth century and is illustrated in several contemporary prints.

The narrow elongated bowl of the early champagne flute was supported by a round hollow knop upon a folded foot measuring one-third greater in diameter than the diameter of the bowl rim. The fold was narrow, hollow, and carried below the surface of the foot. Some flutes were of fine Venetian soda-glass, others from 1665 came from the Greenwich glass-house of St. Evremond's friend, the Duke of Buckingham. Flutes of clear, tough flint-glass were made from about 1678: in this type the knop was solid and the fold of the foot made considerably wider and thick enough to lift the rough punty mark above the table top and thus avoid scratching it.

At 6s. a bottle there was, apparently, a considerable demand for 'brisk' champagne. Poets and dramatists of the Restoration period glamorized it as a gay, exhilarating wine. George Farquhar in his play *Love in a Bottle*, staged at Drury Lane in 1698, described champagne as 'a fine liquor which all the great Beaux drink to make them Witty'.

The consumption of champagne was considerably reduced, however, after ratification of the Methuen Treaty in 1703. This placed a tax of £55 a tun on French wines, while permitting the levy upon the wines of Spain and Portugal to remain at £7 a tun. Matthew Prior in 1716 was still lamenting that 'our warlike men Might still drink thick Port for fine Champagne'. Champagne could now be afforded only by the nobility and wealthy merchant princes, but it still bore little resemblance to the sparkling limpid wine sold today. There were no brands of champagne, merely the name of the vineyard burned into the barrel. It was customary for the purchaser to prevent adulteration by visiting the vintners and watching the wine being transferred to special bottles impressed with his own seal. Advertisements in *The Kentish Post*, 1755, announced 'Champagne quarts 27/- gross' and 'Newcastle Champain quart bottles 26/- gross': these would not be sealed.

This was an age of night revels, and from about 1700 it became customary to toast the reigning belle of the moment in costly champagne. Sir Richard Steele in 1709 recorded that ' "toast" was a new name found by the Wits for a Lady', whose name was supposed to flavour the wine like spiced toast. The flavouring of wines with browned and spiced toast is advised in many English cookery books from 1440 to 1720.

The early toasting-glass was a flute made from the finest flint-glass, the stem being drawn from the bowl to a diameter no thicker than one-eighth of an inch (fig. 158a). The London mode was for the drinker to snap the stem between finger and thumb immediately after drinking the toast, thus preventing the glass from being used for a lesser toast. The great majority of toasting-glasses now remaining have more substantial stems with bowls strong enough to be inscribed with an epigram or verse in honour of the toast. Early toasting-glasses were too fragile to permit more than spontaneous engraving of a name with a diamond ring. The majority of toasting-glasses have plain drawn stems on folded feet: some mid-eighteenth-century examples have extremely slender opaque-twist stems with plain feet hollowed beneath. But by this time, according to Fielding, the custom of toasting had become 'another word for drinking the health of one's friend', and special glasses were no longer used.

Champagne was the favourite wine of the Prince of Wales, afterwards George II, who, like other members of the royal family, was exempt from paying import duty. Other champagne drinkers in powerful positions avoided payment of duty by arranging conveyance with the help of a friendly diplomat. Among these was Lord Chesterfield, one-time Steward of the Household, who toasted the beauties of the day: 'Give me Champaign and fill it to the brim, I'll toast in bumpers ev'ry lovely limb.'

Champagne was the royal drink from early in the reign of George I until the mid-1730's. During this period graceful tazza-shaped drinking-glasses were adopted for champagne. These had expansive bowls, often ogee in form and sometimes with slightly everted lips, supported usually on moulded silesian stems placed between triple-knopped collars. This stem was the glass-maker's version of the mushroom stem brought into fashion by the silversmiths of the period. Other, less frequent, stems were knopped or of baluster shape. In some specimens the bowl was of thinly blown glass, entirely smooth-surfaced, in others the metal of the entire bowl was thicker, the lower part being moulded with closely placed ribs or curved reticulations. The foot was wide, high-domed, and folded, the dome being moulded to harmonize with the decoration on the bowl, the rim of which was usually about one-third larger in diameter. Later examples might have plain feet, usually hollowed beneath. Air-twist stems date from about 1740 and opaque-twist stems from about 1750. Both are rare, however, owing to the negligible consumption of champagne between 1735 and 1745. A trade card of the 1760's illustrates such a glass with a pedestal foot.

Early champagne glasses of the tazza type are referred to in the catalogue of the sale of the Grant Francis Collection in 1935 as 'obviously tavern glasses in which resorts champagne was largely drunk in the seventeenth century'. There is no evidence that the tazza champagne glass had come into use earlier than about 1718, however, and real champagne was far too expensive a luxury for the public taverns of the period. The Government of 1695 estimated that England then supported more than 60,000 taverns. In early Georgian days bottled cider was sold in the taverns under the name of champagne: some contemporary writers refer to the drink as 'bootlegger's champagne'.

Addison in one of his famous *Spectator* essays flayed these purveyors of spurious wines whom he accused of 'by the power of magical drugs raising under the streets of London the choicest products of the hills and the valleys of France, squeezing Bordeaux out of sloes and drawing champagne from apples'. Bottled cider sold to the ignorant under the champagne ticket at a price several times its real worth is referred to in Fielding's *Tom Jones*, 1748. The counterfeit wine was served in ordinary tavern glasses and these might be of green-tinted glass.

During this period, as might be expected, several styles of glass might be used for champagne. For instance, there is the evidence of a trade bill in the collection of Sir Ambrose Heal, issued by Thomas Betts in 1755, which includes '1 pair Neat Ice Champagne Quart Decanters 12/-; 12 Wormed [air-twist] ½ rib^d Champagnes 10/6; and 12 green ½ mo [half-moulded] Egg Champagnes 12/-'. It is very evident, however, that the flute was again the predominant glass for champagne in the second half of the eighteenth century (fig. 157), and it is surprising to note that the considerable authority on drinking-glasses, Francis Buckley, writing in the trade journal *Glass*, November 1932, suggested that they were never used for champagne. In contradiction of this, there is in the collection of Sir Ambrose Heal another trade bill which shows that on 2nd February 1773 Edward Gibbon, the historian, bought from Colebron Hancock, glass manufacturer, Cockspur Street, Charing Cross, '1 doz. of Champain Flutes 8/-' (fig. 30). Again, the conversation piece, 'William Ferguson's Birthday Celebration', painted in 1781 by Johann Zoffany (fig. 156), illustrates four long-stemmed champagne flutes on the table, with opaque-white stems, together with a bottle of champagne. Three additional flutes and four more bottles of champagne are visible in a brass-bound wooden wine-cooler.

The new style of champagne flutes dated from about 1745 when the vogue for the wine began a revival which continued in spite of an increase of duty from 1763 to £73 a tun. This tax of about 1s. 6d. per quart bottle had little effect upon the consumption of champagne in fashionable circles. The deep, narrow bowl of the champagne flute now had a rounded base to which a tall stem was stuck. This was usually plain, but sometimes knopped, and examples are found with moulded silesian stems. The foot was folded and exceptionally wide in diameter, and those made before about 1750 showed punty marks on the underside. Thereafter the foot was plain and hollowed. In some types the stem was drawn. A now rare series with air-twist stems was made during the 1750's and later (fig. 157a): these might have domed and folded feet. The more frequent opaque-twist stem with a plain hollow foot dates between 1750 and 1775. In later examples the feet might be flatter and of smaller diameter than formerly. The drawn stem might be plain or diamond-faceted with the base of the bowl cut to match.

Table etiquette during the second half of the eighteenth century demanded that champagne glasses should be of gill-size but filled only half-full. This fashion was responsible for champagne flutes cut with diamond-shaped facets or with shallow vertical grooves or flutings extending half-way up the bowl. These were quoted by the glass-sellers as 'champagnes with cut-bottoms'. The intention of this decoration was to add increased brilliance to the semi-transparent, semi-sparkling liquor. These and other champagne glasses might be given flaring rims from about 1760 to 1790.

The tremendous vogue for engraving wineglass bowls between about 1750 and 1780 included the ornamentation of champagne flutes with sprays of vine-leaves and grapes. Similar motifs were also applied in white and coloured enamels: such glasses usually have opaque-twist stems. The flute was also associated with strong ale and cider. Unless the glass is engraved with the hop blossom and ears of barley (fig. 161), or with a fruiting apple bough or spray of apple blossom and leaves (fig. 162), it is difficult for the collector to distinguish between the three types. Well-designed flutes made of the finer metal taken from the piling-pot and displaying excellent craftsmanship were undoubtedly intended for champagne.

Little, if any, champagne was imported during the quarter-century ending in 1815, and it is unlikely that any change of form was made in the champagne glass during this period. The flute continued in fashion until after the introduction of the 'disgorging process' in about 1820 which produced a limpid and more lively champagne. This was hailed by Byron in *Don Juan* as 'Champagne with foaming whirls, As white as Cleopatra's melted pearls'.

Within the next few years glass-sellers designed a new glass for champagne, still a scarce and very costly wine. This was known as the coupe, a glass with an expansive hemispherical bowl supported on a tall slender stem. Although the metal was of the finest quality its crystal clarity was obscured by lavish wheel-decoration on stem and bowl. Disraeli was sufficiently impressed by the new design to think it worth mentioning in a letter written to his sister in 1832 that he had taken champagne from 'a saucer of ground glass mounted upon a pedestal of cut glass'. The wide expansive bowl displayed the new liveliness of champagne to its finest advantage, but exposed too much of the wine to the air and tended to make the champagne look flat too soon.

Few glasses of this type may be dated earlier than about 1840 when there was a sensational fall in the price of champagne owing to the discovery of less hazardous methods of fermentation. The wine could now be bought at prices ranging from 11s. to 22s. per dozen quart bottles in bond at London. As production trebled and quadrupled so did the production of fragile champagne glasses. The expensive hemispherical glass was condemned in 1858, however, by the writer of *London at Dinner: or where to Dine* as 'animalculae-catching'. Instead, he recommended the use of 'new-fashioned tulip-shaped glasses' for champagne. Such glasses are still in use and should hold six to the bottle when filled about two inches below the rim.

Figure 156

'William Ferguson's Birthday Celebrations', painted by Johann Zoffany, seen on the right of the group. William Ferguson was adopted by his uncle as heir to the estate of Raith in 1781, and the party is celebrating that occasion. On the table are four champagne flutes, with plain stems rising from hollowed conical feet: three more flutes are visible in the brass-bound wine-cooler.

By courtesy of Viscount Novar's Trustees

Figures 157–9

(157)   Champagne flutes with air-twist stems; *c.* 1750.
   Top left: Inscribed 'Old Glorious and Steady'; multiple spiral stem.
   Top centre: Bell-shaped flute; stem with shoulder and central knops; folded foot.
   Top right: Coarse multiple spiral

All in the Victoria and Albert Museum

(158, 159)   Toasting-glass with trumpet bowl; multiple spiral. The three other glasses have shoulder and central knops.

By courtesy of Messrs Arthur Churchill Ltd

CHAPTER THIRTEEN

STRONG-ALE GLASSES

IN MEDIEVAL DAYS the words 'ale' and 'beer' were synonymous for an intoxicating drink brewed from malted barley. Eventually the term 'beer' fell into disuse until reintroduced during the reign of Edward VI (1547–53) when 'that wicked weed called hops' was added to the brew and the resulting, less potent liquor differentiated as beer. Although hops were grown in England from 1492, Henry VII and Henry VIII prohibited their use in brewing.

Ale was made in qualities of varying strength, some of the more potent types being stored in long-necked shaft-and-globe bottles of a home-produced glass, pale greenish-yellow in colour. The Spanish-made bottle corks were pressed right home in the necks, tied down with pack thread and sealed with a mixture of resin and pitch. Contact with the liquor swelled the corks and ensured a tight fit. Good ale of prime strength was known as nippitate. Fulwell in his *Art of Flattery*, 1576, noted that London-made nippitate, strong and heady, was commonly called huff-cap. Green and Lodge in *Looking-Glass*, 1594, recorded that 'if the ale is strong ale, 'tis huff-cap'. Hum was a strong ale of double strength and, if old and mellow and exceptionally strong, was known as hum-cap because it caused a humming in the head. Strong ales at this period were served in special glasses known as thimbles, and beer in beakers. Sir Hugh Plat, writing in 1594, remarked that 'it is the Hoppe onlie which maketh the essential difference between Beere and Ale', and also noted that beer was drunk from 'streight upright glasses'. This distinction between ale and beer continued until the nineteenth century, when both were defined as 'liquor made from an infusion of malt by fermentation, flavoured with hops etc'.

Improvements in ale-brewing technique lifted strong ale into the realm of fashionable drinks during the 1660's, a position held until the end of the eighteenth century when it began to be superseded by heavy imported wines. This thick, opaque, strongly alcoholic brew was more heady than wine and bore little resemblance to the light ales served in pewter tankards. A guide to brewing published in 1702 gives this hint to brewers of strong ale: 'Thames-Water taken up about Greenwich at Low-water, when it is free from all brackishness of the sea, and has in it all the Fat and Sullage from this Great City of London, makes very Strong Drink. It will of itself ferment wonderfully and after its due purgations and three times stinking it will be so strong that several Sea Commanders have told me that it has often fuddled their Murriners.'

Georgian strong ale, often called stingo, was drawn from the wood and decanted. It was a costly drink: Dicker, the Edinburgh brewer, for instance, charged ten guineas a gallon for his strong ale. It was generally served at midday dinner from glass serving-bottles, flint-glass globe-and-shaft decanters engraved with hop and barley motifs, or shouldered decanters inscribed 'Ale'.

Decanted strong ale is not to be confused with the inexpensive nappy ale, having a foaming head and served in tumblers known as quaffing-glasses. Nappy ales, which might be bottled, were noted throughout the sixteenth century and Devonshire was described as making 'the nappiest ale that can be drunk'. *Apollo* in 1708 advertised the celebrated Nottingham ale as a 'knappy' ale, which was made also at Burton and Dorchester. The *London Daily Post and General Advertiser*, 1738, announced such ales: 'Brew'd to the Greatest Perfection for Keeping by Sea and Land at 1^{s}6^d per Gallon, Beer Measure . . . also in Bottles not less than a Dozen at 7^{s}6^d, allowing 2s per Dozen for return'd Bottles.'

When strong ale became a fashionable drink in the reign of Charles II the thimble-glass was abandoned in favour of short straight-sided flutes of soda-glass. The rounded base of the blown funnel bowl was set and welded directly to the top of a plain baluster stem rising from a foot with a rim folded from below on to the surface of the foot. Rim and foot diameters were approximately equal. In others a conical flute rose from a short hollow-blown knopped stem.

This shape continued in flint-glass from 1676 until the end of the century with knops at first blown hollow as if the metal were the light soda-glass to which the blowers had been accustomed. The short, hollow-blown ribbed and collared stems, pear-shaped, melon-moulded or plain, were quickly found to be too delicate to endure temperature changes and the jolting of contemporary road travel in England. Breakages were costly for flint-glass at this time was sold by the glass-house at 4s. a pound. The hollow button stem was replaced, therefore, by a solid stem similar in form, with mereses joining it to bowl and foot, the latter with its rim folded beneath. This lifted the glass sufficiently above table level to prevent scratching by the rough punty scar beneath.

Short quatrefoil stems were also made until about 1690. These were knops pressed into four flat vertical lobes extending outward equidistantly (fig. 34c) and with strawberry-pinched surfaces. The quatrefoil knop was separated from the bowl by a merese and from the foot by a ball knop.

At this time ale-glass bowls were conical in shape and might be of clear glass but more commonly the lower two-thirds of the bowl was obscured by writhen ornament to conceal the opaque murkiness of strong ale after standing in the glass for a few minutes (fig. 34a). These rare glasses measure about 6 inches in height and modern copies exist. Writhen decoration was the glass-maker's adaptation of gadrooning, at that time a fashionable ornament on domestic silver plate. Usually the writhen decoration is carried to within about an inch of the bowl rim: in other instances it is shorter, the ends being ornamented with an applied flammiform pincered fringe. Stems associated with writhen bowls on ale glasses at this period might be ball or half-ball decorated with spiralling to match. A collection of seventeenth-century flint-glass ale glasses will show height to have varied between 5 and $5\frac{1}{2}$ inches, with few exceptions.

Fryer, in 1698, complained of the small capacity of 'the Glasses as we drinke Somerset ale out of', Somerset then providing the most potent of strong ales. In that year ale glasses cost 8s. a dozen in London: in the same bill ordinary wineglasses cost 5s. a dozen. As table-ware was sold by weight, it may be assumed that ale glasses were half as heavy again as wineglasses and rather more capacious.

In the early eighteenth century spiralling on ale-glass bowls continued until the 1740's, and from about 1725 the twist might cover the entire surface of the bowl (fig. 189). This later series was blown into moulds and in consequence the ribbing was coarser in finish and the bowl so shaped that no difficulty was experienced in removing it from the mould. In the earlier hand-tooled work each spiral widened in harmony with the gradual increase in bowl diameter. The stems might be of baluster shape, double knop or dumb-bell form, joined to the bowl by a single or double merese, and might be surface-spiralled to match the bowl. The foot was conical and folded, its diameter being equal to or greater than that of the bowl rim.

A method of clarifying strong ale was evolved during the late 1730's, and by 1740 the tall ale glass with a clear bowl displaying the now rich amber hue of the liquor had become fashionable. This new style of glass, used only on fashionable tables, had a deep, narrow, round-based bowl (fig. 160), slightly everted towards the rim. The tall stem might be plain (fig. 169), moulded, air-twist (fig. 161), opaque-twist (fig. 164) or facet-cut (fig. 90b), and the bowl was generally decorated with engraved (fig. 161) or enamelled and gilded hop-and-barley motifs. Feet until about 1750 were folded and always considerably wider in diameter than the narrow bowl rims to ensure stability. After about 1750 punty scars were ground smooth and the foot, its rim no longer folded, was conical or domed.

In July 1746 the firm of Cookson and Company, Newcastle upon Tyne, invoiced '1½ dozen Worm'd Ale Glasses, 10½ lb. at 10d per lb. 8s 9d; ½ dozen Plain Ale Glasses 3½ lb. at 8d 2s 4d'. In 1749 the Earl of Carlisle bought '12 ale glasse, new fashion, 2s each'. In the collection of Sir Ambrose Heal is a bill from Thomas Betts, dated 1757, for '6 Enamell'd Shank Flutes', and in the Earl of Carlisle's accounts for 1760 similar opaque-twist glasses with tall narrow bowls are entered as 'six long enamelled ale glasses', at a cost of 4s.

The zenith of ale-glass design was reached between about 1750 and 1775 when twist stems were at the height of public regard. Tall ale glasses were usually made from fine-quality metal and the bowls of many were ornamented with the well-known hop-and-barley motifs to distinguish them from champagne glasses of similar form. Typically, one side of the bowl was engraved with two stalks of barley diagonally crossed and each bearing two or four ears: on the reverse was shown a single hop blossom between two leaves and some tendrils.

Grant Francis in *Old English Drinking Glasses*, 1926, lists ten other variants of the hop-and-barley motif, all more or less common: (1) two leaves on each barley stalk; (2) four leaves on each barley stalk; (3) five leaves on each barley stalk; (4) one ear of barley and one single-leafed hop blossom; (5) one ear of barley and one hop blossom with two leaves; (6) two ears of barley and one single-leafed hop blossom; (7) four ears of barley with a single leaf to each stalk; (8) two hop blossoms with tendrils from the two barley stalks; (9) two ears of barley sideways and no hops; (10) four ears of barley crossed and no hops. Pattern arrangement might differ, but variants other than those listed are rare.

The engraved motifs might be gilded from the late 1750's, and a wide band of gilding encircled the bowl rim. A newly invented method of gilding was used, long-wearing and capable of being burnished to a high lustre. Amber varnish was used as a fixing medium which did not require firing and fixed the gold leaf more evenly than any other method then known. Amber gilding was used only by London glass-decorators until the 1780's.

Hop-and-barley motifs were sometimes painted on ale-glass bowls in white or coloured enamels. Nearly all examples noted have been in a dense

212

152   Sweetmeat glass with cover

153   Covered punch bowl

154, 155   Engraved punch bowls

156 'William Ferguson celebrating his succession to Raith' by Johann Zoffany; 1760's. Illustrating champagne flutes

157–159   Champagne flutes with air-twist stems

160–165   Champagne, cider, and ale flutes

216

166–171   Ale and wine flutes with bucket-bowl cider glass

172, 173   Two cider flutes, each measuring 14½ inches in height; *left*, in soda-glass, *c.* 1660; *right*, in flint-glass, 1800

174 'The Dilettante Society' by Thomas Patch, *c.* 1750. Illustrating cordial glasses

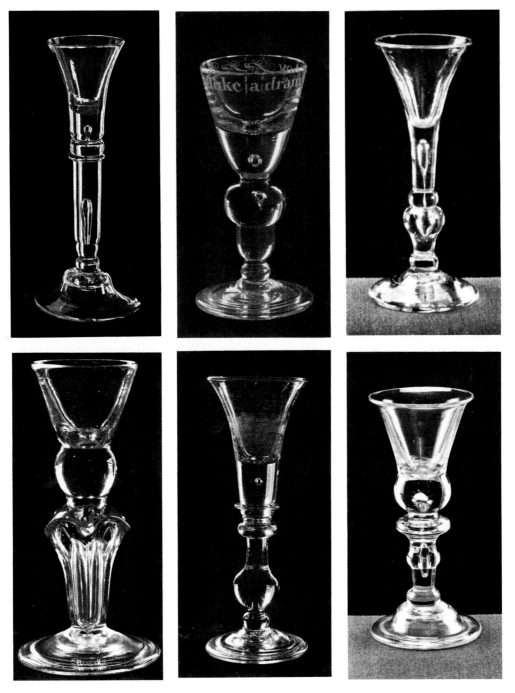

175–180   Cordial glasses of the early eighteenth-century

full enamel thickly applied. Some finer work in a thinly applied wash enamel is rare and possibly earlier; in this, such details as the veining of leaves was accomplished by removing enamel with a needle.

Although deep, round-based, straight-sided flutes were standard bowls for tall ale glasses, other bowl shapes might be used. Flutes engraved with the hop-and-barley motifs might be deeply waisted and drawn with straw shanks, and deep double-ogee bowls might have the upper curve of the bowl encircled with festoons of hop and barley. The funnel bowl was also used in this connection.

A late series of strong ale glasses were those with deep conical bowls cut or pressed with vertical flutes rising from the base. Such a bowl might be set directly upon the plain foot or separated from it by one or two knops. After about 1780 such an ale glass might rise directly from a thick, square, hollow-based foot.

Short-stemmed ale glasses continued concurrently with tall stems, now with crystal-clear funnel (fig. 166) or conical bowl through which the newly won clarity of the liquor could be seen. The stem measured about one inch in length with a beaded or other knop immediately below the bowl: many variants are found. In early examples the feet were folded and of greater diameter than the bowl rims. Plain rims were usual after about 1750 and late examples tended to be smaller than the bowl-rim diameters. Bowls were often engraved with hop-and-barley motifs but no gilded examples have been noted.

From the 1780's ale glasses might have short plain stems, sometimes centrally knopped, supporting barrel-shaped or wide bucket bowls. These were made with strengthened bowl-stem junctions and plain feet and have been noted in sets of a dozen engraved with hop-and-barley motifs.

Glasses in a coarse metal blown with a thick section and closely resembling short ale glasses with funnel-shaped bowls were made in immense numbers for indiscriminate use from about 1780 and continued in production until early Victorian days.

221

Figures 160–5

(160) Champagne flute with gadrooned base to bowl: incised baluster and knop stem; folded foot; *c.* 1740.

In the Victoria and Albert Museum

(161) Ale flute, engraved with hops and barley; air-twist stem with shoulder and centre knops; plain foot; 1740's.

(162) Cider flute enamelled with branch of apples and a moth; compound opaque-twist stem, pair of narrow spiral tapes within a wide spiral tape; plain foot; 1760's.

Formerly in the Bles Collection

(163) Flute engraved with thistle flowers and leaves: compound opaque-twist stem, gauze pillar within single spiral tape; 1760–70.

(164) Ale flute engraved with hop and barley; compound white opaque-twist stem, pair of corkscrews within a single tape; plain foot; 1770's.

(165) Champagne flute, engraved 'Success to the Renown'; compound white-twist stem; plain foot; 1774. The *Renown*, 1,044 tons, was launched in 1774.

By courtesy of Messrs Arthur Churchill Ltd

Figures 166–71

(166) Dwarf ale flute engraved with hop and barley; short knopped stem; wide folded foot; *c.* 1750. Height 6 inches.

In the collection of Mrs William Hopley

(167) Cider glass, its bucket bowl engraved with border of apples; corkscrew mercury-twist stem; plain foot.

In the Corning Museum of Glass

(168) Wine flute engraved with grapes and vine-leaves; short dumb-bell stem; folded foot. Early George III. Height 6 inches.

In the collection of Mrs William Hopley

(169) Flute engraved 'P: Tate' in an elaborate wreath and a violin in a similar wreath; plain stem; folded foot; *c.* 1740–1750. Height 6 inches.

(170) Drawn conical bowl; plain stem. Engraved 'Rights of Man', the title of Thomas Paine's book published 1790. Height 6¼ inches.

(171) Flute with twisted bowl and plain foot.

All by courtesy of Messrs Arthur Churchill Ltd

Figures 172, 173

(172)   A *façon de Venice* cider flute on a blown knop on a folded foot with the fold upward. Engraved in the English style with the diamond-point, the royal arms on the front and the Scudamore escutcheon (illustrated) on the reverse. The whole is ornamented, partly in stipple, with garlands and apple trees. Height 14½ inches; *c.* 1650–70.

In the collection of the Earl of Chesterfield

(173)   Flute with long conical bowl from the base of which is drawn a bifurcated and twisted stem, very rare. Wheel-engraved with sprays of roses, thistles, and shamrocks in vertical panels in commemoration of the union of Britain with Ireland in 1801. Plain flat foot hollowed beneath. Height 14½ inches.

In the Author's collection

CHAPTER FOURTEEN

CORDIAL, DRAM, FIRING, AND TOAST-MASTER GLASSES

HEARTY BEERS, ales, and rough-textured mixed wines sweetened with sugar were the lusty English tipples until Carolean days. Then finer, unblended wines became the fashion and among the brilliant liquors that caught popular fancy were aromatic cordials. These contained about 50 per cent of alcohol and 25 per cent of sugar. Flavoured with fruit juices or herb essences, they were English-made equivalents of the French liqueurs. Direct descendants of Chaucer's 'grate delycious wynes aromatiques', they were known also as compounds, and cost, early in Queen Anne's reign, about 2s. a pint at a time when spirits of wine was being sold at 4s. a gallon.

So potent were undiluted cordials that small quantities only could be dispatched with sobriety. John Bunyan in 1682 wrote: 'I have a cordial of Mr. Forget-Good's making, the which, sir, if you will take a dram of may make you bonny and blithe.' Cordials were sipped in fashionable homes from special glasses allocated to the purpose. A glassful of cordial was called a dram, the term denoting also a similar quantity of strong waters or spirits. The first literary reference so far noted to a cordial glass dates to 1663 when Cowley cried: 'Fetch me the Cordial glass in the Cabinet-Window.'

No cordial glass made before the introduction of flint-glass seems to have survived. The modish design from about 1680 to the early years of the eighteenth century resembled a wineglass with heavy baluster or drop-knop stem supporting a small funnel or bell-shaped bowl rendered even less capacious by a thick base. The stem might display a lustrous elongated air bubble, matching a fellow caught in the heavy base of the bowl: the foot was either plainly conical, folded, or domed and folded. At the turn of the century an inverted acorn might be incorporated into the stem (fig. 176), and the straight stem drawn from a trumpet bowl and tooled at each end to form a knop made its appearance (fig. 175). The straight stem in a three-

225

piece glass might be plain; centrally knopped, either swelling, ball or angular; or with a merese or button knop immediately beneath the bowl and a baluster rising directly from the foot junction (fig. 179).

Cordial glasses from about 1720 became an essential accompaniment to the Georgian tea-table equipage, bucket-bowls usually indicating their original use for this purpose. The drawn stems and bell-bowls typify tavern and domestic cordial glasses. With a long-drawn tear in the stem, a short bowl, and a foot measuring substantially more in diameter than the bowl rim, the slender cordial glass now conveyed an impression of being taller than contemporary wineglasses although in reality of about the same height (fig. 177).

The Female Spectator, 1744, in discussing tea-drinking, recorded that 'tea whether of the Green or Bohea kind, when taken in excess occasions a dejection of spirits and flatulency, which lays the drinker of it under a kind of necessity of having recourse to more animating liquors. The most temperate and sober of the sex find themselves obliged to drink wine pretty freely after it. None of them nowadays pretend to entertain with the one without the other, and the bottle and the cordial-glass are as sure an appendix to the tea-table as the slop basin. Brandy, rum and other spirituous liquors are become a usual accompaniment to tea.'

Tea-table cordial glasses were graceful in design, made from the best metal, and always displayed new decorative features, contrasting with the heavy dullness of the average domestic or tavern type. From about 1725 bowls tended to become shorter and squarer, smaller in diameter, thinner in section, and without the heavy base. Stems became correspondingly longer, usually plainly solid, sometimes with a tooled collar at the bowl junction: others were plainly knopped. Moulded silesian stems (fig. 184) are also found on cordial glasses, early examples being wide-shouldered and sturdy, sometimes with a solid sphere of glass between shoulder and bowl (fig. 178). Tavern cordials throughout the eighteenth century were usually drawn with shallow trumpet bowls and straw shanks. Until the 1750's the stem might contain an elongated tear and the foot was folded.

Cordial glasses with air- and opaque-twist stems (figs. 190a) accompanied the early London-made tea-table porcelain from the mid-1740's. Stems were tall and bowl shapes now included bell, straight-sided bucket (fig. 182), ogee and trumpet (fig. 185), the latter merging into a straw shank. The thin-walled bowls were often engraved, and occasionally the base of a bowl might be encircled with shallow-moulded fluting, or moulded dimpling. Cordial glasses with filigree stems are more frequent than the earlier types.

The fashion for cordial drinking waned from the early 1760's: facet-cut examples are therefore comparatively rare (fig. 186).

Flute cordial glasses with long, deep, extremely narrow tapering funnel bowls, often with drawn stems of about the same length (fig. 190b), were made from about 1740 until 1770. Collectors generally refer to these as ratafia glasses, but no evidence seems available to indicate that this was a contemporary term or that they were used exclusively for ratafia. This was a brandy infusion in which most of the soft fruits were used, black cherries, strawberries, raspberries, currants, and mulberries, all picked at the prime of their ripeness. Ratafia was sold by the bottle in three qualities, fine, dry, and common.

Cordial glasses might have faintly moulded vertical fluting encircling the lower half of the bowl, suggesting that they were intended for those cordials which were inclined to lose their clarity whilst standing (fig. 190d). The bowl might be engraved with a narrow flowered border. The majority, however, had flutes of clear glass engraved with an all-over flower-spray. The un-knopped stems were plain: after 1750 they might be air-twist or opaque-twist. Some stems display a colour-twist and very rarely combined air- and opaque white-twist. Feet were always plain, their diameter measuring more than half as much again as the bowl rims (fig. 182).

Although a glassful of cordial might be termed a dram, dram glasses and the style of drinking known as dramming were particularly associated with 'distilled Spirituous liquors or Strong Waters' — as spirits such as brandy, whisky, rum, and gin were defined by Act of Parliament (George III (3) c. 38, No. 9). The distilling of strong waters was a profitable Elizabethan occupation and in 1613 Overbury referred to the 'new Trade of Brewing Strong Waters'. Burton's *Diary* of 1654 described visits to 'Tobacco-shops and Strong-Water Houses', and the State Papers three years later record searching 'the House of Samuel Rogers a strong-water man'. The *London Gazette* in 1707 mentioned 'Thomas Mathews, late of Newberry, Strong-water Man'.

These strong waters were served in small vessels known variously as dram cups, dram dishes, dram pots, and dram glasses, the latter term dating from the 1660's. There was a distinction between the techniques of dram-ming and drinking, dramming being associated with the gulping of cordials and strong waters.

The earliest style of dram glass was a small, thimble-shaped beaker measuring about $1\frac{1}{4}$ inches in height, either plain-surfaced or decorated with two rows of prunts or raised icicles in Venetian style and supported on four tiny feet. In 1670 John Greene, a city glass-seller, was importing Venetian dram cups without feet.

Dram cups in flint-glass, stronger than those of soda-metal, were so designed as to be less liable to get broken in the rough-and-tumble of strong-water houses. The small cup was joined to a heavy foot by a short, heavily moulded, plain knop or baluster. Dram glasses towards the end of the century became rather more elegantly designed with straight-sided bowls of thick section on flattened or spherically knopped stems merging into thick plain disc feet. By 1710 stems might be short and plain, or might be entirely lacking with the bowl joined directly to the plain foot. Dram glasses of this form in inferior metal and of poor workmanship were made in vast quantities from 1713, after Parliament had removed all restrictions connected with the distillation and sale of spirits, thus setting in motion that devastating craze for drinking strong waters, particularly gin, which caused so much havoc among the poor during the next thirty years.

Short, drawn, trumpet-bowled dram glasses on plain disc feet appeared in about 1720; finer-quality glasses of this type were also made with thinner bowls and well-shaped folded feet, intended for use in the home. During the 1720's appeared the foot with a substantial solid dome to which the bowl was welded. Terraced feet first appeared on dram glasses; radially moulded feet were also used. Other feet were pressed with coarse or fine radial stringing passing over the rim to meet near the punty mark. Although bowl and stem forms show wide variations, the diameter of the feet considerably exceeded that of bowl rims until about 1745. Cost of such glasses at the glass-house in this year was 1s. 6d. for a dozen of fourteen.

Short air-spiral stems were unable to display their beauty to advantage on dram glasses, but a few are known dating to the 1740's. The opaque-spiral was frequently used on domestic dram glasses from the mid-century, and short, knopped stems of clear glass were made for half a century or more after 1770. Contemporary were dram glasses with ovoid bowls on plain stems, rather taller than other types, usually made from thick, poor-quality metal. Dram glasses of the waisted tumbler form, 2 to 3 inches high and filled only to two-thirds capacity, were also made in large numbers from about 1750 until the 1820's.

The thumping glasses mentioned by D'Urfey in 1719 and in continual production throughout the Georgian period were short, stumpy glasses with drawn bowls on thick stems with heavy disc feet. They became known as 'hammering' glasses in domestic circles, and in the taverns as 'firing' glasses, by political and other societies who rapped the thick feet of their

228

glasses upon the table as a form of acclamation in honour of the toast. This produced a sound resembling the firing of a ragged volley of musketry: hence the term 'firing glasses'. The majority appear to date to the second half of the eighteenth century, but the heavy thumping foot can be traced back to 1710 and sets are known engraved with dates of the 1850's.

These glasses were exceptionally sturdy and of strong construction to resist a reasonable amount of pounding. Feet were heavy discs of glass sometimes as much as $\frac{1}{2}$ inch thick, never less than $\frac{3}{16}$ inch, and were appreciably larger in diameter than were the bowl rims (fig. 187). Feet are almost always plain, but occasional specimens have radially moulded, stepped, or square feet. Punty scars are almost invariably present except in fine examples dating from the early 1800's.

The stem, short and thick to prevent fracture by concussion, was at first drawn into a thick baluster or flattened spherical knop. After about 1725 the bowl might rest upon a solid dome of smaller circumference than the foot. This was followed by a centrally knopped stem and a plain, straight stem often enclosing a tear. Air- and opaque-spirals are rare on firing glasses; other fine examples have their stems facet-cut. Early stem forms appeared in firing glasses of later periods, but correct interpretation of metal and other features enables dating to be decided with some accuracy.

Bowls were thick-walled to withstand the shock of firing, although thinly blown bowls of an excellent tough metal have been noted in association with opaque-spiral stems. Bowl forms included trumpet, bell, ovoid, straight-sided, plain ogee, pressed ogee with flat flutes encircling the base, and fluted ogee with decorative cutting around the lip. Bowls were often engraved with society emblems such as those associated with the Jacobite movement. Masonic firing glasses were engraved with emblems of the craft. Sets included a tall 'constable' or master-glass of a capacity six times greater than the smaller ones. These were charged with liquor, the constable standing unused upon the table except on special ceremonial occasions.

The toast-master with his deceptive drinking-glass was an essential feature of eighteenth-century conviviality, when company drinking might be hard and long. Exactly when the office of toaster or toast-master originated is uncertain. A Toasters' Club is known to have been functioning in 1690 and Brown's *Humorist*, 1704, refers to 'the Chief Toaster at a Drinking-Match'.

Few toasters of the eighteenth century could withstand the effects of the continued drinking of highly alcoholic liquors and still officiate soberly. Special glasses were therefore designed for their use, bearing an outward resemblance to ordinary drinking-glasses or long-stemmed cordial glasses, but deceptive as to the amount of liquor they contained (fig. 181). The almost-solid bowl possessed only a small V-shaped depression containing a bare half-ounce of liquor. Toasters were first styled toast-masters in the late 1740's at a time when this official's special glass resembled a tall-stemmed cordial glass with a straight-sided deceptive bowl and a solid, conical foot.

Toast-master glasses should not be confused with the short, deceptive glasses of later in the century and early in the nineteenth century. These, commonly used by tavern-keepers for a somewhat similar purpose, were known as sham-drams. They were generally short, solid-bowled editions of the contemporaneous strong-ale glasses.

Figure 174

'The Dilettante Society' by Thomas Patch, *c.* 1750. The small-bowled cordial glasses have plain stems with highly domed feet. The peak of the high-kick in the bottle base to the left can be seen rising above the liquor.

In the Tate Gallery

Figures 175–80

CORDIAL GLASSES

(175) With trumpet bowl and drawn cylindrical stem tooled into knops at the ends, and containing spherical and elongated tears. High-domed foot. Early eighteenth century. Height 7⅛ inches.

Formerly in the Bles Collection

(176) With solid-based straight-sided bowl diamond-engraved around the rim 'Take a dram old boy', with scrolls; acorn stem on ball knop; flat folded foot; *c.* 1700. Height 5 inches.

Formerly in the Bles Collection

(177) Made in three pieces; drawn trumpet bowl with elongated tear in extension; short inverted baluster between two flattened knops; solid conical foot; 1730's to 1740's.

In the Brooklyn Museum

(178) With straight-sided thistle bowl on solid base; four-sided smooth-shouldered silesian stem; folded foot. George I period.

In the Victoria and Albert Museum

(179) With bell bowl drawn into a tooled neck; baluster between annular and flattened knops; folded foot. Early Georgian.

In the Victoria and Albert Museum

(180) With everted rimmed thistle bowl on solid base containing a spherical tear; necked; with inverted baluster between cushion and flattened knops; domed and folded foot. Early Georgian.

In the Brooklyn Museum

Figures 181–6

(181) Toast-master glass with deceptive, thick-sided thistle bowl on solid base, engraved 'Glorious Memory' and the cypher W III R below the royal crown; plain stem; folded foot. George II period, of Irish glass. Height 7⅞ inches.

Formerly in the Bles Collection

(182) Cordial glass with bucket bowl engraved with laureate bust of William III, the inscription 'The Immortal Memory', and crowned harp; plain stem; plain conical foot. Mid-eighteenth century.

In the Corning Museum

(183) Toasting-glass with clear trumpet bowl; slender stem, opaque corkscrew within two-ply spiral; folded foot; *c.* 1750.

In the Victoria and Albert Museum

(184) One of a pair of cordial glasses with bucket bowls, flower and foliage engraving; reeded silesian stems; plain feet; *c.* 1740's. Height $6\frac{3}{4}$ inches.

(185) Williamite cordial glass with drawn bowl and stem; engraved with equestrian portrait of William III and the inscription 'In Glorious Memory of King William'; domed and folded foot.

By courtesy of Messrs Christie, Manson & Woods Ltd

(186) Cordial glass with ovoid bowl, rim encircled by engraving; facet-cut stem; folded foot. Early George III period.

Figures 187–90

(187) Dram glass with drawn conical bowl, plain cylindrical stem, and plain foot. The rim is engraved 'SUCCESS TO WIL. & MARY'. Joseph Bles illustrates this glass, dating it between 1689 and 1694. Height 4 inches.

In the collection of Sir J. R. Risley

(188) Dram glass with drawn conical bowl; plain stem with air bubbles; low, terraced folded foot with rough punty mark. The bowl, which has a narrow gilded rim, is engraved with the coronet and cypher of Mary, Marchioness of Rockingham, widow of the first marquess. This would have been engraved between his death in 1752 and her own in 1761. Height 4 inches.

In the collection of Lady Kathleen Ward

(189) Ale glass with funnel bowl with writhen twist continuing over dumb-bell knopped stem; ribbed foot. *c.* 1800.

(190) Group in which the heights of cordial, ratafia, and toast-master's glasses may be compared with (*centre*) a contemporary wineglass measuring 6 inches. 1750's and 1760's. (*a*) Cordial glass, its ogee bowl with thickened base, engraved with viscount's coronet; opaque-twist stem with central gauze and two spiral threads; plain conical foot. (*b*) Ratafia

232

glass with deep funnel bowl engraved with a design in flowers and foliage in keeping with fine tea-table porcelain; air-twist stem; plain foot. (*c*) Wineglass with ogee bowl; plain stem; highly domed and folded foot. (*d*) Cordial glass with ovoid bowl, rim encircled with engraved stars; facet-cut stem; plain foot. (*e*) Toast-master's glass with deceptive bowl; opaque-twist stem; domed and folded foot.

CHAPTER FIFTEEN

JACOBITE GLASSES

THE JACOBITE MOVEMENT covered exactly a century, from 1688 when James II abdicated his throne, through the lifetime of Chevalier de St. George, King James III of the Jacobites and known as the Old Pretender, to that day in 1788 when death removed his son, Prince Charles Edward. Around the historic adventures of these three men glass played a rather sinister part, for ardent supporters thought it a duty to toast their health at the risk of liberty. Strange and secret clubs and societies were formed which had an immense influence on the Jacobite movement, their semi-seditious inscribed glasses being closely guarded from prying Georgian supporters.

Frail mementoes of a lost cause, the drinking-glasses which clinked to Jacobite toasts can be classified in chronological sequence. At first they were conspicuous for their fine metal: only the best was good enough for ceremonial glasses intended to honour an exiled Royal House.

With the proclamation of James III of England and VIII of Scotland at the Palace of St. Germain on 16th September 1701, a fervent wave of Stuart patriotism swept these islands. Simultaneously the tear became a popular decoration for drinking-glass stems — apt cypher for a lost throne. First it appeared in the heavy baluster stem, fashionable in the years between revolution and rebellion (1688–1715). Bowls were still without engraved emblems or inscriptions.

Among the two hundred or so heavy baluster forms, one is particularly noticeable: a glass having a deep thistle-shaped bowl with a solid round base, above a stem perfect acorn in shape, through which runs a brilliant tear into a small knop above the foot (fig. 46). This first appeared in 1701, and there seems no reason to doubt that it is the original drinking-glass for sending a cryptic greeting to fellow Jacobites: England's oak and Scotland's thistle, with the tear for the lost throne, are represented.

The British Museum houses the manuscript of a lengthy Jacobite ballad, 'Directions to a Painter'. Written in 1714, it contains these lines:

'At the sad Prospect of his Peoples Woe,
Let the big Tears in our Goblits show.'

The thistle-acorn glass as a Jacobite symbol stood alone until 1710, when the white rose with its six petals expanded into heraldic form, was adopted as their insignia by many of the various societies which came into being during 1709 following country-wide resentment against the impeachment of Dr Sacheverell, the clergyman-politician. The most influential of these clubs was 'The Cycle of the White Rose' founded at Wrexham by Sir Watkin Williams Wynn on the birthday of the Old Pretender in 1710. Meetings were held at three-weekly intervals in the homes of members whose loyalty was beyond suspicion. Diamond-inscribed drinking-glasses were used by certain members from 1724, a custom copied by other Jacobite societies.

When a Jacobite group rose to toast 'the king', their host would lift his charged glass above a bowl of water over which glasses were clinked in acknowledgment that the toast referred not to the king upon the throne but to the exile beyond the seas. It was customary at one period for loyal upholders of the Stuart cause to fling the empty glass over the left shoulder after a Jacobite toast, shattering it to fragments so that the goblet would not serve a baser purpose.

The diamond-engraved series of Amen glasses (fig. 191) appeared on the Jacobite scene no earlier than about 1745: authorities have for long attributed them to a date shortly after the Jacobite rebellion of 1715. Amen glasses are all of the same general style, with a capacious drawn trumpet bowl, usually with a tear in the plain stem, often with an air-twist stem. Amen glasses are engraved with the cipher of James III of England and VIII of Scotland surmounted by a royal crown (fig. 191). The cipher is composed of the entwined script letters I R direct and reversed. The numeral 8 appears either as part of the cipher or immediately below the lower scrolls and above the word 'Amen'. Two verses of the Jacobite paraphrase of 'God save Great James our King' is diamond-engraved in small script on the bowl and a third verse continued on the foot.

The Jacobite rose which appears on so many propaganda glasses has no connection with the sixteenth-century five-petalled heraldic rose of England, itself a combination of the York and Lancaster roses. The Stuart rose dates from 1349 when David II, then a prisoner at Windsor, took for his symbol a white rose. Thus it became a family badge to be used as an emblem by the Old Pretender nearly four centuries later. The rose has always been regarded as an emblem of secrecy and was therefore trebly suitable as a Jacobite emblem.

The Jacobite heraldic rose, with six (fig. 197a), seven or eight petals,

236

181–183   Toast-master, cordial, and toasting glasses

184–186   Three cordial glasses

187–189   Dram glasses and writhen-twist ale glass

190   Cordial, ratafia, wine, cordial, and toast-master glasses

191–196   Engraved Jacobite drinking-glasses

197 Engraved Jacobite drinking-glasses

decorated the bowls of a great number of drinking-glasses associated with the 1745 rising under the leadership of the Young Pretender. Springing from the same stalk may be a single small bud to the left and/or a large bud to the right. No contemporary evidence has yet been discovered by which the underlying meaning of the rose and its buds may be interpreted. The usually accepted theory, however, is that budless roses were engraved during the few years preceding the birth of Prince Charles Edward on 31st December 1720; single-bud glasses after the birth of Charles, but before the birth of his brother Henry, Stuart-styled Duke of Albany and York, on 6th March 1725, when a second and smaller bud was added, remaining there until the twenty-two-year-old Duke became Cardinal Bishop of Frascati in 1747 and the second bud was discarded.

This theory, however, cannot be sustained as Jacobite roses do not appear on flint-glass made much earlier than 1740. A great number, probably the majority, of Jacobite rose glasses have air-twist stems, a feature not found in flint-glass earlier than about 1740. A majority, too, appear to have two buds, whereas the great period for Jacobite propaganda glasses was after the defection of Prince Henry. Flowered glasses having one side of the bowl decorated with a single engraved blossom were popular during the period of Jacobite activity, thus masking the underlying significance of the propaganda emblem. The rose was a fashionable motif of the period and is not necessarily of Jacobite interest unless of the quasi-heraldic form made to escape notice among the naturalistic specimens.

Another theory sometimes put forward is that the seven-petalled roses represent the Old Pretender, and eight petals his son. If this were the case, the eight-petalled rose should be very frequent, but actually it is extremely rare. On that theory, too, the seven-petalled rose might have one bud and the eight-petalled rose no bud at all. But these designs are never seen.

The most reasonable interpretation yet put forward in connection with the presence of the heraldic rose on Jacobite glasses is that the rose represents the House of Stuart, the small bud the Old Pretender, the large bud on the right being added either in honour of the arrival of Prince Charles Edward in Scotland or after James's proposal to 'abdicate' in favour of his son. It seems generally agreed that the rose with the single bud preceded the two-budded spray, both continuing simultaneously after about 1745.

It is interesting to note that when Jacobite roses are accompanied by one bud there are five leaves; two buds, only four leaves; the rose alone, six leaves. Counting rose, buds, and leaves together, they invariably number seven, a numeral hallowed by the Stuarts as having mystic significance.

241

Portraits engraved on Jacobite glass usually celebrate the personality of the Young Pretender who, almost unknown in these islands until 1745, is frequently shown in tartans, a dress he did not wear until he went into hiding. It seems highly probable, therefore, that most portrait glasses were engraved after 1745. The white cockade he is sometimes shown wearing appeared as a Jacobite badge during 1736 (fig. 200). Some portrait glasses have the figure surrounded by sprigs of the cottage garden plant, Jacob's Ladder, occasionally interwoven with sprigs of oak. Obviously portrait glasses were brought out only for guests of proven loyalty to the Cause, otherwise they were reserved for personal use. Few portrait glasses depict the Old Pretender (fig. 202).

Rose and portrait glasses almost invariably display additional emblems, frequently with an inscription, all possessing cryptic significance. Roses are usually found either alone or in company with a butterfly, star, oak-leaf or thistle. Few of them preceded 1746, when a further rebellion was plotted to take place in 1750, delayed until 1752, then abandoned. During the mid-century years vast quantities of propaganda souvenirs flooded the country. These included many cheaply engraved drinking-glasses bearing Jacobite emblems and suitable for household and tavern use. Conventional versions of the rose displaying six or more polished circular petals and unpolished central cross-hatching were engraved on these purely commercial products.

It has been impossible to discover who engraved the diamond-point Amen glasses: not even tradition gives a hint. Regarding wheel-engraved Jacobites, it is obvious that as glass-houses were under the supervision of Excise officers, they were the work of specialist engravers until after about 1752 when objects for Jacobite propaganda entered a commercial phase.

Bles thinks it possible that Collin, a silversmith of Bond Street, was also an engraver of Jacobite glass. It was from Collin's window that the Young Pretender secretly viewed the coronation procession of George III. Hannah Ashburn, 'At the Rose, the corner of Fleet-Bridge', a well-known London glass-seller and fan-maker from about 1740, displayed on her bill-head dated 1745 an elaborate cartouche enclosing a rose and a single bud, together with an open fan similarly decorated. It seems reasonable to assume that glasses sold at this establishment might be engraved with Jacobite emblems. Thousands of paper-leafed propaganda fans similar to the example illustrated on the bill-head were distributed in the Jacobite cause. There is evidence that some glass was decorated by a Derby glass-engraver named Duesbury who continued this work until 1771. A remarkable similarity is apparent in the craftsmanship of early engraved Jacobite roses, indicating that they were of limited manufacture.

Glasses blazoned with a stricken and burgeoning oak (fig. 198e) were issued about 1740 to members of the Oak Society. The burgeoning stock is shown with two vigorous young saplings springing from the roots. Cavaliers had pollarded oak trees as a symbol of mourning for Charles I on the anniversaries of his execution. The emblem therefore refers to the beheaded king and a hope for restoration of the Stuart line. A similar design was diamond-engraved on tall flutes used at the coronation of Charles II. On the right of the tree in the Oak Society version usually appears the formerly unidentified trefoil plant, symbol of revenge. On the opposite side of the bowl is the rose and bud with the Society password *Revirescrit* inscribed above. In 1752 the six-rayed Star of Hope was added and the motto changed to *Redeat*. A glass bearing a six-rayed star may be engraved also with a rose and two buds (fig. 198f).

The symbolism of the oak-leaf derives from the incident of Charles II and the Boscobel Oak. The theory is that the oak-leaf was an emblem for English Jacobites, the thistle an emblem for Scotsmen. There is also a double significance arising from the fact that on the day when Charles II entered London he wore a spray of oak-apples in memory of his escape ten years earlier. The appearance of oak-leaves on drinking-glasses may therefore be taken as foreshadowing a second Restoration. The leaf also had a special Scottish significance. The clans in battle or on great occasions wore a flower or a sprig of greenery in their bonnets and for centuries it had been the Stuart custom to wear a spray of oak-leaves.

The thistle, representative of Scotland and used in much the same manner as the rose to which it is frequently joined, is seldom found as an independent motif (fig. 194). The blue gold-embroidered standard raised by the Old Pretender in 1715 had a thistle blazoned on one side. Glasses engraved with a thistle or a thistle crowned may be regarded as being both Scottish and Jacobite in sentiment. The triple ostrich plume occurs either with portraits of the Young Pretender or independently (fig. 198a). From the time of James I this had been considered the special badge of the Prince of Wales.

Among the dozen or more additional emblems is the jay (fig. 192). This obvious bird emblem for the initial letters of James and Jacobite has not previously been identified. The wheel-engraved jay, with its typical upstanding crest, barred wing, and spreading tail, usually found perched upon a spray of Jacob's Ladder foliage, has always been mistaken for a blackbird because, during the '15, the Old Pretender was referred to in the Jacobite ballad, 'Good luck to my Blackbird where'er he may be'. Because of his shining black eyes the Stuart family had nicknamed him 'Blackbird'. The jay is sometimes shown eyeing a dragonfly resting on the same branch, conveying the idea of St. George and the dragon — the 'usurper' King George being the dragon. The raven too, having served as a badge of the ancient Scottish kings, also appears as a Jacobite symbol.

Jacob's Ladder foliage (fig. 192), a then common garden plant which frequently decorated wheel-engraved glass, was emblematic of Jacobite efforts in assisting the Stuarts in their attempted climb to former royal heights. The Old Pretender, in his Declaration to the Rebels of 1715, quotes the prophecy of Jacob: 'Monarchy shall be hereditary'.

The carnation (fig. 198), used alone or with other motifs non-Jacobite in nature, should not be construed as Jacobite. It is, however, sometimes seen with the quasi-heraldic roses and then represents the royal crown. The *Universal Dictionary* says: 'The word carnation first appears as coronation and may have meant shaped like a corona or crown from its indented petals.' From early Tudor days this flower has been used as a royal badge.

The word 'daffodil' is accepted as a popular corruption of the Greek *Asphodos,* and, as the flower appears only on later specimens, an obvious interpretation is found in classical mythology, where this is the flower that blooms eternally in the fields of the dead. This emblem appears in place of the rose and is shown growing from a sprig of oak.

Yet another occasional flower emblem, the fritillary or snake's-head, has formerly been too hastily identified as the tulip, to which flower no possible association with Jacobitism can be found. It is unlikely that the Jacobites would use a symbol so Orange in its source. The snake's-head emblem, with its characteristic pointed petals, appears only on post-'45 glasses and is thought to refer to the defection of Prince Henry when he joined the Roman Church in 1747. A fritillary is also a butterfly, having markings similar to the flower, and this is engraved on some Jacobite glasses.

Monkshood leaves are sometimes noted around portraits of the Young Pretender. Its Jacobite affiliations are unquestionable and the general symbolism of the monkshood flower is obvious. General George Monck played a leading part in restoring the Stuarts.

The sun and sunflower, which frequently appear on contemporary Jacobite seals, are easily recognizable emblems. The sun was the badge of James II as Duke of York and the sunflower is supposed, in the words struck on a Jacobite medal, to 'look at, love and follow' the sun, thus expressing unswerving loyalty. Hovering butterflies with expanded wings represent prayers for the 'return of the soul' of the Jacobite movement; hovering bees the hoped-for renewal of activity after rest. Both were used during the decline of the Stuart cause. The forget-me-not was occasionally engraved after Culloden: its significance is obvious.

During the fifties and sixties, as Jacobites viewed various examples of compromising conduct on the part of the Stuarts, their enthusiasm waned and expressions of despair made their appearance even on drinking-glasses. Sprays of roses are found with the butterfly converted into a caterpillar and gnawing at the stem. Occasionally a moth caught in a spider's web stretching over other emblems serves to portray their awareness of intrigue.

'No names, no exile!' This cryptic message engraved on Jacobite drinking-glasses came to be associated with emblems. Each of the following inscriptions has a Jacobite significance.

Ab Obice Major: The great often fall. Used after 1745.

Audentior Ibo: I shall go more boldly. This Virgilian motto (Aen., IX, 291) refers to the defeat at Culloden.

Cognoscunt Me Mei: My friends know me.

Fiat: Let it be done. It is widely believed that this was the password of the Cycle Club and that all glasses inscribed *Fiat* in italics originally belonged to members. The word is usually found on rose glasses, infrequently on portrait glasses. English members had oak-leaves engraved on their glasses; Scottish members had thistles.

Floreat: He or the cause will flourish again.

God Bless the Prince: Most glasses with this inscription post-date the '45, when the Jacobites considered Charles Edward as Prince of Wales presumptive.

Health to All True Blues: Inscribed on drinking-glasses of the True Blue Society, a Jacobite club.

Hic Vir Hic Est: This, this is the man, taken from Virgil's praise of Augustus Caesar. It may refer to Charles Edward's arrival in Scotland.

Now or Never: This phrase was used by the Young Pretender in his secret message to adherents in the North of England before his campaign and after Culloden became a propaganda slogan in an effort to incite enthusiasm and support. It appears chiefly on tavern-type goblets.

Premium Virtutis: The reward of valour. These words were probably inscribed on drinking-glasses presented to Jacobites as a reward for some glorious action during the '45.

Radiete, Radeat or Radiat: May he shine. The last two versions are misspellings of the first. Refers to the radiant star of the legend 'Etoile en Soleil', to show that its glory still shone.

Reddas Incolumen: May you return safely. Commemorative of a secret visit the Young Pretender made to London in 1752. It usually accompanied a rose, star, forget-me-not, oak-leaf or thistle.

Redeat: May he come back. Inscribed on Oak Society glasses from 1752 and also found accompanied by the Arms of England and Scotland quarterly.

Redi: I have returned.

Revirescit or Reverescit (figs. 108 and 198): He is renewed. This was the password of the Oak Society and always accompanied the burgeoning oak.

Success to the Society: Probably inscribed on stock glasses issued by merchants to the numerous small societies and clubs which sprang up in the taverns of Northern England, Scotland, and the Welsh Marches.

The Glorious Memory: Refers to the days when the Stuarts occupied the throne. This is an abbreviation of the Orange Toast and was used for the purpose of disguise on Jacobite glass.

Figures 191–6

JACOBITE GLASSES, *c.* 1750

(191) Amen glass with drawn trumpet bowl, plain stem, and plain foot. Bowl engraved in diamond-point with the royal crown surmounting the cypher J R through which runs the figure 8, and the complete Jacobite anthem in four verses, two verses being on the bowl and two on the foot, ending with the word 'Amen' in a scrolled cartouche. The bowl is further engraved with the inscription 'To His Royal Highness the Duke' and 'To the Increase of the Royal Family'. The verses of the anthem inscribed are as follows:

> God Save the King, I pray
> God Bliss the King, I pray.
> God Save the King.
>
> Send Him Victorious.
> Happy and Glorious.
> Soon to reign over us
> God Save the King.
>
> God bliss the subjects all.
> And save both great and small in every station.
> That will bring home the King,
> Who has best right to reign,
> It is the only thing
> Can save the Nation.
>
> God Bliss the Prince of Wales,
> The true born Prince of Wales.
> Sent us by Thee.
>
> Grant us one favour more.
> The King for to restore.
> As Thous has done before.
> The Familie.
>
> God Save the Church, I pray,
> And Bliss the Church, I pray,
> Pure to remain.
>
> Against all Heresie,
> And Whigs Hypocrisie,
> Who strive maliciously
> Her to defame.

By courtesy of Messrs Christie, Manson & Wood Ltd

247

(192) Ogee bowl, straight stem, and heavy plain foot. Body wheel-engraved with the conventional rose, crested jay, and leaves of Jacob's Ladder plant.

In the Author's collection

(193) Ogee bowl, plain stem, and folded foot, its diameter measuring nearly half as much again as the bowl rim. Bowl engraved with rose and two buds and flying crested jay.

In the Author's collection

(194) *Fiat* glass with drawn trumpet bowl and plain stem on plain foot greater in diameter than the bowl rim. Bowl engraved with rose and two buds and flowering thistle; foot engraved with Prince of Wales's feathers.

In the Brooklyn Museum

(195) *Fiat* glass with bell bowl, double-knopped air-twist stem, and solid conical foot. Bowl engraved with rose and two buds and flowering thistle.

In the Brooklyn Museum

(196) Waisted bucket bowl, air-twist stem — gauze and pair of spirals — on solid conical foot. Bowl engraved with six-rayed Star of Hope and rose with two buds.

In the Brooklyn Museum

Figure 197

ENGRAVED JACOBITE AND WILLIAMITE DRINKING-GLASSES

Top row: Jacobite glasses. (*a*) *Fiat* glass with waisted bowl engraved with rose and two buds, oak-leaf, and star; plain stem with knop containing tear-drops; domed foot with wide flange. (*b*) Portrait glass with deep rectangular bowl engraved with a medallion containing a full-face portrait of Prince Charles Edward in tartans and wearing the Order of the Garter; slender air-twist stem on plain foot. (*c*) *Redi* glass with drawn trumpet bowl and air-twist stem on plain foot; bowl engraved with six-petalled rose, two buds, and a double oak-leaf; foot twice inscribed 'Redi'. (*d*) *Audentior Ibo* glass, the pointed funnel bowl engraved with a full-faced portrait of Prince Charles Edward wearing bonnet and tartans, flanked by a rose and one bud and a thistle; air-twist stem with two knops on conical foot.

Bottom row: (*a*) *Fiat* glass with pointed funnel bowl engraved with rose and one bud and an oak-leaf; air-twist stem with double knop and plain foot. (*b*) Williamite glass with drawn trumpet bowl containing a long tear on a plain folded foot; engraved with grape and vine-leaf motifs and the inscription 'The Glorious Memory of King William'. (*c*) Round funnel bowl engraved with rose and bud, thistle, and around the rim 'Success to the Society'; on opaque-twist stem and plain foot. (*d*) *Fiat* glass with drawn trumpet bowl and air-twist stem on plain folded foot; bowl engraved with rose and bud and an oak-leaf.

By courtesy of Messrs Christie, Manson & Woods Ltd

248

Figure 198

JACOBITE DRINKING-GLASSES, *c.* 1750

Top left: Fiat glass with a pointed funnel bowl engraved with a six-petalled rose and two buds and an oak-leaf; plain stem containing a single tear. The high foot is engraved with the Prince of Wales's feathers.

Top centre: Portrait glass, the round funnel bowl engraved with a full-face portrait of Prince Charles Edward in tartans, between a rose and thistle spray, on an air-twist stem with a wide folded foot.

Top right: Rose glass with pointed funnel bowl, engraved with a seven-petalled rose and two buds, and a butterfly, on a corkscrew mercury-twist stem on a plain foot.

Lower left: Disguised Jacobite goblet, the round funnel bowl engraved with roses and buds, carnation, sunflower, butterflies, acorns and oak-leaves suspended from rings; a two-knopped air-twist stem with conical foot.

Lower centre: Oak Society goblet, its round funnel bowl engraved with a rose and two buds, a stricken oak with two burgeoning branches, trefoil, and the motto *Revirescit* on a two-knopped air-twist stem with conical foot.

Lower right: Portrait goblet, with round funnel bowl engraved with Prince Charles Edward wearing the Order of the Garter and facing left in a floriate wreath between a seven-petalled rose with two buds and a thistle and bud, with a star. On a double-knopped air-twist stem with a plain foot.

All by courtesy of Messrs Christie, Manson & Woods Ltd

Figures 199–203

JACOBITE GLASSES

(199) *Redeat* glass, with pointed funnel bowl, double-knopped air-twist stem, and conical foot. Bowl engraved with eight-petalled rose and two buds.

(200) *Audentior Ibo* glass, with pointed funnel bowl, double-knopped air-twist stem, and conical foot. Bowl engraved with full-face portrait of Prince Charles Edward in tartans wearing bonnet with cockade, and the Order of the Garter, and a rose with one bud and a thistle.

(201) *Fiat* glass with pointed funnel bowl and straight air-twist stem, on domed and folded foot. Bowl engraved with rose and two buds and oak-leaves.

(202) Goblet with capacious cup-shaped bowl on plain stem. Engraved with portrait of the Old Pretender wearing a chaplet in a circle surmounted by a royal crown and inscribed in a scroll: 'Though he fall, he shall not be utterly cast down, for the LORD upholdeth him

249

with his hand. P37. v20.' The goblet has the dark quality of early flint-glass, and Mr Joseph Bles, its former owner, thought the inscription was engraved shortly after the battles of Sheriffmuir and Preston Pans in 1715. Height 8 inches.

(203) With deep ogee bowl, facet-cut stem, and plain foot. Bowl engraved with the Star of Hope and a crown above a full-face portrait of Prince Charles Edward in armour and wearing the Order of the Garter.

CHAPTER SIXTEEN

SERVING BOTTLES, DECANTERS, SQUARES, AND CARAFES

D ECANTERS HAVE PLAYED a distinguished part in the ritual of the English wine-service. Decanting, the gentle pouring of the wine from the original cask or bottle so that the sediment should not be disturbed, is probably as old as the crushing of grapes into wine. The English decanter traces its immediate descent from the white-enamelled earthenware serving bottles in which wine might be tabled throughout the Stuart period. These handled serving bottles, raised on foot rings and with string-courses encircling their short necks immediately below the mouth, were inscribed in blue with the names of their contents, such as claret, white wine, sack, and so on, with sometimes the addition of a cypher. These were of small capacity and few specimens are known dated later than 1662, although Doctor Plot referred to their manufacture in the 1680's. John Worlidge in 1678 noted that such bottles were apt to leak, liable to taint, and, being rough in the mouth, were difficult to cork.

More usually, however, the wine was poured into drinking-glasses from wine-bottles taken direct from the cellar. These, known to collectors as shaft-and-globe bottles, were of coarse dark glass with an almost spherical body and a long neck encircled below the mouth with a knife-edged string-course, and with a narrow kick or intruding base.

The shaft-and-globe bottle was made contemporaneously with the rather more costly onion- or balloon-shaped bottle with a short tapering neck and high kick. This, with minor variations, was made until the 1720's when wine-bottle sides were straightened, making the wide body almost cylindrical. The neck was lengthened and the kick became higher. By 1740 the body was narrower and taller. Until the 1820's the wine-bottle might bear on its shoulder a glass seal impressed with a heraldic device, cypher or initials, and the date. When acting as a serving bottle upon the table a silver bottle-ticket might be suspended with a chain from its neck (fig. 91).

When George Ravenscroft evolved transparent flint-glass in 1675,

251

serving bottles were among the table-ware he made. They appear in his trade list of 1677 as with or without loop handles and glass stoppers. To facilitate filling, the mouth was expanded into an almost hemispherical funnel with a spout lip immediately opposite the handle.

Many of these serving bottles appear to have been lavishly ornamented with applied decoration in the Venetian fashion and listed as 'extraordinary work' at greater cost. Thick threads applied to the body might be trailed into a trellis design, or the surface tooled into a similar pattern, listed by Ravenscroft as 'bottles all over nipt diamond wais'. Body decoration included also trailed chainwork, vertical strapwork, ribbing, pincered wings, strawberry prunts. Elaborate frills encircled the lower neck and the body rested upon a heavily gadrooned foot ring. The base was intruded in the form of a cone, known as the kick, with a rough punty mark at the apex. The loop handle with curled ends might be given a rope-like twist: usually it was left plain. The stopper was hollow, highly domed, and topped by a solid knop finial, frilled decoration concealing the join. A projecting rib encircled the interior of the neck upon which the stopper rested loosely.

In quart-size and weighing exactly one pound, serving bottles in extraordinary work cost dealers 4s. apiece. If the body were merely ribbed the price was 3s. Such serving bottles continued to be made until early Georgian days.

More commonly serving bottles in flint-glass were of shaft-and-globe form (fig. 204) with incurved shoulders, intruding base, and an applied ring encircling the neck a little below the mouth. In the British Museum is a pint-size example, its body 'nipt diamond wais', bearing the Ravenscroft seal and mounted on a gadrooned foot ring. The majority, however, were plain-surfaced with the mouth flaring slightly outward (fig. 209). It is probable that few shaft-and-globe decanters were made in flint-glass earlier than about 1690, when they were referred to as decanters to distinguish them from wine-bottles.

The earliest use of the word 'decant' so far noted was by Wotton in reference to fruit juice in 1633. Thorpe quotes an advertisement of 1690 illustrating a lip-spouted earthenware jug described simply as a 'decantor'. Flint-glass decanters are included among the tariffs levied on English goods exported to France during 1701, and Oxford University accounts contain frequent references to 'pairs of decanters' between 1702 and 1709. *The Tatler,* dated 9th August 1710, printed the following advertisement: 'At the Flint Glass-House in White Fryars are made and sold all sorts of decanthers of the best Flint.' *Kersey's Dictionary*, 1715, defines decanter as 'a Bottle made of clear Flint-glass, for the holding of Wine, etc., to be pour'd off into a Drinking-Glass'.

Plain-surfaced shaft-and-globe decanters continued to be widely used until the accession of George III. Minor variations in form are found, but appear to lack any chronological significance, although later examples are usually without string rings. Their height ranges from 7 to 9 inches. Unless it bears commemorative engraving such as Jacobite emblems, metal must be the deciding factor in dating a shaft-and-globe decanter. Pre-George II glass, for instance, often contained impure lead oxide causing the high kick in the base to appear almost opaque. The collector must remember the existence of thinly blown Victorian decanters similar in form, but with shoulder curves more accentuated.

The straight-sided mallet-shaped decanters of the Queen Anne (fig. 210) and George I periods were rather more capacious, height for height, than the shaft-and-globe type, in spite of the kick rising in a high cone. The sides might slope slightly inward forming an angular shoulder at the neck junction and occasionally in other examples the body was pressed into a hexagonal or octagonal form. Some examples have been noted with a loop-handle, and others with a spout lip to assist pouring. It is unusual to find the mouth interior ground to receive a glass stopper.

The mallet decanter was superseded by a group in which the body was shaped on plan into four deep lobes, this pressed quartrefoil design dating between 1725 and the mid-century (fig. 211). The long neck might be encircled, immediately below the mouth, with two, three, or four joined rings. Both mallet and quatrefoil decanters may be found in a heavy metal displaying a slightly blue tint. During the 1730's two interesting series of flint-glass decanters were made: those with vertically grooved cylindrical bodies, and the square-bodies type with vertical grooves at the corners (fig. 212). The necks of both are encircled by rings.

The inclusion of a neck ring on any of these early decanters was inconsistent: it might be absent from the shaft-and-globe as early as 1690, yet encircle the neck of a similar decanter made half a century later.

In decanters properly so termed, the mouth interior was ground for the reception of a glass stopper: unground examples may more exactly be called carafes. In contradiction of the opinion of those authorities who give 1718 or various later years for the introduction of stopper-grinding, the process was fully described by John Worlidge in 1675. 'With a Turn [lathe] made for that purpose you may grind glass-stopples to each Bottle, that no liquor or spirit shall penetrate its closures: always observing to keep each

Stopple to its bottle which is easily done by securing it with a piece of pack-thread, each stopple having a button on top of it for that end and a glass ring round the bottle neck. These stopples are ground with the powder of the stone smyris, sold in the shops by the vulgar name of Emery, which with oil will exquisitely work the glass to your pleasure. First grind them rough with coarse emery, then make them smoother with fine. The mouths of your bottles are similarly ground in the Turn.'

Not until after 1745 were stoppers and decanter-mouths ground as a matter of routine. This process was carried out with a lathe resembling that used by engravers, the abrasive medium being emery powder and water. The stopper, fixed in a wooden chuck, was rotated in the lathe and tapered to the required dimensions. It was then introduced into the bottle-mouth, the workman carefully grinding one into the other, reducing the speed and gradually supplying finer and finer emery until a perfect fit was achieved. A few turns of the stopper with the hand completed the process. This method was continued throughout the collector's period.

No plain-bodied shaft-and-globe decanter of the seventeenth century seems to have survived complete with its glass stopper, which would have been hollow-blown. Stoppers were moulded solid after about 1700, and by 1710, although hollow ones were made throughout the century, the ball finial might be enriched with a single air tear or several spherical air bubbles. From about 1725 the bubbles might be comma-shaped. Stopper ends made before about the middle of the eighteenth century display punty marks — later they were ground flat. The celebrated Chastleton shaft-and-globe decanters are fitted with cut spire-finialled stoppers and are engraved with Jacobite emblems. They were made for Henry Jones, who died in 1761.

Decanter-mouths varied with the period. Except for collared lips on some of the later mallet-shaped series, mouths were invariably plain until about 1750 and a trifle thicker at the lip rim, adding necessary strength to the slightly tapering mouth entrance which was ground so that the stopper would fit with air-tight precision.

The sale of wine by the bottle was prohibited in taverns and inns from 1636 by a law which remained on the statute books until early in the nineteenth century. By the 1680's innkeepers were selling wine in carafes (fig. 29). These were usually stopperless serving bottles made from cheap glass, often green-tinted. In 1775 a quart of Dorchester ale served in a carafe cost 6d. Made in flint-glass, carafes were used as containers for water, one carafe and a pair of goblets being set before each two guests. They were advertised in flint-glass, plain and cut, until about 1800 as water crafts, half-pint carrosts, and carraffs.

England's fast-increasing wealth during the middle years of the eighteenth century brought unaccustomed refinements to many homes. Tableware in flint-glass of the improved quality then being made quickly captured the market. The flint-glass decanter became an object of beauty, given an honoured place in the home, while those it replaced, dull and heavy in comparison, were relegated to the kitchen. When cracked or broken they were traded to hawkers who disposed of the fragments as cullet. For this reason decanters and carafes in early forms are extremely rare.

Shouldered decanters (fig. 221) were fashionable from the late 1740's to about 1770 and continued to be made until the end of the century. One is illustrated with a steeple stopper on the trade card of John Harwood, Norwich, issued in 1792. According to the books of the Whitefriars Glasshouse they were known as Newdegate decanters and were of two types: (a) narrow-shouldered with outward sloping sides and (b) broad-shouldered narrowing towards the base. Carafes were also made in these forms. Early examples were wide-bodied and retained both kick and punty mark: these are rarely found in shouldered decanters made later than the early 1750's. Later the kick was reduced to a slight upward depression in the base and the punty mark was ground smooth. Like their predecessors these decanters were without lips and their stoppers ball-finialled. In September 1746 the Newcastle firm of Cookson and Company invoiced four such decanters of three pints capacity at 9d. per pound, their total weight being 12 pounds and the cost 9s. The wholesale price of each was therefore 2s. 3d. undecorated. Some examples after the mid-1780's were large-bodied and short-necked, having two plain neck rings. Few decorated examples may be dated later than the 1780's, however. A small group of early shouldered decanters have bodies grooved horizontally with seven to nine very shallow corrugations carefully polished. These are known to collectors as Norwich rings.

Shouldered decanters tended to become more slender-bodied by about 1750 and the ground stoppers supported plain cone-shaped finials. A print issued by Carrington Bowles in 1747 illustrates a pair of narrow-shouldered decanters, each with a plain cylindrical flat-topped finial to its stopper. Other prints issued during the following half-century display this feature, but curiously enough no such stoppers appear to remain. At this period the stopper was recessed in the decanter mouth, a ball-knop containing clusters of air beads often separating the ground stopper end from the finial.

255

From about 1750 the bodies of shouldered decanters might be enriched with wheel-engraving in naturalistic devices, dominated by floral sprays, birds, insects, and vine motifs. Engraving during the 1760's consisted of formal ornament, including trellis, husk, and sprig motifs. Festooning rope-work, usually fully polished and resembling light cutting, belongs to this decade. An advertisement in the *Weekly Mercury*, April 1771, refers to 'London and Bristol Glass . . . flower'd and cut pint and quart decanters; a variety of neat enamel'd wine glasses'. In the December issue of the same journal James and Arthur Jarvis advertise 'Cut, plain, sprig'd, and engraved quart decanters and a few plain half-gallon decanters; quart, pint and half pint carrosts'.

Tougher, more brilliant flint-glass was in production by about 1750, following the introduction of the tunnel leer for annealing. Shouldered decanters then became a field for all-over cutting with diamond facets (fig. 214). At first the facets were flat, then hollowed. Body facets were wider than long, shoulders were cut with wide, upward curving flutes, and necks with long narrow facets. Because fashion decreed the metal to be thinner than formerly, facets could only be shallow. Some of the most scintillating of facet-cutting came from the workshops of the London glass-sellers Thomas Betts, Jerome Johnson, John Akerman, and William Parker. By 1760 shouldered decanters might be blown with thicker bodies to accommodate deeper facets.

The body of a shouldered decanter during the 1760's, and possibly earlier, might have its base encircled with a double row of facets, short vertical flutes, or a plain zigzag, and its shoulders and neck enriched with scale or polygonal facets, or small detached circular discs later known as printies. The space between this decoration was engraved with an all-over design, usually of flowers and foliage, sometimes with star festoons, rarely with a commemorative scene.

Labelled decanters (fig. 221) date from the mid-1750's. The earliest reference to this decoration found by Francis Buckley is Jonas Phillips's advertisement in the *Norwich Mercury* dated 26th December 1755: 'new-fashioned Decanters with inscriptions engraven on them viz. Port, Claret, Mountain, etc., etc., decorated with vine leaves, Grapes, etc'. Other advertisements refer to them as 'flower'd and lettered decanters'. Ten years later they were generally advertised under the trade name of 'label decanters'.

The engraved labels covered a wide variety of liquors such as beer, burgundy (both rare), old hock, rum, punch, port, ale, white wine,

256

198 Engraved Jacobite drinking-glasses

199–203   Engraved Jacobite drinking-glasses

204 'The Brothers Clarke of Swakeleys' by Gawen Hamilton, *c.* 1750. Illustrating shaft-and-globe decanter and wineglasses

205 'A Literary Party at Sir Joshua Reynolds's' by James E. Doyle. Illustrating old-fashioned mallet-shaped decanter and a pair of new-fashioned taper decanters

Lisbon, Greek wine, cider. The lettering was enclosed in a cartouche re-sembling in shape the contemporary bottle-tickets in silver and enamels, the illusion being completed by encircling the decanter shoulder with engraved chain work. The cartouche carries engraved mantling above, vine-leaves and grapes below. The engraved labels for ale and beer bore hop and barley motifs instead of the vine: cider displayed apples and foliage. Sometimes the inscription was gilded, and rarely the ornament too (*see* Chapter 9). The opposite side of the decanter might be ornamented with floral sprays or other motifs.

A series was issued in which the labels were applied in white enamel and a few remain in coloured enamels. The greater part of this decoration was carried out by enamellers employed by the London and Bristol glass-sellers adapting standardized designs taken from the engravers' pattern book. The productions of Newcastle upon Tyne in this medium were the work of the Beilby family, perhaps entirely so. Beilby work displays skilful origin-ality, the lettering being incorporated with groupings of vine-leaves and grapes, flowers and other motifs, including the Beilby symbol of a butterfly (*see* Chapter 9). Enamellers also decorated shouldered decanters with coats of arms in full colour.

Few collectors are aware that a later series of labelled decanters was issued during the Regency period. The bodies of these are in the prussian shape, with three rings encircling the neck, and pear-shaped or target stopper-finials. They were made by the glass-houses of Birmingham, Stourbridge, and Sheffield. Labelled decanters of blue glass with gold lettering are discussed in Chapter 21.

The shouldered decanter is almost invariably without a lip to the mouth. Occasionally a decorated example of the late 1760's is found with a flared mouth, the lip being slightly turned back on itself for about $\frac{1}{4}$ inch, providing the first real mouth lip to be found on a decanter.

The spire-finialled stopper which superseded the ball type in shouldered decanters was introduced in about 1750 by Thomas Betts, the King's Arms Glass Shop, Charing Cross, London, under the name of 'Betts' Gothic Spire' during the minor mid-eighteenth-century vogue for Gothic orna-ment. The spire stoppers used on undecorated decanters were smooth-surfaced cones; with engraved decoration it was usual to cut the spire into pyramid form. When associated with decanters displaying any form of cutting the spire finials were usually cut to harmonize: with all-over faceted decanters the spire was enriched with small diamonds.

Towards 1760 stopper-finials might be in the form of flat, vertical discs,

261

plain-surfaced but slightly convex, their edges notched with lunar cutting, usually six to each face. After about 1760 convex diamond-cutting might decorate both faces of the disc. These stoppers are found more usually with the narrow-shouldered decanter (fig. 221). Towards the end of the era of the decorated shouldered decanter came the flat pear-shaped stopper-finial. Stoppers with plainly flat heart-shaped or clover-leaf finials belong to this period.

The mid-eighteenth-century vogue for champagne prompted some ingenious glassmen to evolve the shouldered decanter with a cylindrical pocket for ice extending from the side into the body, and a pair of such decanters in quart size was invoiced by Thomas Betts in 1755 at 12s.

'New-fashioned decanters' were advertised in 1765, too late to be associated with any form of shouldered decanter. This announcement, then, probably heralded the arrival of the taper decanter (fig. 223) with body more slender and shoulders more sloping than any former type. Its slim elegance was considered a fashionable refinement. Its base might be cut with a circuit of narrow vertical flutings, known to the collector as comb-fluting, and the body was decorated with shallow swags, stars, and other motifs associated with the classical style. These were in lightly applied cutting little removed from polished engraving, the neck being faceted either in a scale pattern or with diamonds. From about 1770 the neck might be cut with long flutes extending from shoulder to mouth and these might be notched (fig. 213). Cut decanters were now being widely advertised. Mouths of early taper decanters were without lips: after about 1770 the mouth might be slightly turned back on itself for about $\frac{1}{4}$ inch. Collectors will find little difficulty in distinguishing the heavily cut flint-glass taper decanters belonging to the 1820's and later.

Taper decanters of the 1760's were supplied with lunar-cut disc stoppers. As the body became slimmer the finial followed suit and became a flat, vertical lozenge or pear-shape such as was also associated with the shouldered decanter. Face-cutting on disc finials then became less elaborate than formerly, the edges usually being plainly bevelled.

'Curious barrel-shaped decanters cut on an entirely new pattern' (fig. 220) were advertised by Christopher Haedy in the *Bath Chronicle* of 21st December 1775. This shape was evolved by reducing the base diameter of the taper decanter so that shoulder and base were of similar dimensions and accentuating the bulge, thus giving the body a form resembling that of a contemporary wine-barrel. The body was cut with vertical lines to resemble staves: these were carried up the neck to the mouth. Incised rings encircling the body suggested hoops. Early barrel decanters were lipless: then came the lip, which soon became wider, and for the first time was made with a flat surface. Stopper-finials were either pear-shaped or of the target type. This barrel-shaped decanter has been known variously as the Indian club and the oviform type.

Competing with this slender decanter was a broad-shouldered type in which the sides were given a greater inward slope than formerly, the lower portion being encircled with comb-fluting extending about half-way up the body, the neck shortened and ornamented with three widely spaced rings, and the mouth expanded into a broad, flat lip which might slope towards the neck interior. The design emphasized horizontal lines, but although lacking the delicate grace of the earlier shouldered decanter this form continued in production until the 1830's.

Misleadingly called the barrel decanter by collectors because its silhouette slightly suggests a barrel, this was known to its makers as the prussian decanter. One specialist in this type of decanter was the firm of John Keeling, Dudley, whose trade card of 1784 illustrated such a decanter under this name. By about 1780 the flutes on such a decanter were usually blown-moulded, that is, the body was blown in warm earthenware moulds strengthened with iron bands and set into the floor of the glass-house. Early moulded fluting was usually finished on the cutting-wheel, but not invariably so. In an early-nineteenth-century series the flutes were made sloping to the left, such decanters being hand-cut until after 1802 when they might be blown in the open-and-shut mould invented in that year by Charles Chubsee of Stourbridge.

The prussian decanter of the eighteenth century might be engraved or lightly cut on the lower neck and upper body. Deep cutting was rare until the introduction, early in the nineteenth century, of an improved flint-glass (Chapter 3) which gave a hitherto unsurpassed brilliance to deeply cut decanters. This was followed by the entry of steam power into cutting-workshops in about 1806. Deep cutting by hand-operated cutting-wheels was costly, a week of seventy-two hours being hardly sufficient to cover the body of a quart decanter with small diamonds in relief. Steam-driven cutting-wheels revolved at a greater, more forceful speed. The 1809 trade card of W. Wilson, Steam Mills for Cut Glass, 40 Blackfriars Road, London, illustrates a lavishly diamond-cut prussian decanter with a disc stopper. The actual cutting was still carried out by hand.

Bands of relief diamonds encircling the decanter shoulder, with a herring-bone fringe beneath, were among early steam-mill productions. Gradually the band became deeper until the whole body was enveloped in deep cutting, as many as a dozen different types being used on a single decanter. The combinations of cut designs on decanter bodies are too numerous to classify here.

The prussian decanter brought with it a new shape in stopper-finials. This was the horizontal or mushroom-shape, the finial in many examples being separated from the ground stopper by a polished ball knop (fig. 228) or the stem cut. The curve of the mushroom top was moulded in gadrooned or radial grooves quite independent of the style of ornament on the body. Remaining as a legacy from earlier decanter forms were various vertical disc finials, such as the target type (fig. 222). This might have a large central boss or radial ridges on each face and either a cut or a moulded edge; alternatively it might be facet-cut on each face, or might be lightly impressed with trellis or other simple patterns. Such stoppers are found in prussian decanters made until the 1820's, when a heavy moulded pinnacle or globe finial became usual.

The cylindrical-bodied decanter (fig. 228) with perpendicular sides meeting the base at right angles had appeared by 1790, cut with inch-wide vertical flutes which continued over the shoulder; the neck was encircled with three rings. This type of cylindrical decanter was characteristic and continued in production until the 1830's. From about 1805 the shoulders might be ornamented with diamond-cutting in relief and the neck with horizontal prismatic cutting. Cylindrical decanters became more elaborate as a result of the efficiency of steam-driven cutting-wheels. The lower body might be encircled with comb-fluting, below a band of small diamond-cutting; or horizontal prismatic cutting might encircle the lower part with a band of diamond-cutting above, a plain shoulder, and horizontal prismatic cutting encircling the neck; there might be all-over prismatic cutting; and from 1810 step-cutting on shoulder and neck would contrast with body bands of varying prismatic designs (fig. 228). Variations numbered many hundreds.

Until about 1820 the cylindrical decanter was usually provided with a mushroom-shaped stopper. The body might then become any one of a wide variety of ungainly designs and the finial of the stopper hemispherical. Tall pinnacle stoppers date from the same period.

Regency days saw a brief vogue for lips with rims matching the neck rings below, feathered and cut rings excepted. The lip flared widely and horizontally outward from the neck of the heavy cylinder decanter, the flare beginning immediately above the upper neck ring. This style of decanter continued until the 1830's saw the close of England's great port-drinking days and the end of the collector's period as regards decanters.

Seven forms of neck rings have been recorded: plain round, plain double, plain triple, feathered, triangular, square, diamond-cut. The feathered ring (fig. 222d) is a double ring impressed with shallow transverse lines. Some late-prussian decanters had two neck rings only, usually the plain triple design (figs. 222b and g). After about 1817 applied rings might occasionally be omitted, the neck itself being cut with encircling prisms and other ornament (fig. 228f). Occasionally a decanter may be found in which the neck rings do not match.

Rings on a decanter neck were applied by rotating the red-hot decanter and dropping a thread of hot glass which became welded to the neck by contact. The whole was then reheated at the furnace mouth and a tool resembling a pair of spring sugar-tongs, with a die at the end of each arm, was pressed upon the hot ring, giving to it the required shape and size. The decanter was reheated for the addition of each subsequent ring. While shaping the mouth lip the rings were sufficiently heated to ensure that they would not fly off during annealing. The joints are always faintly visible as hair cracks having the appearance of flaws.

Cutting on decanters was carried out by hand until 1833 when John Gold of Birmingham invented a machine for cutting, grinding, smoothing, and polishing flint-glass decanters. Plain surfaces, grooves, elevated surfaces, and ornamental cutting were as efficiently produced by this machine which decorated several decanters at a time with all the appearance of having been hand-cut.

Decanters were generally sold in pairs or, from about 1760, might be in matching sets of four, six, twelve or twenty-four. The accounts of All Souls, Oxford, for the year 1703, record that glass decanters cost 5s. a pair: by 1721 the price had increased to 6s. a pair. The Earl of Carlisle paid 4s. 5d. for a pair of quart decanters in 1745; 6s. 6d. a pair for quart ground-glass decanters in 1749; 7s. for a pair of cut and stained decanters in 1776; and a set of four cut decanters cost him 18s. in 1785. W. Naylor, a glass-seller of Cavendish Square, advertised decanters at the following prices in 1805: cut-glass 7s. to 50s.; engraved 21s. to 42s.; moulded 7s. to 10s.

Square decanters appear to have been made consistently from about 1725 at first in a remarkably heavy metal. These might be small containers for perfumes or medicines, pint and quart sizes for spirits, and half-gallons for wines. Squares made before about 1760 are found in two distinct types: thin-walled and thick-walled. They were usually fitted with solid glass stoppers, ground, and with ball finials which might be enlivened with air bubbles. From about 1760 the stoppers usually supported flat vertical finials. Squares cost 2d. a pound less than decanters.

The majority of early squares, intended chiefly for the rough and tumble of everyday service and for use while travelling, were crudely finished. In 1769 an advertisement in the *London Evening Post* had for disposal 'a quantity of square decanters for public houses, to be sold cheap'. Squares for the toilet table were of fine quality and usually enriched with gilding (*see* Chapter 9). Spirit squares were high-shouldered and exceptionally short-necked. Those fitted with metal mounts and stoppers are seldom of English flint-glass.

By the middle of the century squares were made in sets of two, four, six or eight, enclosed in attractive chests. These were often fine pieces of cabinet-work little removed from the boxes in which silver tea canisters were stored. So similar are plain-faced squares that it is difficult to date them closely: they can be grouped only by their metal and any distinguishing feature, such as an engraved crest or other personal motif, or the presence of gilding or enamelling.

Spirit squares from about 1780 might be lightly cut and sets of three fitted into silver, Sheffield plate, or mahogany *gardevins*. Others were sold by the set of four fitted into a mahogany or satinwood case. From about 1810 they might be finely diamond-cut after the style of the modern tantalus bottle, with faceted ball-finialed stoppers.

Figure 204

'The Brothers Clarke of Swakeleys', painted by Gawen Hamilton, *c.* 1750. On the table are six wineglasses with conical bowls and knopped stems a stopperless shaft-and-globe decanter in flint-glass, and two wine-bottles in dark green glass. On the marble-topped serving table is a silver wine-fountain and below is a wine cistern.

In the collection of the Hon. Mrs Ionides

Figure 205

'A Literary Party at Sir Joshua Reynolds's', painted by James E. Doyle, showing a banquet of fruit and wine served on such occasions at 47 Leicester Square, London. The sitters (*left to right*) are James Howell, Dr Johnson, Sir Joshua Reynolds, David Garrick, Edmund Burke, Pasquale Paoli, Dr Burney, Thomas Warton, and Oliver Goldsmith, who died in 1774. With the exception of Dr Johnson, who has a capacious goblet with a hollow pedestal foot, each has a wineglass with a drawn flute, a plain stem, and an expansive foot. On the table, between Reynolds and Garrick, is an old-fashioned mallet-shaped decanter, and the servant is carrying a pair of contemporary taper decanters with neck rings and bull's-eye stoppers.

From an engraving in the collection of the Royal Society of Arts

Figures 206–9

FLINT-GLASS DECANTERS

Those with handles and expanded mouths display much crizzling and are considered to be examples of Ravenscroft's early work.

(206) Body decorated with bold vertical ribs forming diamonds, and seven vertical trails pinched alternately horizontally and vertically; spouted neck encircled with wavy collar; foot closely indented and with high kick in the base; swan's-neck handle; *c.* 1675. Height $8\frac{3}{8}$ inches.

By courtesy of Mr Howard Phillips

(207) Decanter of similar shape without spout and decorated with trailing; blown stopper with solid finial; *c.* 1675. Height 11 inches.

By courtesy of Messrs Sotheby & Co. Ltd

(208) With pressed flutings around lower part of body; 1675–80.

In the Victoria and Albert Museum

(209) Globe-and-shaft decanter, neck encircled with string rim; *c.* 1735.

In the Victoria and Albert Museum.

267

Figures 210–16

DECANTERS

(210) With mallet-shaped body pressed into octagonal form, with angular shoulder, long neck, and everted mouth fitted with an unground stopper having a ball finial containing air beads. Bladed neck ring. Rough punty mark beneath; *c.* 1730.

(211) Quart-size with vertically grooved cylindrical body, angular shoulder, long neck with triple rings and thickened mouth. High kick beneath; *c.* 1730.

(212) Pint-size, the square body shaped with two vertical grooves at each corner. Deep shoulder with thickened mouth and bladed neck ring. High kick; *c.* 1730's.

(213) Tapered decanter with widely fluted base and neck, the flute crests closely notched, and the body wheel-engraved with coat of arms; pear-shaped stopper edged with lunar-cutting fitting into everted mouth; 1780's.
In the Corning Museum of Glass

(214) One of a pair of broad-shouldered decanters ornamented all over with facet-cutting; diamond-spire stopper; hollowed base; 1770's.
In the Corning Museum of Glass

(215) Broad-shouldered labelled decanter in green glass with diamond-cut spire stopper; gilded cartouche of grape and vine-leaf motifs with scrolls and chainwork around neck to give the effect of a bottle ticket in gold; 1770's.
By courtesy of Mr Howard Phillips

(216) Narrow-shouldered decanter for Greek wine, ornamented with fruiting vine motif, its vertical disc stopper notched with lunar cutting; *c.* 1770.
In the Corning Museum of Glass

Figure 217

Decanter with narrow shoulders richly engraved with an equestrian portrait of King William III, the Irish harp, and the Stuart rose. In a ribbon framing the portrait are the words 'The Immortal Memory of the Glorious King William'; 1760's (*see* fig. 218).

Figure 218

Reverse of fig. 217, wheel-engraved all over with a bouquet of flowers. This decanter has not been ground to receive a stopper. Height 11½ inches; 1760's.
Formerly in the Joseph Bles Collection

Figures 219, 220

(219) Enamelled armorial decanter, with hollowed base; the stopper has a ball finial containing air beads. The coat of arms is painted in coloured enamels, the ornamental cartouche of grapes and vine-leaves in white enamel. Labelled 'Claret' on the reverse. The butterfly motif enamelled on the neck is the signature mark of William and Mary Beilby, glass decorators of Newcastle upon Tyne; *c.* 1770.

In the Corning Museum of Glass

(220) Barrel-shaped decanter with body in the form of a wine-barrel, cut with vertical lines and encircling rings to suggest staves and hoops.

In the Corning Museum of Glass

Figure 221

A collection of labelled decanters with broad and narrow shoulders, stoppers all recessed in the mouths. None is engraved on the reverse. 1760–75.

Top row: Engraved with cartouches composed mainly of grape and vine-leaf motifs.

Bottom row: (*a*) Engraved with hop and hop-leaves. (*b*) Engraved with grape and vine-leaf motifs. (*c*) Enamelled in white with grapes and vine-leaf motifs, and the Beilby butterfly on the neck; this example shows a tendency towards the barrel-shaped design which followed. (*d*) Engraved with hop and barley motifs. (*e*) Engraved with grapes and vine-leaves.

By courtesy of Messrs Delomosne & Son Ltd

Figure 222

Irish decanters made at Cork, blown-moulded in thin metal, bases of bodies encircled by comb-fluting untouched by the cutting-wheel; stoppers with moulded target finials, except in first example.

Top row: (*a*) Impressed beneath the base 'Cork Glass Co' in raised letters; plain neck rings. (*b*) Engraved with rose, shamrock, and thistle motifs in commemoration of the Act of Union 1801; two plain triple rings; slight kick in base. (*c*) Engraved with inscription 'The Land we Live in' above vesica motifs; plain round neck rings. (*d*) Engraved with agricultural motifs; three feathered neck rings.

Bottom row: (*a* and *b*) Pair impressed beneath the base 'Cork Glass Co' in raised letters; encircled with engraved vesica pattern containing eight pointed stars and ovals filled with cross-hatching. (*c* and *d*) Pair impressed beneath 'Waterloo Co. Cork' in raised letters; plain triple rings.

All by courtesy of Messrs Delomosne & Son Ltd

269

Figure 223

A collection of decanters assembled during the 1940's, none costing more than five shillings.

Top row: (*a*) Tapered, with short neck, encircled by two bands of engraved ornament; pear-shaped stopper-finial with bevelled edge; 1770's. (*b*) Blown-moulded short taper, base encircled with comb-fluting and engraved with a flower-foliage spray and bird; tool-moulded broad sloping lip (a rare feature) with pear-shaped stopper-finial with bevelled edge. 1780's. (*c*) Prussian shape with plain body, three rounded neck rings and a target stopper; *c.* 1800. (*d*) Blown-moulded with deep vertical flutings, three rounded neck rings; stopper with target finial in slightly everted mouth lip; 1790's. (*e*) Long-necked taper, smooth surface with punty scar beneath; stopper with pinched target finial; 1780's. (*f*) Taper decanter, base encircled with cut comb-fluting, body engraved with simple festoon work; stopper-finial a vertical disc with serrated edges.

Bottom row: (*a*) Narrow shoulder, body with all-over geometric designs in shallow flat-cutting, cut facets on neck; pear-shaped stopper-finial with lunar notching; 1770's. (*b*) Barrel-shaped decanter such as were first advertised in 1775, cut with flutes to resemble staves and encircled with incised lines suggesting hoops; pear-shaped stopper-finial with bevelled edge. (*c*) Blown-moulded wide-taper decanter with comb-fluting encircling base, wide hollow flutes around shoulder and neck, with two triangular neck rings; wide pear-shaped stopper-finial with bevelled edge. (*d*) Prussian-shaped decanter with cut comb-fluting encircling base and band of relief diamonds above, and three rounded neck rings; stopper with target finial and serrated rim; 1820's. (*e*) Blown-moulded and hand-finished, the interior surface having slight depressions following the shape of the design; two plain treble neck rings; vertical stopper-finial with lunar-cut edge; 1820's. (*f*) Blown-moulded in two-piece open-and-shut mould and finished by cutting the moulded designs on the wheel; pear-shaped stopper-finial pinched with trellis work; 1820's.

Figures 224–7

(224–6) Ship decanters, all taken from pairs, made of thick heavy metal and designed with expansive bases to give stability. (*a*) Body encircled with cut comb-fluting, plain shoulder, neck cut with wide flutes and encircled with three square neck rings; stopper with bull's-eye finial, *c.* 1800. (*b*) Plain body engraved with a seaman's head, fluted shoulder and neck; the three wide neck rings are tooled into the metal and cut; stopper with flat heart-shaped finial; *c.* 1810. (*c*) Exceptionally wide base, encircled with broad flutes cut from the instep and continuing up the neck over the four triangular neck rings to a widely flared mouth fitted with a pear-shaped stopper cut with bevelled edge and printies; 1820's. (*d*) From a set of three, quart-size, body cut with flutes above and below a plain band; four plain round neck rings; widely spreading mouth rim, and target stopper; 1820's.

(227) (*a*) Narrow-shouldered body encircled with shallow-cut columns rising from terraced plinths; stopper with disc finial notched with lunar-cutting; 1770's. (*b*) Base encircled by

270

perpendicular blazes; shoulder cut with pillar flutes, and neck with horizontal prismatic cutting; mushroom stopper with cut stem; 1820's. (*c*) Taper decanter, its base encircled with hollowed flutes; bevel-edged pear-shaped stopper; 1780's. (*d*) Prussian-shaped decanter with encircling band of strawberry diamonds above a band of swirls; prismatic cutting on neck; mushroom stopper.

All by courtesy of Messrs Delomosne & Son Ltd

Figure 228

DECANTERS OF GEORGE IV AND WILLIAM IV PERIODS

Top row: (*a*) Body cut with band of relief diamonds between bands of horizontal prismatic cutting, the lower bands having two panels of vertical prismatic cutting. The two lower neck rings have diamond-cutting, with a triple ring above. Mushroom stopper with plain shank. (*b*) Body base encircled with a short comb-fluting, a band of wide hollow flutes, and a band of relief diamonds, and the lower neck encircled with horizontal prismatic cutting; three triangular neck rings, exceptionally expansive mouth, the stopper having a compressed cushion finial. (*c*) Body all-over cut with relief diamonds, the neck with horizontal prismatic-cutting. (*d*) Body encircled with comb-fluting, a band of wide hollow flutes, a band of relief diamonds, and the neck encircled with hollow fluting; three neck rings cut with relief diamonds. (*e*) Body encircled with band of strawberry-cutting with comb-fluting below, and wide hollow flutes above; three cut neck rings and flattened mushroom stopper-finial.

Bottom row: (*a*) Base encircled with prunties, with a band of perpendicular blazes above; three triple neck rings; shallow mushroom stopper with plain shank. (*b*) Vertical-sided body with pillar-fluting, shoulders and neck cut with horizontal prismatic cutting, cushion stopper-finial. (*c*) Vertical-sided body with hollow flutes, three cut neck rings, mushroom stopper with cut shank. (*d*) Vertical-sided body with hollow flutes, two cut neck rings and cushion stopper. (*e*) Base of body encircled with comb-fluting, shoulder cut with festoons of fine diamonds and splits; three plain rounded neck rings; target stopper with bevelled edge. (*f*) Base encircled with wide hollowed flutes, below a band of relief diamonds, two square-cut neck rings; mushroom stopper.

By courtesy of Messrs Delomosne & Son Ltd

Figure 229

These decanters, with the exception of the two tapered specimens dating to the 1780's, were made during the early decades of the nineteenth century. The collection gives some idea of the wide range of patterns then available. Deep cutting on thick metal provided unsurpassed brilliance in artificial light.

By courtesy of Messrs Delomosne & Son Ltd

271

CHAPTER SEVENTEEN

SWEETMEAT GLASSES AND SALVERS

ELIZABETHAN, STUART, AND GEORGIAN cookery books made much of dessert. A repast of sweetmeats, fruit, and wines was served either as a separate meal or as a continuation of the principal meal, and was known as a banquet. Venner in 1620 noted the prevalence of 'banquets between meals, when the stomach is empty', and in 1657 the Goldsmiths' Company recorded that their wardens and assistants should be given 'a small banquet of fruit, according to the custom of the day'. As late as 1800 Southey noted the drawing-room 'as the common place for banqueting or of eating the dessert'.

Markham in his *English Housewife*, 1615, instructed his readers that in the service of dessert 'four preserved fruites shall be disht up first, four pastes next, four wet suckets after them, then four dried suckets'. A similar procedure was prescribed in 1688. At each place was a small plate measuring about 6 inches in diameter and known as a banqueting dish: this might be of silver, pewter, glass or earthenware. The Duke of Rutland's MSS. record that in 1598 glass plates were hired for sweetmeats at dinner: in 1602 a quantity was bought with 'graven rims' costing 6s. 2d. a dozen. Similar entries are frequent until 1615. Banqueting dishes or 'glass saucers for holding sweetmeats' continued to be made until early Victorian days. Georgian banqueting dishes were shallower than those formerly used and in shape resembled small silver waiters. Examples are now extremely rare.

When flint-glass began to grace the tables of the rich during the 1680's it was the signal for dessert to be served with increasingly lavish ostentation. Special glasses were evolved which in their maturity became symbolic of eighteenth-century hospitality.

Following the Hanoverian succession dinner-tables became more attractively and interestingly equipped. Desserts in their clear glass containers were made colourful and raised above table level on stemmed salvers of silver or glass, placed one above the other. The earliest reference so far noted to this style of dessert service was recorded by Lady Grisell Baillie in connection with a supper given by Mr Cockburn in December 1719:

273

'in the midle of the table there stood a pirimide of sillibubs and orang cream in the paste, above it sweet meats dry and wet'.

When in March 1727 she dined with Lord Mountjoy, ten at table, arrangements for the service of dessert had become more ornate. Down the centre of the table stood a row of three-tier pyramids built with glass salvers having ½-inch brims. The lower salvers displayed glasses of dry sweetmeats such as French plums, apricots, almond biscuits. The second tier supported four fruit jellies and wet sweetmeats with covers and 'betwixt them high glasses'. On the third tier were glasses of white comfits surrounding 'a tall scalloped glass, corner brim'. At each end of the table was placed a pair of silver salvers each holding several matching cornered brimmed sweetmeat glasses. When, in the following June, she stayed for ten days with Sir Robert Walpole at Twickenham, an epergne always occupied the centre of the table and dessert each day consisted of a variety of sweetmeats, jellies, and syllabubs.

By the time Mrs Hannah Glasse had written *The Compleat Confectioner* in 1753, the 'dressing out of a dessert' had become a polite accomplishment for ladies living in the country. In London a member of the household staff might be experienced in the art of confectionery for social occasions; otherwise a professional confectioner was engaged. Georgian dessert from the mid-1730's was not served in the dining-room. After finishing the earlier courses, guests would move to another apartment, usually the drawing-room, where the desserts were displayed in all their colourful magnificence. The guests were not seated, but conversed as they stood or strolled about in the manner of a modern cocktail party. Horace Walpole, writing in 1758, referred to a banquet attended by the Prince of Wales at which 'even on the chairs were pyramids with troughs of strawberries and cherries'.

Mrs Glasse planned and described in her book 'the dressing out' of several dessert arrangements. In a typical example the centre of the table was ornamented with 'a high pyramid of one [stemmed] salver above another, the bottom one large, the next smaller, and the top one less; these salvers are to be filled with all kinds of wet and dry sweetmeats in glass, or little plates, colour'd jellies, creams, etc., biscuits, crisp'd almonds and little knicknacks, and bottles of flowers prettily intermix'd, and the little top salver must have a large preserved fruit in the centre'. At each end of the table were glasses of ice-creams in different colours, whipped syllabubs, clear jellies, and lemon cream all in their appropriate glasses for individual serving.

274

Recipes for the preparation of a wide range of wet and dry sweetmeats will be found in the pages of late-Stuart and early-Georgian cookery books, such as the volume published in 1682 by Giles Rose, master cook in the kitchen of Charles II, and the *Royal Cookery Book* compiled in 1710 by Queen Anne's master cooks in the palace kitchens at St. James's, Kensington, Hampton Court, and Windsor. Wet sweetmeats included ice-creams, custards, trifles, jellies, syllabubs, and similar desserts served individually in small glass vessels: dry sweetmeats included suckets (candied fruits), comfits, boiled sweets, dried orange chips, and other confections contained in stemmed bowls.

English glass-workers experimenting with flint-glass during the 1680's listed glasses for dry sweetmeats among their fashionable table-ware. Endeavouring to imitate the fragile *façon de Venise*, they produced ware very similar in form, but far more substantial and 'clear as crystal'. The bowls of these early sweetmeat glasses were straight-sided, with everted lips folded inwards, and with gadrooned surbases supported upon hollow pedestal feet. By 1690 pedestals had been superseded by short, stout baluster stems rising from domed and folded feet.

The bowl of a Queen Anne sweetmeat glass was usually hemispherical in shape, with a gadrooned surbase matching similar moulding encircling the bowl of the foot. The stem was short and might be either an inverted or true baluster. In late William III examples a thin knop was inserted between baluster and bowl; by 1705 a matching knop might be placed between the baluster and the dome of the foot. From about 1710 the expanded part of the baluster might contain a tear. The moulded silesian stem in its early form, short and square on plan, is found dating from about 1710, usually topped by a moulded bowl. Squat bell-shaped and double-ogee bowls were associated with short-stemmed sweetmeat glasses from about 1715. Surface moulding seldom decorated short-stemmed sweetmeat glasses after about 1720, although some provincial glass-houses possibly continued the style into the reign of George II.

Short-stemmed sweetmeat glasses resembling small tazza-shaped standing dishes were made until about 1760 (fig. 243). These had shallow, lipped bowls supported on short baluster stems rising from spreading domed feet. Nat Berry in his 1726 price list refers to these as 'sweetmeat stands'. Some were made with wavy rims. These were succeeded by sweetmeat glasses with tooth-lipped rims which were in considerable provincial use between about 1745 and 1775. Although they were often made of excellent metal they were poorly finished. The bowl was either plain-surfaced or moulded with wide base fluting. Teeth were spaced irregularly around the rim, being alternately rounded at the end and sheared off more or less squarely. The stem was usually of the air- or opaque-twist type: frequently there was a knop or an inverted baluster immediately beneath the bowl and a second knop above the thick flat foot. This was moulded on upper and lower surfaces with eleven radial grooves. As with all other forms of table glass there were numerous variations of this basic type.

Tall-stemmed glasses for dry sweetmeats came into use in or shortly after 1715 and were sometimes termed sucket glasses. Their capacious, smooth-surfaced bowls might be hemispherical or double ogee in shape, with everted rims. Such bowls continued throughout the sweetmeat-glass period: rims might be scalloped from about 1720, and five years later arch-and-point repeats, and the plain zigzag, described by Lady Grisell Baillie as 'cornered brimmed', started a vogue lasting for about twenty-five years (fig. 231). Interior and exterior surfaces of scalloped rims were ground to produce a sharp edge: later scalloped edges were blunt and less deeply ground. Stems were of the shouldered silesian type, collared at each end, rising from spreading, domed, and folded feet.

The bowls of sweetmeat glasses from about 1730 might be rib-moulded, the decorative radial ribs sometimes being notched on the grinding-wheel. Rib-moulding had a half-century vogue, ribbed sweetmeat glasses being advertised as late as 1772. Diamond and hammered-surface moulding decorated the bowls of some sweetmeat glasses between 1730 and 1750 (fig. 239). Some of these were provided with highly domed covers surmounted by moulded finials, early examples containing a group of tears. Those remaining intact show that the ornamental moulding matched on covers, bowls, and feet.

Looped-rim sweetmeat glasses (fig. 230) and those with open basket-work of trailed glass rising vertically from the bowl in two, three, or even four tiers, were fashionable throughout the reign of George II (1727-60). Pinched endings at the bowl rim and basket-work junctions were concealed beneath rosette embossments or strawberry prunts. High looping was associated with shallow bowls. Looped and basket-work sweetmeat glasses are usually supported by shouldered silesian stems rising from high-spreading domed and ribbed feet. A few examples are known with air-twist or opaque-twist stems.

Bowls of sweetmeat glasses from about 1730 might be enriched with flat geometrical cutting and shallow slicing (fig. 238). Lunar slices were cut alone or in company with other simply ground motifs composing simple

206–209   Flint-glass decanters: those with handles are considered to be examples
of Ravenscroft's early work

210–212   Mallet-shaped decanters, early George I

213–216   Decorated decanters of the 1770's

222 Irish blown-moulded decanters made at Cork, bases of bodies encircled by comb-fluting

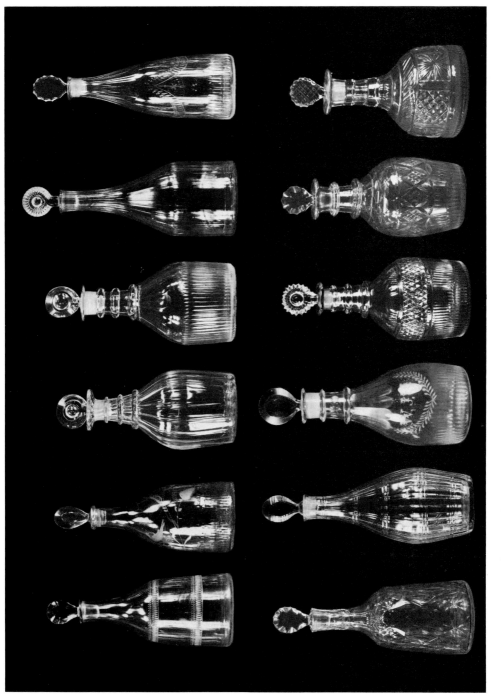

223 A collection of decanters assembled during the 1940's, none costing more than five shillings

designs. A series dating between 1730 and 1750 is cut with triangular facets placed to form diamond-shaped compartments, From about 1735 the upper part of double-ogee bowls might be encircled with shallow-cut double arches, with flat triangular facets below (fig. 236). Such bowls are usually associated with shouldered silesian stems which might be cut with vertical flutes. A beaded knop at first joined stem to bowl. This was quickly superseded by the insertion of triple rings at either end of the silesian stem. After about 1750 a large round knop was placed between stem and bowl. A few specimens are known with light baluster and knopped stems, and rare also are the air-twist stems of 1740–60 and the opaque-twists of 1750–75.

Vertical flutes or a band of convex diamonds might enrich sweetmeat bowls from about 1770. Plain flat pyramids in low relief date from that year to about 1785. Bowls then tended to be made deeper and enriched with large diamonds cut in deep relief. Most of the early cut motifs recurred during the period 1770–85.

Stems of fashionable sweetmeat glasses from the 1740's might be enriched with facet-cutting, but few remaining examples may be dated earlier than about 1760. Early facet-cut stems were cusped, an adaptation of the centrally knopped plain stem (fig. 236c): this form continued until the 1780's. Until 1770 stem diamonds were small and might be long and narrow, squarish, or hooked at the top. Straight stems enriched with facet cutting (fig. 240) were made from about 1750, and were succeeded by hollow-diamond faceted stems. Fluted stems appeared on sweetmeat glasses during the 1780's.

The feet of sweetmeat glasses throughout the period were generally highly domed, their upper surfaces being either plain or, more usually, radially ridged and sometimes ornamented with moulded bosses (fig. 236b). Smooth-faced domes might be decorated with slicing in fan-shaped panels. Instead of being circular the foot rim might be polygonal and the dome shaped to match. Foot rims were seldom cut in symmetrical lunettes before 1765. The foot was almost invariably small in proportion to bowl diameter. Sweetmeat glasses with cut bowls fitted with covers are illustrated on certain trade cards issued as late as 1785.

Some tall sweetmeat glasses with clear, smooth-surfaced bowls bear a striking likeness to champagne glasses made between about 1720 and 1740. These drinking-glasses possessed thinly blown bowls with plain, unfolded rims, and the diameter of the foot exceeded that of the bowl rim. Sweetmeat glasses with their everted and folded rims are obviously unsuited for drinking-purposes and should not be confused with champagne glasses.

285

The wet sweetmeat glasses included those used for jellies, ices, creams, and syllabubs. Jelly glasses (fig. 244) which constitute a distinct group in English table glass, might also be used for ices and creams. The deep, trumpet-shaped bowl may rise directly from a domed or high instep foot, or a flat, expansive knop may be introduced between them.

Jelly served individually in glass containers is first recorded in *The Accomplisht Cook* by Robert May, 1678. Fashionable cooks are directed to 'serve jelly . . . run into little round glasses four or five to the dish'. Thin plain footless bowls, basin-shaped and with folded lips, were sold in sets of eight which in 1698 would cost 1s. Because hot jelly was poured directly into them, their sides were appreciably thicker than the open-flame oil lamps which they closely resembled in shape and size. After about 1700 the lower part of the body might be moulded with gadrooning and a rim foot might be added.

Various cookery books published during the reign of Queen Anne required jelly to be 'poured into narrow-bottomed Drinking Glasses', clear indication that the footed, trumpet-bowled jelly glass had yet to be designed. 'New-fashioned jelly glasses' were advertised during the early years of the Hanoverian regime. These were in a stemmed design with a pair of swan-neck or double-loop handles on the trumpet-shaped bowl which was given vertical or twisted ribbing and gracefully waisted. Early in the 1720's, however, the desire for a more capacious and stable vessel suggested the removal of the stem, by joining the bowl directly to a highly domed foot which might be plain-surfaced, radially ribbed or panel moulded. This was the basic form of the Georgian jelly glass although there was considerable variation in details.

By 1730 a large flattened knop, upon which moulding could be concentrated, was introduced between bowl and foot. Plain knops were usually enriched with clusters of silvery air beads. Jelly glass bowls might be plain and thin of section or of thicker metal displaying moulded ornament such as vertical or twist ribbing, purled diamonds, or a diaper in hexagons or diamonds. Domed and spreading feet might be moulded with radial ribs, but more frequently the surface was plainly smooth. A single handle of the swan-neck type was fashionable between about 1730 and 1750: the plain single-loop handle dates from about 1740 and was in use until the end of the century. The majority of jelly glasses, however, were made without handles.

Joseph Highmore's 'Scene from Pamela', painted in 1744, shows five jelly glasses with trumpet-shaped bowls and domed feet standing upon a

286

glass salver or middle stand. The glasses contain jelly topped with 'clouted cream' as was customary at the time.

Jelly glasses from the mid-eighteenth century might have their bowl surfaces either plain or decorated with moulding, cutting, or engraving. Moulded bowls now tended to be somewhat shorter than the plain-surfaced blown type, which might be wider across the mouth than formerly. Bowl rims are occasionally noted with a wavy outline when viewed on plan, and a rare series of bowls was hexagonal. The flat knop joining bowl to foot decreased in size and importance during this period and in the fourth quarter of the century might be omitted entirely. The foot might be low-domed, but more usually was slightly conical, plain, and thick.

Shallow slicing might decorate jelly glass bowls from about 1750, and the rims might be cut with scallops. This ornament is illustrated on trade cards as late as 1790 and continued on elaborately cut jelly glasses throughout the Georgian period. Jelly glasses with vertical ribs cut with notching date from about 1770: examples from about 1785 have thick square feet. Bowls with pressed flutes appeared in about 1780, but cut flutes date from about 1790. After 1800 they were associated circular moulded feet: trade catalogues illustrate them with and without loop handles. From 1790 double-cut diamonds and other forms of deep relief cutting enriched the bowls of fashionable jelly glasses, some of which were supported by thick square feet with high solid domes, star-cut beneath.

Large numbers of stemless glasses with hybrid conical bowls set directly upon flat disc feet were used by confectioners for the sale of ice-cream and other similar delicacies 'consumed on the premises'. Trade cards illustrate them as early as 1760 and engravings until the 1830's. Beginner-collectors often mistake these for jelly glasses: they are of poor metal and their thick disc feet irregularly shaped.

Whipped syllabub, the dessert, was a Georgian innovation having little in common with the well-known Tudor and Stuart syllabub drink. The earliest reference to syllabub glasses appears in the Duke of Bedford's accounts for June 1676: 'ribb'd flintt sulibub glasses, marked'. These had covers and were sold at 1s. 6d. each, but no records exist suggesting their shape. At that period syllabub was a drink of the posset type and described by the Oxford Dictionary as 'made of milk or cream, curdled by the addition of wine, cider, or other acid, and often sweetened or flavoured'.

Some confusion has been caused by some earlier writers applying the term 'syllabub glass' to a vessel with a curved spout, a pair of heavy, applied handles, and a cover. Such glasses were made by the early flint-glass men in imitation of earlier pottery examples. They might measure more than 9 inches in height and were used for serving purposes: they may conveniently be classed under the more general term of posset cups (fig. 25).

Whipped syllabubs are not referred to in pre-Georgian cookery books. Afterwards they are frequent and varied. *The Compleat Housewife*, 1732, gives a typical recipe: 'Take a quart of cream, not too thick, and a pint of sack, and the juice of two lemons: sweeten. Put into a broad earthen pan and with a whisk whip it, and as the froth rises take it off with a spoon and lay it in your syllabub glasses: but first you must sweeten some claret or sack or white wine, and strain it, and put it into eight glasses, and then gently lay on your froth. Set 'em by: do not make 'em long before you use 'em.'

Whipped syllabub was, then, a wet sweetmeat served in special glasses. Some authorities affirm that syllabub glasses and jelly glasses were of one and the same design. As early as 1725, however, 'Whip-Sillibub' and 'Jelly-Glasses' were consecutive items on a glass-seller's bill. The term 'whip syllabub' is used consistently in advertisements until 1751, after which the word 'whip' is omitted. An advertisement issued by Phillips of Norwich refers to 'Glass Salvers and Pyramids of all sizes, Syllabub, Jelly, and Sweetmeat Glasses', clear indication of differentiation between syllabub glasses and jelly glasses, and of their association with salvers and sweetmeat glasses.

At Oxford in 1733 six syllabub glasses cost 2s. and three dozen jelly glasses cost 6s. Undecorated flint-glass table-ware at that time retailed at 8d. a pound. Syllabub glasses appear ,then, to have been about twice the weight of jelly glasses and it may be assumed that they were proportionately larger. This is confirmed by trade cards of the 1760's and 1770's which illustrate syllabub glasses of about twice the capacity of their jelly glasses.

Bowl decoration and the feet of syllabub glasses followed those of contemporary jelly glasses: but form and size differed. Glasses designed for whip syllabub possessed deep, wide-mouthed bowls of the double-ogee type, the lower portion being longer and narrower than was usual in drinking-glass bowls (fig. 242). This lower portion contained the sweetened wine while the widening shoulders of the ogee offered support for the airy froth. Two qualities of syllabub glass were advertised in 1772: common ribbed and best diamond-cut. Many had short knopped stems rising from scalloped feet cut to match their bowl rims.

The display of desserts on glass pyramids was fashionable from about 1715. Such a pyramid consisted of a series of two, three, or four stemmed salvers in gradually diminishing sizes piled one upon the other (fig. 28). The earliest detailed description of a pyramid set was found by Francis Buckley in the account books of Cookson, Jeffreys, and Dixon, Newcastle upon Tyne, under the date of 2nd September 1746. This consisted of 'four salvers, one top branch, five top sweetmeats, and thirty-two jellies and custards'. The total cost was £2. 2s. 4d. Pyramids for desserts continued throughout the century. Jonas Phillips, a glass-seller of Lynn, in 1768 advertised 'the grandest and best Pyramids ever made in England'. Sweet-meat glasses intended for use on pyramids were made with feet perceptibly smaller in diameter than their bowl rims to prevent overlapping, thus avoiding accidents when they were lifted from the salver.

Glass salvers are recorded among the dining-table equipage as early as 1620. The workers in flint-glass soon included these in their range of table-ware, for the Duke of Bedford's accounts dated 1682 refer to '1 fflint salver 1/6'. Until about 1690 the flat circular plate rested directly upon a hollow pedestal. These pedestals were superseded by short stems of baluster form rising from high, spreading domed feet, which might be folded. With these, from about 1700, were stems containing various shapes of knops. Both baluster and knopped stems are seen on salvers illustrated on trade cards of the mid-eighteenth century. Moulded silesian stems in their several variations were used from 1720 and commonly supported salvers for more than a century. Coarse rib-twist stems belong to the period 1740–60 and are usually of inferior-quality glass. Air-twist and opaque-twist stems are rarely found on salvers. The pyramids and salvers illustrated on trade cards and bill-heads between 1765 and 1790 show a reversion to the hollow pedestal stem often enriched with sliced cutting (fig. 27). In the 1760's they were advertised as 'new fashioned salvers'. Few of these appear to remain, however, and small salvers are also uncommon.

An early Stuart example, excavated in 1914 and now in the London Museum, shows that the under-surface of the plate might be impressed with an outline design composed of circles. In flint-glass both surfaces were smooth, except in the case of the cut salvers of the early George III period. A shallow gallery encircled the upper rim of the salver plate throughout the period of their manufacture. For a period during the 1730's and 1740's the gallery might project both upward and downward. Trade cards indicate that in a series made from about 1750 the gallery projected only below the plate — obviously following a contemporary style in pewter in which the projection concealed the rough under-surface of the plate.

Cut-glass salvers of the George III period might have the under-sides

289

of their plates cut with stars or other flat geometric patterns and after about 1765 their upturned rims might be scalloped. These were supported on low bell-shaped pedestal feet, at first plain-surfaced and with their spreading foot rims folded. Later the pedestal became a field for cutting and the foot rim might be scalloped to match the plate edging. Sometimes the lower salver of a high pyramid was supported by a spool-shaped foot with a diameter approximately half that of the plate itself. From about 1770 the upper tiers might rise from a heavy glass salver some 10 pounds in weight, its circular plate revolving on a metal pivot fixed into a massive bell-shaped pedestal. The early-nineteenth-century salver with a stem cut in flutes and a square foot marked the final phase of this design. Considerable numbers of salvers with moulded silesian stems were made for use as cake-stands during the first half of the nineteenth century.

Glass salvers were also carried by liveried servants, the moulded silesian stem offering a firm grip (fig. 33). Upon the plate stood either a selection of desserts in their appropriate glasses for handing to the assembled guests, or glasses filled with wine. When wine was offered the servant carried a bottle by the neck in his other hand. The term 'waiter' has not been noticed in this connection earlier than 1740. A newspaper advertisement of 1772 announced 'Glass Salvers or Waiters, chiefly from 9 to 13 inch, to be sold in Pyramids or Singly, with Orange or Top Glasses'.

The orange or top glass stood centrally upon the topmost salver of a pyramid. It resembled an ordinary sweetmeat glass in all features except that the stem was tall enough to lift its more capacious bowl well above the five or six sweetmeat glasses which surrounded it. Top glasses were piled with candied orange chips, a popular confection of the period. In 1715 these chips were costly to buy at 72s. a pound, but by 1745 they could be bought at 10d. a pound; in 1771 they had risen to 2s. a pound. Collectors often refer to these glasses as captain or master glasses.

Contemporary with pyramid sets consisting of stemmed salvers, there was, from about 1760, a less popular but more stable type of pyramid consisting of three to five circular glass plates of diminishing sizes, through the centres of which passed a slender tapering stem 2 to 4 feet in height. In early examples the stem was of silver supported by a widely spreading silver pedestal base. Examples have been seen with deeply cut glass pedestals supporting stems of brass or bronze. Glass stems, somewhat thicker than their metal prototypes and fitted with metal collars upon which the glass plates rested and revolved, appeared during the 1780's. The stem passed through the topmost plate to end in a decorative finial. This type of pyramid was probably a Stourbridge product: several were noticed on sale in that district during a brief visit. Sweetmeat stands or centre-pieces, decoratively cut so that their radiance scintillated in the light of wax candles, appeared early in the reign of George III.

An innovation introduced a few years earlier for dry sweetmeats was the glass epergne. This consisted of a strongly made top glass, 18 inches high, with a moulded stem and a plain double-ogee bowl with a scalloped rim. From projecting hooks or branches welded to a knop immediately below the bowl there might be suspended six or more hemispherical glass baskets (fig. 235). Later the central column might rise from a heavy pedestal-stemmed salver.

Such stands were made throughout the second half of the eighteenth century in styles of ever-increasing lavishness. In the majority of designs several curved branches notched or facet-cut extended from metal fittings attached to a tapering stem cut to match. A spreading domed foot might be decorated with shallow geometric cutting matching a fixed bowl at the top. The loose hanging baskets were designed and cut to harmonize, and additional ornament might include pendant lustres.

After about 1790 the lower portion might consist of an urn, pineapple, or other moulded shape rising from a scalloped moulded foot, or of a dome on a heavy square foot, star-cut beneath. A glass-and-metal attachment supported the central sweetmeat bowl and a number of curved notched branches terminated in smaller matching bowls. Hanging from each branch was a pendant lustre and these were linked by strings of smaller lustres.

Figures 230–4

SWEETMEAT GLASSES

(230) Ribbed ogee bowl, rim decorated with trailed loops having pinched endings; moulded silesian stem, mereses above and below; radially ribbed foot; *c.* 1740. Height 6¼ inches.

By courtesy of Messrs Christie, Manson & Woods Ltd

(231) Waisted double-ogee bowl with arch-and-point rim, moulded silesian stem between mereses; expansive domed and folded foot; *c.* 1720. Height 6 inches.

In the collection of Mrs William Hopley

(232) Double-ogee bowl, rim encircled with trailed loops and strawberry prunts; opaque and air-twist coil stem; folded foot; *c.* 1760. Height 6 inches.

By courtesy of Messrs Christie, Manson & Woods Ltd

(233) Pan topped bowl with everted folded rim: stem composed of rudimentary baluster supporting an annulated knop; domed and folded foot.

In the Victoria and Albert Museum

(234) Moulded and ribbed ogee bowl with everted lip; four-sided silesian stem: plain foot.

In the Brooklyn Museum

Figures 235, 236

(235) Sweetmeat epergne: heavy moulded pedestal, with thick radially ribbed conical foot; vase stem, notched; large bowl containing brass fitment for eight notched branches terminating in shallow fluted dishes with wavy rims, and a central pillar supporting a double-ogee bowl. Early George III period.

(236) Sweetmeat glasses.
Left: Ogee bowl cut in the vandyke style with scalloped rim; composite stem, with massive moulded stem between mereses, and a large beaded knop; cut foot with lobed rim; 1780's. Height 6½ inches.
Centre: Saucer-topped bowl cut with large hollow diamonds and scalloped rim; eight-sided moulded pedestal stem; moulded and ridged domed foot; *c.* 1760. Height 7⅛ inches.
Right: Waisted bucket-topped ogee bowl, decorated with sliced cutting and scalloped rim; facet-cut knopped stem; domed foot with scalloped rim to match bowl; 1780's. Height 7 inches.

Formerly in the Bles Collection

Figures 237–40

SWEETMEAT GLASSES

(237) Shallow bowl with gadrooned base and everted rim; baluster stem with knop above; folded foot.

(238) Waisted ogee bowl; eight-sided silesian stem; high moulded foot; bowl and foot rims scalloped; bowl cut with shallow diamonds.

Both by courtesy of Messrs Arthur Churchill Ltd

(239) Moulded double-ogee bowl; knopped air-twist stem with collar above, domed foot moulded to match bowl.

By courtesy of Messrs Cecil Davis Ltd

(240) Ribbed double-ogee bowl; facet-cut stem; plain foot; rims of foot and bowl scalloped; 1780's. Height 7 inches.

Figures 241–4

SWEETMEAT GLASSES

(241) Stemmed salver with rim projecting above circular plate; silesian stem between mereses; highly domed and folded foot. With two syllabub glasses and a master glass.

By courtesy of Messrs Delomosne & Son Ltd

(242) Syllabub glass with deep ogee bowl; flattened air-beaded knop; domed and folded foot.

By courtesy of Messrs Arthur Churchill Ltd

(243) Double-ogee bowl with white *latticinio* and fringed lip; white opaque-twist stem knopped at each end; radially moulded foot.

(244) Jelly glass with diamond-moulded body joined directly to domed foot. Height 3¾ inches.

Both by courtesy of Messrs Arthur Churchill Ltd

CHAPTER EIGHTEEN

WINEGLASS COOLERS
AND FINGER-BOWLS

S UCH A WIDE and fascinating field is offered to the collector by glass associated with the table that its minor accessories have tended to be neglected. In particular the various receptacles for water or iced water, associated with the service of wines and dessert, have received less attention than is merited by either their past importance or their present attractiveness.

Pungent spices flavoured and scented many of the unappetizing dried and salted foods which necessarily found a place on the seventeenth-century dining-table. To counteract the fiery tang which followed the lavish use of piquant sauces prepared in noble homes by the Yeoman of the Saucery, diners 'cooled their mouths with lumps of ice'. These were served on small glass plates, a custom vigorously condemned in 1723 by Sir Richard Steele as 'fashionable though vulgar'.

Wines at this period were preferred as cold as possible, but their servers had to contend with the sultry atmosphere created in the dining-room by braziers of red-hot charcoal and lustres burning candles by the dozen. In particular it was found that the stout goblets of flint-glass inevitably attracted the heat. This was counteracted by placing wineglass bowls in iced water, and within a few years a special receptacle had been evolved for this purpose.

This vessel's inception was recorded in 1683 by the Oxford diarist Anthony à Wood: 'This year in the summer-time came up a vessel or bason notched at the brims to let drinking vessels hang there by the foot, so that the body or drinking place might hang into the water to cool them. Such a bason was called a "Monteigh" from a fantastical Scot called Monsieur Monteigh who at that time or a little before wore the bottome of his cloake or coate so notched.' Bailey in his *Dictionary* of 1721 defined 'Monteth' as 'a scollop'd Bason to cool Glasses in'. Dr Johnson in 1773 preferred the spelling 'Montith' and described it as 'a vessel in which glasses are washed'.

Monteiths are wrongly regarded by many collectors, and museums too, as punch-bowls. As affirmed by Anthony à Wood, monteiths are wineglass coolers. The semi-circular depressions in the rim form rests for wineglass stems whose bowls are suspended downward to be chilled in iced water, the feet resting against the outer surface of the rim.

Early monteiths were of silver, occasionally of gold, and before 1690 they were being copied in pewter, in copper, and in delft ware. Monteiths in flint-glass, and in porcelain and cream-ware, belong to the eighteenth century. The earliest were circular bowls which might measure as much as 14 inches across, with eight U-shaped notches in the rim, and a moulded foot ring. From about 1750 the rim had a wavy edge and notches were wider and shallower. Oval examples, dating from about 1760, were in pairs and might accommodate eight, ten or twelve drinking-glasses each.

In fashionable society the use of monteiths appears to have become outmoded following the appearance of individual wineglass coolers at the coronation banquet of George III and Queen Charlotte, although these had been introduced to the English dining-table during the 1750's. Writers on table etiquette later in the century instructed butlers to place one to the right of each person. Early in the nineteenth century directions were more explicit: 'hock and champagne glasses are to be placed in the cooler, two wineglasses upon the table'. Wineglass coolers continued in use until early-Victorian days for in 1851, Redding, on page 370 of his book *Wines*, instructs butlers to 'lay wineglass coolers on the table with the glasses reversed in them' (fig. 245). After use the glasses were returned to the iced water until again required.

Wineglass coolers were known to their contemporary users as water-glasses and until about 1790 it was customary for them to be accompanied by glass water-plates. A glass bill in the Brandsby household accounts for 1764 shows water-glasses to have been bought for the first time at 7s. 6d. each, accompanied by water-plates at 6s. each. At these prices they were obviously cut in the style of water-glasses and plates illustrated on various glass-sellers' trade cards of the period: plain flint-glass vessels were sold by dealers in this year at 8d. a pound. The earliest advertisement recording such ware was found by Francis Buckley in *Aris's Birmingham Gazette* of 1764. Here, listed among the stock of John Taylor, a glass-seller of Coventry, were 'Water Glasses and Plates'.

In this and other advertisements reference was also made to water-glasses among the drinking-vessels, a duplication of terms which has caused some confusion among collectors. These water-glasses, to which many references are made during the first half of the eighteenth century, were tall and narrow, rather resembling tumblers, and used for rinsing the mouth at table. Tobias Smollett in his *Travels*, 1766, complained that he knew 'of no custom more beastly than that of using water-glasses in which polite society spirt, and squirt, and spue the filthy scourings of their gums'. Such water-glasses, which of necessity would be neither wide nor heavy, were predecessors of finger-bowls.

The rims of early individual wineglass coolers were scalloped, the edges of their plates being cut to match. Such wineglass coolers were flat-based, their straight sides having a distinct outward slope. As finger-bowls, plain and vertical-sided, became established as an essential part of the table-ware service, wineglass coolers were made to match, but rather deeper, and with one or two lips in the rim to form rests for the wineglass stems. Many were encircled with narrow fluting rising from the base half-way up the bowl. 'Glass finger-cups and wineglass-coolers' were differentiated in an advertisement of 1800, prices ranging from 2s. to 8s. each.

Handsome table services of deeply cut flint-glass consisting of two hundred to five hundred matching pieces, combining dessert and wine-service ware, glittered upon candle-lit tables during the Regency and George IV periods. Wineglass coolers and finger-bowls were included in such equipages. Both are found in the Marquess of Londonderry's unique cut-glass armorial service made for the third marquess in 1824 by the Wear Flint Glass Company at a cost of two thousand guineas.

Finger-bowls (fig. 246 top) are now so essentially associated with gracious living that it is, perhaps, surprising to find their introduction dating to no earlier than about 1760 — their name merely to early-Victorian days. No evidence is available supporting the widely held view that finger-bowls were a dining-table accessory by the time of the Jacobite rebellion in 1745, when it was customary for adherents to the Stuart cause to toast 'the king over the water'. Fielding in *Tom Jones*, published 1749, relates that in Squire Western's household there was a standing rule requiring 'the women to come in to dinner with the first dish and to go out after the first glass', a toast to the exiled Prince Charles. Squire Western ostensibly toasted 'the King' while holding his charged glass above a water-filled wineglass cooler.

When finger-bowls were introduced to the dining-table, Jacobites were enabled to hold their glasses individually 'over the water' while drinking a loyal toast. Because of this emblematic gesture finger-bowls and wineglass coolers were banned from royal banquets after it had been noticed at the

297

coronation banquet of George III that guests with Jacobite sympathies held their glasses 'over the water' during the loyal toast. The embargo continued until 1905 when Edward VII restored finger-bowls to their place on the royal table.

A book on table etiquette published in 1788 instructed butlers 'to put on those glasses [finger-bowls] half-full of clean water, when the table is cleared, but before the cloth is removed for dessert'. From 1820 it was fashionable to use dilute rose water. The hostess of 1849 was informed that 'finger-glasses precede the dessert, but it is sometimes customary to hand two-compartment dishes, the outer section containing rosewater, the inner eau-de-Cologne. These are passed down each side of the table: into these the guest may dip the corner of his napkin and with it refresh his lips and the tips of his fingers.'

Glass finger-bowls were introduced as 'wash hand glasses', a term noted in contemporary advertisements until about 1775 when the name 'washer' was preferred. By 1780 they were known variously as finger-cups, finger-basins, and finger-glasses. The name finger-glass remained in use for more than half a century before they were styled finger-bowls.

Until the close of the eighteenth century finger-bowls served the double purpose of cleansing the fingers and rinsing the mouth at the end of a meal. Sophie von la Roche, visiting London in 1786, noted in her diary that she was 'quite delighted' when dining with the Von Reventlows at Richmond, Surrey, to observe on the table 'blue glass bowls for rinsing the hands and mouth in at the end'.

Fashionable glass-sellers stocked these dining-table accessories in clear flint-glass, blue glass (fig. 285), and for a time in opaque white glass. It appears that the first to be devised were in flint-glass: the sides were almost vertical with a slight outward slant, about $3\frac{1}{2}$ inches deep, and with a medium kick in the base which met the sides squarely. The surface was entirely plain unless engraved with a crest or other personal emblem.

Finger-bowls, and wineglass coolers too, from the late 1770's, still straight-sided and often with a slight outward flare towards the rim, might be encircled with short shallow grooves rising from the base in formal arrangements. These were known as 'cut bottoms' and in 1790 cost 1s. 8d. each. Bowls of this pattern were blown into shallow gunmetal moulds with fluted walls. The upper diameter of such a mould was, of course, slightly greater than that of the base, permitting the moulded glass to be removed easily. The vertical flutes thus moulded were finished on the cutting-wheel. This pattern continued in production until the mid-nineteenth century. The space above the grooves from about 1780 might be encircled by an engraved garter or a narrow band of shallow facets.

During this period and until early in the nineteenth century finger-bowls of a deep blue glass were made at Bristol and at other glass centres. These might be enriched with gilded decoration, but this has seldom withstood the wear of generations. In shape and size blue finger-bowls resembled those of clear flint-glass. William Cowper in 1784 wrote to a friend staying in Bristol: 'Your mother begs that you will buy her eight blue, deep blue, finger-size glasses.' The use of the word 'finger-size' suggests a resemblance in shape but difference in size between these and wineglass coolers.

Early in the nineteenth century fashionable finger-bowls tended to become slightly incurved at the rim and the base corner was boldly rounded. The glass was now thicker in section to accommodate diamond-cutting in deep relief: others, of course, followed the earlier forms.

The lower part of the bowl might be encircled with bands of relief (see Chapter 8), and such cut decoration might be combined with lozenges and stars. Upright flutings and pillars, pillars with arches, stars and splits, and rows of semi-circles were variously combined to add interest to the sparkle. Other aids to refraction on cut finger-bowls of this period included the slanting lines called blazes, leaf festoons, fans, printies and pomegranates. The rim of an elaborately cut finger-bowl was usually scalloped and the under-base enriched with a star, of which there were several forms. From about 1820 the sides might be vertical and widely fluted and the intervening sharp points left plain or notched.

Throughout the eighteenth century finger-bowls had been entirely blown, with the exception of 'cut-bottoms'. In 1802 the blown-moulding process was introduced by Charles Chubsee, enabling the exterior surface to be decorated mechanically, by means of an open-and-shut mould, with geometrical and curved motifs displaying clean, smooth edges almost equal to those on cut-glass. The geometrical patterns included encircling bands copiously decorated with horizontal, vertical, and diagonal ribbings; flutings; motifs composed of concave circles and ovals; diamonds; and diamond diapering in combination with ribbing and fluting.

Baroque decoration in this medium dates from about 1825. This included elaborate designs composed of fanciful, delicate curves in high relief with the addition of hearts, shells, trefoils, and the guilloche motif. Roman and gothic arch patterns, all in high relief, date from about 1840.

Blown-moulded finger-bowls, other than 'cut-bottoms', may be recognized by hair-line ridges where the molten glass has been forced into the fine crevices between the mould sections. Fire-polishing, however, rendered these marks very indistinct, often almost invisible. This process of reheating finished glass-ware was an English invention which all but obliterated tool and mould marks and at the same time produced a polished surface suggestive of blown flint-glass. The edge of the rim was hard and sharp, however, in contrast to that of the blown bowl which was always beautifully rounded.

Coloured finger-bowls in a multitude of patterns were made from about 1845, purples, amethysts, ultramarines, Bristol-blue, reds, and greens predominating.

224–226   Ship decanters all taken from pairs, made of thick heavy metal, and blown with thick bases
to give stability

227   Cut decanters (*left to right*), narrow-shouldered body, 1770's; with horizontal
prismatic cutting, 1820's; taper, 1780's; prussian shape, 1820's

228 A collection of cut decanters of George IV and William IV periods

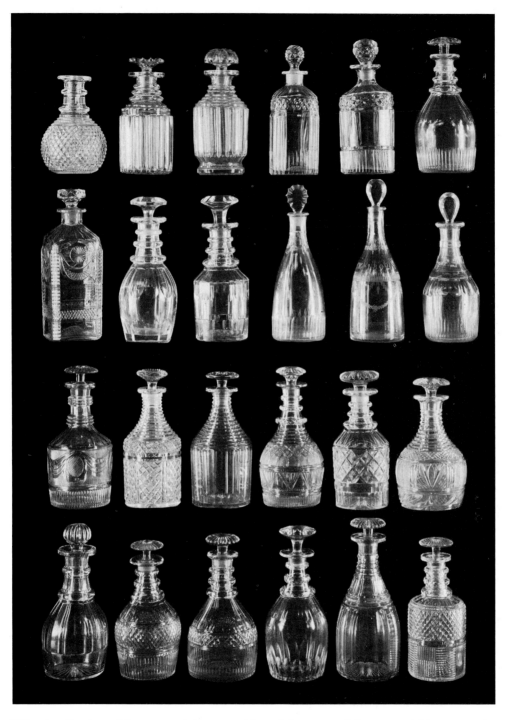

229   A collection of decanters giving some idea of the range of design available during the
early nineteenth century

230–234   Sweetmeat glasses

235 Sweetmeat epergne

236 Sweetmeat glasses

237–240 Sweetmeat glasses

241   Stemmed salver   242   Syllabub glass

243   With white *latticinio* bowl   244   Jelly glass

SWEETMEAT GLASSES

307

245 'The Toast', by Henry Alken, 1824. Illustrating wineglass coolers containing upturned wineglasses

Figure 245

'The Toast', drawn and etched by Henry Alken, aquatinted by G. Hunt, and published in 1824 by Thomas McLean, 26 Haymarket, London. The table displays the flint-glass ware used for everyday drinking. The drinking-glasses are of the fashionable tapered style seen in a variety of long and short bowl forms. Wine-bottles and cut-glass decanters, with cylindrical bodies vertically fluted and banded with deep relief diamonds, and mushroom stoppers are in use together. Each place is set with a wineglass cooler and at the near and far corners of the table they contain upturned wineglasses.

By courtesy of Mr Frank T. Sabin

Figure 246

FINGER-BOWL AND TWO-LIPPED WINEGLASS COOLERS

Top left: Finger-bowl moulded with gadrooning and encircled with a plain rim; *c.* 1830.

Top right: Wineglass cooler with moulded fluting finished by hand-cutting, and with the edge of the rim ground flat; *c.* 1830.

Bottom left: Wineglass cooler with hollowed base encircled by wide cut fluting and a narrow band of diamond-cutting in relief; early nineteenth century.

Bottom right: Wineglass cooler with cut comb-fluting encircling base and a ribbon of trellis-work; early nineteenth century.

In the Corning Museum of Glass

CHAPTER NINETEEN

CANDLESTICKS, TAPER-STICKS, GIRAN-
DOLES, AND GIRANDOLE-CANDLESTICKS

FOR SHEER BEAUTY beneath the candle's mellow flame, flint-glass candlesticks have no rival. Hollow-stemmed and with high domed feet they made their first appearance during the early 1680's, dull competitors of the heavy rock-crystal candlesticks which had been imported for more than half a century as costly *objets d'art* and of which few have survived. These flint-glass candlesticks were made by the old Venetian method of blowing them entirely hollow from deep socket to high pedestal foot. Having no place for the punty rod, the blown candlestick, whilst being shaped, had to be gripped around the stem: the tool marks may generally be detected. The stem was composed of a series of knops and a wide baluster might be incorporated in the design. This was supported by a high pedestal foot expanded downward to a wide flat-spreading rim as a precaution against accidental overturning. The deep, cylindrical socket was lipped. Blown candlesticks have been noted with feet measuring no more than $2\frac{1}{2}$ inches in diameter, too small to be used with any degree of safety. It has been suggested that these fitted into metal stands.

Stems were invariably solid by 1685, the high pedestal foot supporting a true baluster, the swell of which might contain air bubbles, a knop above, and a deep socket. By the end of the seventeenth century, the stem of inverted baluster form was usual, its swell supporting a straight-sided socket, the base of which might be encircled with gadrooning in the style of silver candlesticks. A taller candlestick was secured by placing a true baluster above an inverted baluster with a knop separating stem and foot.

The baluster continued, more slender than formerly, until the 1730's. At the same time and until the middle of the century other stems were built from characterless assemblages of knop forms, air-beaded or plain, or from series of slightly flattened balls of equal diameter (fig. 248 left). Collared knops date from about 1715. A short vogue for a stem with a large, solid-moulded ball set between heavy ringed collars in the early 1730's was followed by the

311

stem with a large hollow sphere centrally placed between a series of knops.

Sockets appear always to have been finished with rolled lips (fig. 247 centre) and were usually plain, but from about 1710 might be moulded with vertical ridges. After 1730 the socket tended to be slightly waisted immediately below the lip. During the 1730's socket lips might be slightly expanded to catch candle drips: this feature was soon enlarged into a saucer or sconce (fig. 249). Loose saucer-sconces with necks fitting closely into plain-rimmed sockets had appeared by 1740 (fig. 254), usually more widely spreading than the fixed sconce. The great days of the loose sconce, however, belong to the early period of cut-glass. Wax candles only were burned in glass candlesticks; wax-refining processes were improved during the 1730's enabling a thinner, less costly candle to produce the same amount of illumination as former designs. The result was that pre-1740 candlestick sockets were of greater diameter than those made later although it must be remembered that examples with loose sconces were exceptions — easily distinguishable, even when now lacking such sconces, by the absence of the rolled lip (fig. 258).

The feet of flint-glass candlesticks varied little in form until the middle of the eighteenth century. Early pedestal feet were superseded by highly domed feet, the upper surface decorated with radial moulding (fig. 250). These were followed by smooth-surfaced round (fig. 248b), sloping (fig. 248a), and squarish (fig. 254) domes with spreading rims which might be folded back on themselves for nearly half an inch, providing extra strength at the part most liable to be chipped. The surface of the spread was usually plain but might be terraced or ornamented with concentric rings (fig. 253): these rings might be continued upon the dome. Domed feet of this period were seldom symmetrical as they were shaped entirely by hand, and they invariably possess rough punty marks beneath.

Candlesticks with moulded stems of the shouldered or silesian type (figs. 249-54 and Chapter 4) date between about 1710 and 1740. Ridges might be pressed vertically (fig. 249), or the flutes curved gracefully (fig. 252): impressed bosses might ornament the shoulders. A variety of knops, collars, multiple rings, and air-beaded balls might be introduced above and below the shouldered motif. Short silesian stems, one placed inversely upon the other with a flattened knop between, were fairly frequent (fig. 250). Some late examples were adapted to the fashion for cutting flat vertical fluting, being enlivened with shallow diamond facets. Few of these have survived.

Sockets on shouldered stems pre-1730 were vertically ribbed; plain sockets from 1730; cut sockets and loose sconces after 1740, but rarely earlier than about 1750. Socket lips were usually rolled and from 1730 might be expanded to catch the candle drippings. Feet were domed and usually moulded with radial or vertical ridges.

Running parallel with the later shouldered stems was the now rare rib-twisted baluster stem with highly domed foot and plain socket (fig. 248d). Plain or air-beaded knops might be placed above and below the stem. Incised balusters, one placed inversely above the other, might be separated by a series of collared knops and a centrally placed ball knop.

Glass candlesticks were highly ornamental pieces of table-ware between about 1740 and 1780, stems being decorated in three ways: air-twist (fig. 258), enamel-twist (fig. 259), and facet-cutting (figs. 261-66). The air-spirals developed from the neatly arranged clusters of tears which might ornament socket bases of the 1730's. They were advertised as 'wormed candlesticks' and had a twenty-year vogue. The air-spirals in early examples were inexpertly drawn with multiple rings or knops containing air-beads at both ends. When perfection in air-spirals was eventually achieved, elaborate twists were preferred in a single-knopped stem (*see* Chapter 5).

Stems enlivened with white enamel twists of all varieties, single and compound, were fashionable from about 1750 to 1775, but were made until about 1790. The earliest were broad tape-like spirals (fig. 260). The fault found with most enamel-twist stems is their rigidity of outline. Coloured twists appeared in candlestick stems after about 1760, but few of these remain.

Sockets of air- and enamel-twist candlesticks might be either plain or fluted, with rolled lips, or with widely expanded fixed sconces, or with removable sconces. Highly domed feet continued in use with plain, flat, wide rims, advertised as 'spreading domes'.

Candlesticks of cut-glass exist in greater profusion than earlier types by reason of the loose sconces which, after 1750, almost invariably completed the design of their deep sockets. Loose sconces were now sold as spares to replace breakages, chiefly caused by carelessly permitting candles to burn down into the glass and crack it. Before the days of the loose sconce the entire stick was damaged beyond repair.

The earliest candlestick advertisement to be noted by Francis Buckley appeared in the *Daily Advertiser*, December 1742, when Jerom Johnson announced 'diamond-cut and scalloped candlesticks'. Their absence from glass-sellers' lists until the 1740's suggests that they were not highly popular. They were not costly: in September 1746 Cookson & Co., Newcastle upon Tyne, invoiced '6 Candlesticks, best, at 3/- each' and later in the year a 'pair of Worm'd Candlesticks at 10d. lb.' A 'four-branch sconce' was invoiced at £1. 11s. 6d. Enrichment in the form of diamond facets and the greater durability ensured by the fitting of loose sconces carried them to the tables of the gentry.

The early diamond-faceted stem was straight-sided with a plain surfaced knop at each end containing a cluster of air beads (fig. 262). Soon, however, knops were cut to match the stem. Then came the central knop or cusp (fig. 264), followed by the double baluster with a central ball knop facet-cut (fig. 265). Numerous other knop arrangements are also found. By about 1770 facet-cut stems on candlesticks became tall and pillar-like, suggesting the prevailing classical influence and sometimes decorated with convex diamonds. At about the same time diamond faceting might be combined with plain vertical fluting.

Highly-domed feet, smooth-surfaced and with flat, medium-wide rims, supported some early faceted candlesticks (fig. 261) and continued to be made until the early 1760's. In others the domes might be moulded with radial ridges as in earlier styles, but with the flat foot rims scalloped. From about 1760 insteps might be ornamented with large diamonds cut in relief, plain diamonds double cut, flat geometric cutting, or any of the curvilinear motifs (fig. 264). The sliced edges of scalloped foot rims matched those of the loose sconces above (fig. 266), which by 1770 might sometimes expand to a diameter approximating half that of the foot (fig. 265).

Sockets on early faceted stems might be either plain or spirally fluted, but by 1750 scale pattern or flat diamond faceting was usual. The loose sconce might be scalloped as on earlier types. In cut stems foot scalloping was introduced to match that on the sconce above.

Glass candlesticks with stems resembling slender classical columns were contemporary with tall faceted stems tapering towards sockets cut in flat facets and expanded into fixed and scalloped sconces (fig. 263). The vogue for these and for the classical type with stem moulded in vertical flutes and finished with ornamental rings at top and bottom continued until about 1785. Others were plain, hexagonally stemmed, highly polished. Classical stems were never knopped and were generally supported on spreading domed feet with terraced or stepped rims, advertised at the time as 'Norwegian feet'. Similar feet are sometimes found on moulded stems of the pre-1740 period.

Less expensive candlesticks began to appear during the 1770's, made by a specialist set of glass-workers known as 'pinchers'. These workers were noted as a separate branch of the glass trade as early as 1777, and the

Birmingham *Directory* of 1780 lists eleven firms under this classification. They pressed feet, bodies, and cylindrical sockets separately, joining the red-hot sections into single entities measuring from 9 to 12 inches in height.

At first the sturdy body of such a candlestick followed the fashionable barrel shape, ribbed vertically to resemble staves and encircled with shallow incisions to represent hoops (fig. 271a). In later examples these rings might be omitted, the ribs accentuated and continued up the socket, and notched. The loose sconces were moulded with widely dished rims, the edges of which might be notched. In the 1780's and later the body might be urn-shaped, the lower portion decorated with thick gadrooning and the upper part with wheel-cutting. Others were cut all over with shallow diamonds, the cylindrical sockets being diamond faceted. Advertisements of the late 1780's and early 1790's refer to these as vase-shaped candlesticks.

This style of candlestick was supported on a thick square foot, sometimes terraced, and with a dome-shaped hollow pressed beneath and usually gadrooned to increase refraction. By about 1780 the base of the socket might be expanded into a shallow flange of about the same diameter as the foot, with a scalloped rim from which depended six single- or double-lustre drops. Contrary to general belief early specimens are not of Irish origin.

Such candlesticks, lavishly cut with diamonds in relief, were made from about 1800 to 1820, the diamonds being pressed and wheel-finished. Circular feet with radially moulded surface and star-cut beneath were a Regency development.

Miniature glass candlesticks, 4 to 6 inches in height with deep, narrow sockets, often without rolled lips, appeared early in the eighteenth century, following all the characteristics of glass candlesticks proper. These were known at first as tobacco candlesticks, and were used with specially refined candles as pipe-lighters by smokers. By 1740 they were being referred to as pipe-lighters by smokers. By 1740 they were being referred to as tea-candlesticks or taper-sticks (fig. 34).

Glass candlesticks were joined during the early 1740's by elaborate table chandeliers of flint-glass holding two or more candles and known at the time as lustres or candlestands (figs. 267-70).

Chambers's *Cyclopaedia*, 1753, records that 'larger and more stately candlesticks contrived for holding a great number of candles are called *branches* or *girandoles*, and when made of glass lustres'. These lustres eventually became magnificent in their display of glass drops, then known as icicle drops. For more than twenty years lustres or table chandeliers

315

could only be 'bespoke', so great was the demand for this resplendent work and so few were the cutters capable of its execution, which included grinding, scalloping, faceting, and notching. Glass-sellers undertook to clean glass lustres when soiled: in 1753 Thomas Betts charged 5s. for this service. Table chandeliers were regularly advertised as glass lustres from 1760 to the ultimate exclusion of glass candlesticks, which continued to be made, however.

In foot and stem and in the socket from which the curving branches and central spire shaft emerged, the design closely resembled that of the contemporary sweetmeat stand. At first the branches were twisted and but slightly cut, but from about 1760 they might be lavishly cut and notched, and the tall spire centre-shafts topped with scalloped canopies (fig. 267). Rayed star finials rising from the apex of the canopy or from vertical extensions welded to the upper curves of branches were important features of early table chandeliers (fig. 268).

Such table chandeliers might also be enlivened with one or more disc reflectors or illuminaries which, according to Ince and Mayhew writing in 1763, were cut so that their 'several rays will reflect the candles in so many different colours as to render it very beautiful'. Some were cut in diamond form, others in fluted radial bevels. Eight-rayed star finials with diamond-cut ball centres belong to table chandeliers of the 1770's: they were often accompanied by pendant rosettes on the branches.

A square foot, its moulded dome supporting a heavy vase-shaped or baluster stem with a shaft rising to a domed canopy, often with a scalloped rim, and topped by a bevelled crescent finial, dates from about 1770. The square foot began to be replaced during the 1790's by the inverted saucer-shaped foot which might be enriched with any of the contemporary styles of diamond cutting. The domed canopy was replaced by a shallow saucer similar in shape to the foot and from its rim hung strings of short lustre drops each carrying a lengthy terminal lustre. Clever grouping of the lustres produced some astonishingly brilliant effects. Branches might now be plain with their upper surfaces notched, while the finial might be shaped and cut to resemble a pineapple or more frequently as a large covered urn decorated with relief cutting. This central finial was sometimes replaced by a third socket matching the pair below.

Table chandeliers of the early nineteenth century were less extravagantly designed than formerly and lost their attractive illuminaries. Every available glass surface was covered with cutting in deep relief. Step cutting on the foot might accompany a step-cut pillar. In the Regency period the foot might be flat and the canopy a horizontal disc of flint-glass, its diameter approximating that of the foot and its upper surface cut to match.

For the most part the lustre drops had now become elongated into a drooping slenderness, and were placed with almost geometric precision. Lustre drops were pressed in flint-glass, being pinched out of lumps of softened glass. The rough-formed drops were then ground. Contrary to general opinion few, if any, lustre drops were made in Ireland: makers of chandeliers in that country appear to have incorporated Birmingham lustre drops into their best work. English-made lustre drops swell to points on one side or on both: they are more richly faceted than the Irish which are rather deeper tinted than English and always round or almond-shaped, and are flat when viewed sideways. Lustre drops and prisms with sharp angular bands for greater reflective brilliancy were the invention of John Gold in 1840.

John Barrett, from 1784, was responsible for glass table chandeliers, the design consisting of a deep, expansive bowl raised upon a sturdy pedestal foot and containing a centrally fixed shaft supporting a canopy and lustres and four branches each terminating in a candle socket. The bowl was filled with water, thus preventing hot candle-wax from falling upon the table or upon the cut-glass where it looked unsightly and might cause breakage if carelessly removed. The servant snuffing the candles also skimmed off any wax floating upon the water.

Closely allied to table chandeliers were the less elegant glass two-branch candelabra with which they were produced concurrently from about 1770. Such table and sideboard illuminants had been made in flint-glass early in the eighteenth century: a four-branch example in the Victoria and Albert Museum dates from Queen Anne's reign. Few examples are known, however, which may be dated earlier than about 1770 when the Birmingham and Newcastle workers in pinched glass extended the scope of their trade, furthering the production of less costly candelabra in competition with the finer, more sparkling table chandeliers.

The early candelabra in this medium measured about 12 inches in height with a square, heavy foot supporting a solid vase-shaped body. From the top of the stem rose a solid socket terminating in a high moulded finial, sometimes shaped as a pineapple, but more usually in one of the various vase designs. Twin branches supported sockets with fixed sconces above wide circular flanges from which hung about six pairs of widely spaced lustre drops.

The influence of Matthew Boulton, who was first to use the term 'candelabra', was reponsible for some handsome candelabra in glass on ormolu stands and measuring from 24 inches to 30 inches in height. These date from the 1780's, the glass bodies still remaining for the most part vase-shaped. From the top of the body sprang a pair of curving branches and a tall slender vertical pillar which might terminate in a third socket or in a decorative finial immediately above a flange. Each of the three flanges was draped with lustre drops which appeared in longer festoons and more closely spaced than formerly. The height of the central spire was such that the strings of lustre drops were about twice the length of those hanging from the branches.

Glass candelabra from about 1805 became a field for cutting in deep relief. The stem rose from an inverted saucer foot: socket flanges on the branches were of similar shape and encircled with strings of lustre drops placed as close together as possible, each terminating in a long pointed prism. From the top of the body extended a moulded and cut pillar, shorter than the former spires, supporting a similar flange above which rose a tall, heavy, diamond-cut finial.

During the Regency period and beyond there was a fashion for candelabra with step-cut feet and bodies, each lustre pendant being composed of one small drop and one long prism. The body-branch-finial junction might be encircled with pendant lustres. From 1820 flat circular feet were usual.

It has not always been appreciated that the vase-candlestick was the real forerunner of the girandole-candlestick, although the less spectacular piece long continued as a distinct design among glass candlesticks. The vase-candlestick was introduced in about 1775 and continued to be made until the 1820's with a square foot supporting a solid vase-shaped body, the lower part in the form of an inverted cone. In many instances a circular flange extended a short distance from the base of the plain, cylindrical socket. The vase at first was barrel-shaped, vertical lines and encircling rings suggesting staves and hoops. This design was introduced in decanters by Christopher Haedy who advertised it as 'new-fashioned' in 1775. Trade cards of the 1780's illustrate vase-candlesticks with barrel-, pineapple-, and vase-shaped stems. In a series issued during the 1790's the socket rose directly from the top of the vase without any intermediate flange. Vase-candlesticks were made until the end of the Regency period, feet, stems, and sockets closely following fashionable forms and cutting motifs.

The girandole-candlesticks developed as a natural result of such a candlestick design when some glassmen expanded the flange and hung it with dangling lustres. In this way the vase-candlestick could the more fittingly accompany and enhance the more majestic girandole, and the name 'girandole-candlestick' was introduced to distinguish it.

By 1780 the flange had been expanded and shaped with a slight upward curve and a scalloped rim from which hung several pendant lustres extending about half-way down the body. Such a lustre usually consisted of two drops, the upper one measuring about one-third the length of the one hanging below. In the centre of the flange was a short thick strengthening ring supporting a cylindrical candle-socket. As with contemporary vase-candlesticks, the earliest of these lustred designs had barrel-shaped bodies. From the mid-1780's the body might be cut with vertical flutes, the crests between the flutes being notched. The majority of existing examples of this period, however, are pinched with coarse gadrooning on the lower half of the vase.

During the 1790's the cylindrical candle-socket was superseded by a tall urn-shaped style with a vertical or horizontal rim deeply scalloped and its surface diamond-cut in deep relief. The flange, now more expansive, fitted closely over the neck of the vase where a brass fitment was attached enabling it to be revolved when the socket was in position. Towards 1800 the flange was made saucer-shaped with a shallow rim and was encircled by a closely spaced fringe of long, slender lustres extending almost to the square foot below.

The girandole-candlestick early in the nineteenth century became more resplendent with diamond-cutting in deep relief and long icicle lustres which tinkled pleasantly against each other in the slightest draught. The fashionable type stood on a high inverted saucer foot which was a field for all-over diamond-cutting in deep relief. The vase-shaped stem supported a flange of equal diameter, deeply saucer-shaped with the opening upward, and cut to match. An urn-shaped socket rose from a sturdy facet-cut knop within the flange and might be fitted with an expansive horizontal rim or a large saucer-shaped sconce. Foot, body, flange, socket, and sconce were all lavishly cut with diamonds of all varieties in deep relief. The outer rims of foot, flange, and sconce had matching borders, often being left plain or edged with short narrow flutes. During the Regency period of 1811 to 1820 the flange might be scalloped. This period, too, saw a series of double-cascade girandole-candlesticks in which the wide rim of the socket was further extended and encircled with lustres reaching almost to the revolving flange below, which still retained its own set of longer, matching lustres.

With the reign of George IV the design of fashionable girandole-candle-

319

sticks again altered. The foot was flat and radially moulded on the upper surface, the stem composed of a vase-shaped unit with a large knop above — ultimately of two large knops, the lower one being the greater in diameter. The flange was omitted, and the sconce, with up-turned, fan-scalloped or shell border, was expanded to a diameter equal to or greater than that of the foot. Foot, stem, and flange might be encircled with horizontal prism-cutting. Long, thin icicle lustres extended almost the length of the body. Final phase of the design was a retention of the cascade effect after the basic purpose of candle-holder was lost. These chimney lustres, possessing no candle-sockets, were for ornament only.

Figures 247, 248

(247) Candlesticks. (*a*) With deep socket and highly domed foot both decorated with horizontal mouldings; the central knop containing air bubbles is placed beneath a wide angular knop and above an annulated knop; *c.* 1730. (*b*) With deep plain socket on stem composed of acorn knop, bladed knop, ball knop, and double annulated knop, on spreading domed and ringed folded foot; *c.* 1730. (*c*) With deep, fluted socket supported by knops, one with tears, on eight-fluted silesian stem with diamond points; reticulated spreading domed foot; *c.* 1750.

By courtesy of Messrs Christie, Manson & Woods Ltd

(248) Taper-sticks. (*a*) With plain socket supported by a five knopped stem, the lowest and largest knop containing air bubbles, on a flared folded foot. Height 6¼ inches; *c.* 1720. (*b*) Moulded socket on inverted baluster and knop containing a tear-drop; domed and ringed foot. Height 4¾ inches; *c.* 1720. (*c*) Cordial glass, to show how this may be confused with a taper-stick with plain stem on folded foot. Height 4 inches. (*d*) With deep socket on a fluted inverted silesian stem rising from a domed and reticulated foot. Height 5 inches; *c.* 1730.

By courtesy of Messrs Christie, Manson & Woods Ltd

Figures 249–54

CANDLESTICKS

With moulded stems of the shouldered or silesian type; early George II period.

(249) True silesian shape with vertical ridges, air bubbles in knops above and below; expansive domed foot with pressed decoration, and diamond motifs on instep; plain socket with expanded rim.

(250) Two short silesian units placed inversely one upon the other, with mereses at each end; the shoulders enriched with cutting; spreading domed foot with pressed diamond motifs on instep; plain socket with rolled rim.

(251) Composite stem with inverted silesian unit between annulated knops, plain ball knop at top and multiple ring knop at base; on plain pedestal foot; socket with rolled rim.

(252) Stem composed of short silesian units placed head to head with annular knop between; mereses at each end; spreading domed foot with pressed vertical ridges and diamond motifs on instep; socket also pressed into ridges and rim expanded into a sconce.

(253) Inverted silesian stem between two air-beaded collared knops; domed foot with encircling ridges on the flange; plain socket with folded rim.

321

(254) Taper-stick with composite stem a silesian unit between a pair of units consisting of mereses, knops containing air tears and drop knops; plain domed foot; deep socket with widespread saucer sconce.

All in the Victoria and Albert Museum

Figures 255–60

EARLY GEORGIAN CANDLESTICKS

(255) Knopped stem containing a central doubly cushioned knop, collared knop above, and knop with air bubbles below, on low pedestal foot with ridged top; plain socket with lip.

(256) Knopped stem with, from top downwards, ball knop, ball knop with air bubbles, two ball knops, double cushioned knop, on domed and terraced foot; plain socket with lip.

(257) Knopped stem with acorn knop, annular knop, ball knop with air bubbles, and ridged knop, on spreading dome foot, the flange pressed into ridges; plain heavily lipped socket.

(258) Knopped air-twist stem on annulated knop with spreading domed foot pressed into vertical ridges; socket lip expanded into grease sconce; *c.* 1745.

(259) Air-twist in straight stem with mereses at each end, on spreading dome foot with flange pressed into ridges; waisted, heavily lipped socket; *c.* 1745.

(260) Composite stem consisting of opaque white section with knops below, on plain domed foot; socket fitted with a plain grease sconce; *c.* 1750.

All in the Victoria and Albert Museum

Figures 261–6

CANDLESTICKS AND TAPER-STICKS WITH FACETED STEMS

(261) Stem and knop diamond-faceted; plain domed foot; lower part of socket encircled with diamond facets; 1750's.

(262) Straight stem, diamond-faceted between flattened knops with tears, on domed foot moulded with radial ridges and sliced edges; socket cut with long diamonds; loose sconce facet-cut; 1750's.

(263) Diamond-facet cut stem with knife-edged knop above and cut cyst below, on domed and scalloped foot with instep ornamented with large diamonds; 1760's.

(264) Knopped stem on domed foot with flat geometric-cutting; scalloped rim with sliced edge; socket cut with long diamonds; 1760's.

(265) Double-baluster stem with knop between, on low domed and scalloped foot with sliced edge; socket cut with short diamonds; 1760's.

(266) Baluster stem supporting spool-shaped knop with facet-cut socket and fixed sconce; 1770's.

All in the Victoria and Albert Museum

Figures 267, 268

TABLE CHANDELIERS OR GIRANDOLES
WITH SIMPLE PENDANT LUSTRES

(267) Two-branch type, with plain domed foot and thick knopped stem supporting a capacious socket from which rises a tall, plain-faced spire centre-shaft supporting a scalloped domed canopy with a crescent finial. From the sockets spring four facet-cut branches, two terminating in candle-sockets with expansive loose sconces, the other two with canopies and starred finials; *c.* 1770.

By courtesy of Mr W. G. T. Burne

(268) Four-branch type the square foot supporting a cut vase-shaped stem with an expansive saucer-flange and a socket from which rises a cut and notched spire centre-shaft terminating in a scalloped domed canopy with a rayed star finial. From the socket spring six facet-cut branches: three curve downward and terminate in candle-sockets made in a piece with deep, expansive scalloped sconces: the other two curve upward to canopies matching the central motif, and spire finials. 27 inches high; *c.* 1790.

By courtesy of Mr W. G. T. Burne

Figures 269, 270

(269) Two-branch table chandelier or girandole with a square foot and a cut stem with faceted knop and a socket supporting a tall, canopied spire topped by a solid vase-shaped finial. From the socket also spring two downward-curving notched and cut branches terminating in candle-sockets fitted with loose sconces, and from the same point rise two curved, notched, and cut ornaments, known as snakes, their heads supporting lustres; *c.* 1780. Height 28 inches.

By courtesy of Mr W. G. T. Burne

(270) Two-branch girandole in glass and ormolu, one of a pair. Square foot, stem with horizontal prismatic cutting supporting downward-curving ormolu branches and a vertical rod passing through a diamond-cut baluster and terminating in a skeleton canopy with pendant lustres, and a tall diamond-cut finial; *c.* 1820. Height 18 inches.

By courtesy of Mr W. G. T. Burne

323

Figure 271

GIRANDOLE-CANDLESTICKS

A collection arranged in approximate chronological order, and numbered left to right. (1, 2, 5, and 6) Square feet with pinched stems. (1 and 2) Barrel-shaped with vertical lines and encircling rings to suggest staves and hoops. (5) Bulbous with notched fluting. (6) Baluster shape and notched. All with slightly depressed radiating flanges hung with lustres and from which rise cylindrical candle-sockets; 1780–1800.

(7 and 12) With flange extended or saucer-shaped and supporting urn-shaped sockets with expansive sconces; 1790–1810.

(8, 13, and 14) Flange extended and socket sunk into the top of the stem; Regency period.

(9, 10, and 11) With sconces expanded into flanges resembling elaborate saucers with up-turned rims, encircled with long thin lustres; radially moulded feet; from 1821.

By courtesy of Messrs Delomosne & Son Ltd

Figure 272

Girandole-candlesticks with candle-shades: Height about 20 inches; 1820's.

By courtesy of Mr W. G. T. Burne

246   Finger-bowl and two-lipped wineglass coolers

247 Candlesticks

248 Tapersticks with, *right centre*, a cordial glass

249–254   Candlesticks and, *lower right*, a taperstick, with moulded stems of the shouldered or silesian type

255–260 Early Georgian candlesticks

261–266 Candlesticks and tapersticks with faceted stems

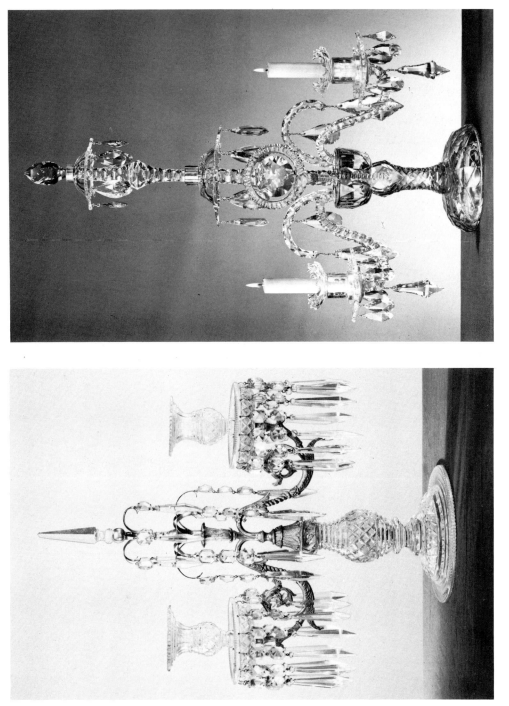

267, 268 Table chandeliers or girandoles with simple pendant lustres

330

269, 270 Table chandeliers or girandoles

331

271 A collection of girandole-candlesticks arranged in approximate chronological order

CHAPTER TWENTY

TUMBLERS, FRUIT AND SALAD BOWLS

'THENCE HOME, taking two silver tumblers which I have bought', confided Pepys to his *Diary* in the summer of 1664. To carry a pair of silver tumblers enclosed in a small gilt-enriched leather case had become fashionable with the nobility and gentry accustomed to coach travelling with its nightly discomfort of boarding and lodging in wayside taverns. Doctors had advocated that liquor should be taken only from silver vessels, thus assuring protection from the ills even then associated with drinking from tavern pewter: the few newly established coaching inns provided a side table with silver plate for wealthy patrons.

Such a tumbler was raised in a single piece from the silver plate: the thickness of its rounded base was made proportionately greater than that of its vertical sides, so that even if the vessel rocked from side to side when placed or jolted upon the table it would not turn over — hence its name. The diameter of a tumbler usually exceeded its depth, which varied from $1\frac{3}{4}$ to 3 inches, and the smooth outer surface was usually engraved with a coat of arms, crest, or name and date encircling the lip. Those accompanying silver travelling sets, including knife, fork, spoon, and tooth-pick, were usually engraved with an all-over scenic design — often sporting in character — or with a closely scrolled design of flowers and foliage. Examples are known worked with repousse and chased ornament, usually large flowers and a cartouche engraved with a coat of arms.

Silver tumblers were an essential part of coach-travelling equipment until the 1730's and hallmarks show them to have been made until the 1760's, Georgian examples usually being carried in silver-mounted shagreen cases. Silver tumblers must be differentiated from the deeper beakers in which the base was inserted and the body joined vertically with an invisible seam.

Inevitably, as with other drinking-vessels in silver, the form of the tumbler was adapted to glass. In the British Museum is preserved an important series of orders, instructions, and drawings sent by the London glass-seller John Greene to Allesia Morelli of Venice between 1667 and 1672. These Venetian drinking-glasses, which numbered some 23,000 pieces in

333

173 types, were specified by Greene to 'be made of verij cleere white sound metall and exact according to the patterns both for size and number and of noe other sorts or fashions'. This shows them to have been made specially to patterns preferred by Englishmen at that period.

Among this wide variety of drinking-vessels were many tumblers, four types being ordered: plain, enamel-speckled, vertically and horizontally ribbed, as well as in nests of six and twelve 'verij well fitting' one within the other. The drawings show that in size they approximated silver tumblers, diameter and depth being about equal, the sides sloping almost imperceptibly outward from the slightly rounded base. They were marked as being for beer, claret, and sack, tiny tumblers being described at the same time as for brandy. Tumblers of Venetian glass were by no means inexpensive, for in addition to losses caused by breakages during transport they were subject to a substantial import duty. Beakers, tall and narrow, were specified separately under that name.

After flint-glass had been patented by George Ravenscroft tumblers were made in this newer, stronger metal, but were thicker in section. Venetian tumblers continued to be imported, however, and in 1698 Bullivant declared 'I put a straw into a Venice glass tumbler'. By about 1700 the flint-glass tumbler was made a little more capacious, while retaining the same proportions and shape. The base was given a medium kick, just enough for the rough punty scar associated with blown flint-glass to be raised slightly above the table top.

Not until the early 1740's were glass tumblers designed with more sharply sloping sides and of a height rather less than double the base diameter and varying between 3 and 5 inches, with 8-inch giants by no means infrequent. The heavy-based waisted tumbler had come into use by 1750, small examples measuring between $2\frac{1}{4}$ and 3 inches in height being known as dram glasses and given exceptionally thick bases for hammering (fig. 275).

Tumblers for table use were now made without a kick, the thick base being ground flat on a horizontal revolving stone. This refinement, known to the trade as 'cut bottoms', increased the cost: less expensive blown-moulded tumblers were made with a kick and rough punty mark. These were customarily smooth-surfaced but many were made with broad or fine spiral flutes, the glass-blower manipulating the twist immediately after removal of the glass from the mould. Diamond moulding also had a vogue and from about 1770 the so-called Norwich or Lynn ringed tumbler was made, its body encircled with six to eight horizontal depressions which might be cut.

334

Undecorated tumblers were advertised at 9d. a pound in 1769. The Sitwell accounts at Rennishaw contain various entries for tumblers bought from the Whittington Glass House, near Chesterfield. In 1791 '2 doz^n $\frac{1}{2}$ Pint Tumb^{ls} cut Bott^{ms}' cost 16s., and in 1795 the price had increased by 6d. a dozen. At the same time '1 doz^n Qua^r Pint Tumblers cut Bott^{ms}' cost 3s. 6d. Flat bottoms continued until after 1805 when it became fashionable for a radiating star to be deep-cut beneath.

Collectors sometimes confuse tumblers with the water-glasses for so long an essential feature of the English table and used for rinsing the mouth at the end of a meal. They were differentiated in eighteenth-century advertisements such as that inserted in the *Norwich Mercury*, August 1758, by Phillips's Glass Warehouse, St. Andrews, Norwich, and quoted by Francis Buckley: 'Pint, Half and Quarter Pint Tumblers, and a great variety of Water Glasses.'

Tumblers decorated with cutting were first noted in England in 1709 when the *London Gazette* referred to the importation of a consignment of German cut-glass in which cut-glass wine tumblers were included. These were no doubt lightly ornamented with small shallow-cut diamond-shaped German facets. For the next half-century flint-glass tumblers might be lightly touched with such cutting and with large diamonds and triangles in low relief. From the late 1750's all-over shallow cutting became somewhat deeper and a wider variety of motifs was used. Frequent advertisements now appeared offering 'cut pint, half and quarter pint tumblers'. The cut bottoms were first applied to tumblers ornamented with cutting.

Finger fluting encircling the lower half of tumblers dates from the same period, at first flat and broad, little more than the surface of the glass being ground away. As the century progressed the flutes were cut deeper and width varied considerably. Between 1790 and 1820 the crests of finger fluting might be notched. Deep relief cutting is found on heavy tumblers from about 1790, some fifty varieties and combinations of motifs being found after 1805 (fig. 276).

Tumblers ornamented with hand-cutting from this period were of a thick section metal of a clarity never before achieved. Typical was the design of ten to eighteen flat flutes extending upwards from the base to cover about one-third of the body, with a wide band of diamonds in deep relief above, and the rim cut with a circuit of blazes — also known as the herring-bone fringe. After about 1820 printies might replace diamonds, and blazes were separated from each other by a narrow prismatic band. The fashionable size was the 'large half-pint'. Those made for use where liquor was sold were made to contain exactly half a pint.

Tumblers ornamented with wheel-engraving were greatly admired: few examples have been noted in which the diamond-point has been used. Until the late 1730's wheel-engraving was confined almost entirely to coats of arms, the reverse remaining undecorated or engraved with a crest. An alternative was a name and inscription encircling the rim. The accuracy demanded in armorial engraving made it a most difficult task. By 1750 it became customary for regimental messes to have their glass table-ware engraved with the regimental badge.

'Flower'd pint, half, and quarter pint tumblers' was a frequent phrase in advertisements such as appeared in the *Weekly Mercury*, April 1771. 'Flowered' was the trade term for tumblers engraved with naturalistic flowers in a style much resembling those on contemporary porcelain and dates between the 1740's and 1780's. At first a single flower such as a rose, carnation, or daisy or other wild flower was considered sufficient, the reverse remaining blank or being engraved with a crest or cypher. During the 1750's other flowers such as sunflower, tulip, and passion flower might also be used while the reverse of the bowl was engraved with a bird, butterfly, moth, or other insect. Wide bands of large parcel-polished flowers engraved below the rim date between 1750 and 1775.

Pictorial engraving, fashionable between about 1760 and the 1780's, included pastorals in the Chinese taste, landscapes, and classical, allegorical, historic, and social scenes. Naval subjects with three-masted ships in full sail were special favourites and continued until the 1820's (figs. 273-4). Sporting scenes might be inscribed with names, places, and dates. Fox-hunting scenes of the 1770's and 1780's were more frequent than others, many having a fox in a landscape with the words 'Tally Ho' engraved beneath in such a way that it was intended to be seen within the glass. Steeplechasing, stag-hunting, fishing, shooting, cock-fighting, and hare-coursing scenes usually date to the early nineteenth century, as do tumblers commemorative of horse-racing successes engraved with the portrait and name of the winning horse.

Trade tumblers included those engraved with the arms of the various trade guilds such as the Weavers, the Turners, the Stationers, the Butchers, and so on. Often a hop-and-barley motif is found on the reverse, but more frequently the name of a member of the company together with his date of admission. Others might be less expensively included in the 'Success' series of tumblers, such as 'Success to the Swordmakers'. Tumblers were also inscribed and dated for christenings, marriages, fairings, and other memorable occasions.

336

Golden bands might encircle the rims of tumblers, narrow until about 1750, then wider. Below such a band there might be an engraved crest or cypher also gilded: traces of gold are sometimes to be detected by careful inspection. Wheel-engraving might be gilded to add radiance, particularly in the case of flowered rim borders. The *Bristol Journal*, 1773, referred to 'new fashion'd tumblers neatly burned with gold flowers'. When such gilding was used it formed the sole decorative medium, but is now scarce on tumblers owings to its inability to stand hard wear.

Enamelling in white and in colours enlivened tumblers during the third quarter of the eighteenth century. At a glance white-enamelled decoration might resemble deep wheel-engraving for which at first it was a cheap alternative, but with coloured enamels some fine illuminated effects were possible. In the most magnificent specimens coats of arms in vivid colours were delineated by enamellers whose advertisements appeared in newspapers of the period, the number of such announcements suggesting that there was a great demand for coloured armorial work. White enamelling consisted at first of a thinly applied wash enamel made from Venetian opaque-glass; from about 1770 a dense full white enamel was thickly applied.

Trick tumblers were a passing vogue from time to time, but few now remain. These date from the 1760's when a tumbler rim might be engraved with a border of baroque floral ornaments, the flower heads having perforated centres in a parcel-polished design. These perforations were invisible until liquor began to trickle down the chin of the unlucky drinker. A later series was engraved with a border of rosettes with central perforations, and in the early nineteenth century the rim might be encircled with a double row of prismatic flutes cut in such a way that piercing would not be discerned. Dice tumblers date from about 1780: the upper part was engraved while the thick base was made hollow to enclose three dice.

Tumblers intended for a cheap market from the 1750's were shaped in one-piece, open-top gunmetal moulds and then expanded by blowing. From the early 1760's the lower part of the mould interior might be intaglio-cut with a circuit of slender flutes. The lower part of the tumbler was thus encircled by a series of flutes rising vertically from the base. Early in the nineteenth century tumblers might be made by the two-piece open-and-shut mould capable of producing in a single operation both the form of the vessel and a range of decoration similar to that found on hand-cut tumblers. These tumblers may be detected from the free-blown and more costly tumblers by the presence of two almost imperceptible ridges on the

337

surface of the glass or two'slight breaks in the pattern. Also, too, the inner surface is not perfectly smooth but slightly rippled. From about 1820 the three-piece mould was evolved, leaving three ridges on the surface of the tumbler.

Surface patterns became innumerable after about 1816, but usually these may be placed in one of three general design categories: geometric (diamonds, flutes); baroque (scrolls and fan motifs in high relief); patterns based on arch shapes. The baroque and arch decorations were usually in higher relief than the geometric. The base of a tumbler is usually plain, but might be patterned in any one of some three dozen designs which have been grouped into seven classes: rays, circles, rays and circles, flutes and circles, circles and printies, circles of diamonds, circles of petal shapes.

Roman pillar moulding on tumblers dates from 1835 when the process was patented by James Green and licensed to glass-houses. This produced vertical columns projecting from the outer surface whilst the inner surface remained smooth. Pillar moulding might extend only half-way up the tumbler with other decoration above and a star beneath the base.

Blown-moulded tumblers as a general rule were made with a diameter approximately two-thirds their height, and the majority were given wide finger flutes. Pointed flutes indicate the gothic influence of the period following 1830. Barrel-shaped tumblers were also made, incurved top and bottom, with flutes shaped like staves and with encircling rings as hoops.

Blown-moulded work was chiefly carried out in clear flint-glass, but from the late 1840's a wide range of tumblers was made in delicate colours, purples, amethysts, ultramarines, ambers, and greens predominating. Coloured tumblers proved unpopular, however, and few were made after the mid-1850's.

Pressed tumblers date from about 1840, the process again drastically reducing manufacturing costs. They may be recognized by mould-marks in the form of sharply defined hair-lines or threads that appear as if applied to the surface. The inner surface is smooth as if it were blown, and motifs in relief are more clearly defined than in blown-moulded glass. Pressed-glass tumblers, too, have a granular texture tending to give them a somewhat matt appearance. By the mid-1840's it had been discovered that the more facets included in the design and the smoother the inner surface, the greater the scintillation under lamp- or gas-light.

Patterns bore a close resemblance to those found on cut-glass tableware of the period, with strawberry diamonds, fine-cut diamonds, and fan-escalloped rims. Low relief work was associated with such motifs as scrolls, various adaptations of the acanthus leaf, the anthemion and floral and gothic ornament. One collector has accumulated more than five hundred blown-moulded and pressed tumblers, all of entirely different patterns.

For nearly two centuries brilliant cut-glass has been prized as a perfect foil for fresh, richly coloured fruits. Today, antique glass bowls for fruit and for salad are as valuable as they are handsome. But while now attributed almost exclusively to the Irish glass-houses, particularly Waterford, it must be conceded that the majority, no doubt, were made in England, where they originated. As early as 1765, according to Francis Buckley, cut and plain fruit bowls were being exported to Ireland from Bristol.

Forerunners of these bowls were to be observed on the fashionable Georgian dessert-table by the 1750's when the flamboyant banqueting epergne in silver was topped with an expansive boat-shaped basket of fruits. In some instances the basket might be fitted with a loose lining in flint-glass: from about 1770 this was in Bristol blue. On less pretentious occasions the need for a colourful centre-piece was met by displaying the fruit in a boat-shaped bowl, decorative cut-glass taking the place of richly tooled silver. This was known as a fruit dish until the late 1770's, then as a fruit bowl. Cut-glass fruit dishes were included in the auction-sale advertisement of the glass stocked by John Marshall, a glass-cutter of Old Market, Bristol, in 1774. The wording of some advertisements suggests that such bowls served equally for fruit or salad.

Fruit and salad bowls in cut-glass may be grouped into six main classes, with virtually no difference between English and Irish productions: boat-shaped bowl with loose pedestal, 1780–1800 (fig. 277); round bowl with pedestal foot, 1790–1810 (fig. 282 centre); boat-shaped bowl with stem, 1790–1830's (fig. 279); hemispherical bowl, 1790–1810; bowl with turned-over rim, 1800–30 (fig. 281); kettle-drum bowl, 1820–40 (fig. 283 left and right).

Some early fruit bowls were made in two pieces, the boat-shaped bowl measuring 12 or 18 inches from tip to tip, resting on a separate stand. This consisted of a hollow pedestal foot supporting a shallow oval container to receive the base of the bowl. The bowl rim was scalloped and crested, often with the arch-and-point motif, and the body ornamented with bands of large shallow-cut motifs. The pedestal was cut in a single geometrical design and the oval rim of the bowl support encircled with narrow flutings.

In a series of fruit bowls dating from the early 1790's a shallow circular

339

bowl was welded to a widely spreading pedestal foot, its clear surface remaining uncut (fig. 282 centre). The bowl rim might be scalloped and crested, the body cut with festoons and large diamonds with star centres. Other bowl edges were notched and the body shallow-cut with a circuit of leaf festoons or diamond facets.

In the majority of instances, however, the flint-glass fruit bowl was welded to a stout stem rising from a heavy square foot. Boat-shaped examples for the luxury trade continued to be made until the 1830's (fig. 279). The pointed ends might rise considerably higher than the sides and the edges were usually scalloped, that is, ground to a sharp edge from the outer surface. The rim of such a bowl might be shaped with an arch-and-point outline, crested, or fan-cut. The body might be cut with a band of large relief diamonds such as square hob-nail cutting with a faceted wreath or cut-leaf festoons below, the lower part remaining undecorated. The stem might be plain, ringed, knopped, or flat-cut, with a thin flat strengthening collar below the base of the bowl. The stem rose from a thick, heavy square foot, which had a domed top and was either solid or hollow beneath (fig. 282 left). The hollow might be impressed with gadrooning as an aid to refraction. Sometimes the foot was stepped. Such feet and stems were moulded by that branch of the glass trade known as pinchers.

In other specimens the foot was square, oval or round, the top drawn out into swirling gadroons to form a stem which was welded directly to the strengthening collar beneath the bowl. By 1820 a thick round or oval foot had been introduced, with a wavy outline and a conical top, its surface moulded with graceful inward-tapering gadrooning. Diamond-shaped or oval feet might be associated with boat-shaped or oval bodies. This style was followed from about 1830 by the thin, flat circular foot, often with a star or radial fluting cut beneath.

Less costly were the hemispherical fruit bowls with wavy scalloped rims. These were sparsely decorated with shallow-cut motifs or a circuit of leaf-cutting with star-cutting above. At first they were supported by plain stems rising from square feet. By the early 1800's the stem was shorter and usually ringed, the square foot more expansive, the strengthening collar beneath the bowl thicker and larger in diameter, the bowl shallower and encircled with rows of zigzag cuttings, or shallow leaf-cutting below a circuit of large diamonds.

The hemispherical bowl was succeeded by the fruit bowl with a turned-over rim (fig. 281): such bowls might be made in matching sets of three — one large and a smaller pair. The deeply flanged or turned-over rims have

340

been wrongly stated by some writers to be a purely Irish characteristic: this design was probably the innovation of an English glass-house in about 1800. The bowl was blown with a hemispherical base and the rim turned over and downward to a depth of rather more than one-third that of the bowl, thus increasing rim diameter by one-third to one-half. This flange on early examples is rarely symmetrical. The foot was either square or round with similar features to those supporting boat-shaped bowls. The stem might be plain with a single knop, or ringed, or the top of the foot might be swirled with a ringed stem above.

The bowl might be circular or oval and the area below the rim might be left plain or cut with two or three closely spaced circuits of shallow facets or flat wreath-cutting, the outer rim being decorated with circuits of narrow prisms (fig. 281). Later bowls were more carefully finished than early examples, and might be cut all over with flat printies or with large diamond or hexagonal facets, and the flange was folded over symmetrically. A late version was the straight-sided blown-moulded bowl, the lower half encircled by wide flutes or flat-cutting. The straight stem in such a specimen might include a centrally placed applied knop resembling the double or triple rings which encircled decanter necks. Formed knops, as distinct from shaped bulges in stems, date from about 1820.

The kettle-drum fruit bowl (fig. 281 left and right), a design and term probably originating at Waterford in about 1820, was made with a shallow recess in the base of the bowl in which surplus dressing might collect when the bowl was used for salad. The recess was usually less than half of the bowl diameter and might occupy up to one-fifth of its full depth. The recess was usually plain and the outward shoulder might be plain or flat-cut, with a band of diamond-cutting composed of diamonds in relief cut smaller and less deeply than formerly. The body of the bowl was consequently thinner in section than if large relief diamonds were used. Such diamond-cutting usually consisted of two or three of the many varieties available, such as strawberry-cutting encircling star-cutting, or strawberry, cross, and hobnail cutting. Separating this band of ornament from the shoulder and rim cutting were narrow bands of prismatic cutting. Rims, fan-cut, or of undulating outline and no longer scalloped, were variously decorated, typical work consisting of short narrow upright flutes, twisted-cutting, and fan-cutting.

By about 1830 the stem had become shorter and rose from a flat circular foot, in the form of a thick plain or centrally knopped spool with a strengthening collar at each end. The recess might now be enlivened with bands of

341

prismatic cutting, the body with a field of hob-nail cutting, and with a fan-cut rim, scallop-edged. Separating diamonds and rim decoration was a narrow band of prismatic cutting. During the 1830's the base recess tended to disappear and prismatic cutting or mitred rings, or wide vertical fluting decorated the entire lower half of the bowl. Pillar moulding associated with diamonds was now common. The bodies of fruit and salad bowls were all hand-blown or blown-moulded: machine-moulded examples date from about 1840.

Figures 273-6

TUMBLERS

(273) Engraved with three-masted man-of-war in full sail and inscribed 'Prince George Admiral'. This was probably given by the Prince, later William IV, to Admiral Digby under whom he served as a midshipman on H.M.S. *Prince George*, a vessel of 1,955 tons and 95 guns, launched 1772. Height 8 inches.

(274) Engraved with a three-masted warship and inscribed 'The Glorious 11th Octr 1797' and 'Success to the British Navy'. Commemorating the Battle of Camperdown and the destruction, by Admiral Duncan, of the Dutch fleet when attempting the invasion of Ireland. Height 4 inches.

Both by courtesy of Messrs Arthur Churchill Ltd

(275) Masonic firing glass in the form of a deep-waisted tumbler with a thick base. The Masonic emblems and the scrolls of flowers and leaves are in yellow and white enamels; 1770's. Height 3 inches.

(276) Heavy tumbler cut with large diamonds in relief; *c.* 1800. Height 5 inches.

Both in the Corning Museum of Glass

Figures 277-80

CUT-GLASS FRUIT BOWLS

(277) Two-piece, boat-shaped bowl supported by hollow pedestal stem; scalloped and crested rim; body cut with band of large diamonds with star centres, and festoons; short fluting encircles bowl base and pedestal top; 1780's. Height 12 inches.

By courtesy of Messrs Cecil Davis

(278) Circular bowl, its rim cut with vertical prisms and its body encircled by rows of long horizontal hollows; on three plain feet, a rare feature; *c.* 1800. Height 8 inches.

Formerly in the Bles Collection

(279) Boat-shaped bowl; knopped stem; square foot, hollow beneath and impressed with gadrooning; scalloped rim; 1790's.

By courtesy of Messrs Delomosne & Son Ltd

(280) As above, bowl cut with vesica pattern, and given a taller stem, with a flat strengthening collar below the bowl base; early nineteenth century.

By courtesy of Messrs Delomosne & Son Ltd

Figures 281–3

STEMMED FRUIT BOWLS

(281) Bowls with turned-over rims; knopped stems with strengthening flanges against bowl bases; square feet hollowed and gadrooned beneath. Outer rims cut with circuits of narrow alternating prisms, and the bowls with closely spaced circuits of shallow facets.

(282) (*a*) Boat-shaped bowl; spreading stem on plain square foot; cut with a band of large diamonds with star centres; notched rim. (*b*) Shallow round bowl cut with a circuit of leaf festoons; spreading pedestal foot; notched rim. (*c*) Plainly hemispherical bowl with turned-over rim; knopped stem; domed square foot.

(283) (*a*) Kettle-drum body encircled with shallow horizontal facets; shoulder cut with band of strawberry diamonds; knopped stem; domed square foot hollowed and gadrooned beneath. (*b* and *d*) Toilet bottles of the 1830's. (*c*) Turned-over rim cut with a circuit of strawberry diamonds; body cut with wide flutes and circuit of large diamonds; knopped stem. (*e*) Kettle-drum body cut with horizontal prisms; shoulder with a band of strawberry diamonds; rim with narrow vertical prisms; knopped stem; round moulded foot.

By courtesy of Messrs Delomosne & Son Ltd

CHAPTER TWENTY-ONE

BRISTOL-BLUE GLASS

BRISTOL WAS LONG CELEBRATED for its splendid flint-glass, particularly for those beguiling radiant blues that have long fascinated collectors. Very little, if any, Bristol-blue glass was made between about 1800 and about 1820, when it again came into vogue under the name of 'king's blue'. This was a loyal gesture to George IV at the time of his coronation in 1821 when he was presented with a lavishly gilded spirit set in blue glass, consisting of decanters and glasses on a rectangular plateau.

This semi-transparent glass must not be confused with the vivid blues made from about 1800 to the mid-1840's in a variety of discordant tints. In recent years there has been a tendency for these often graceless productions to be classed as Bristol-blue. The extension of this term from the specific to the generic is greatly deplored.

The original Bristol-blue was so named by custom because, apart from the fact that such glass was made at Bristol, the superfine smalt capable of imparting the exceptionally strong and brilliant blue colour could be obtained only from Bristol, where, for a short time after 1763, supplies were in the hands of a single merchant. Little or none was available in England until that year.

Blue glass had graced the English table, however, for more than three centuries, early examples being opaque. Sir John Fastolf (1377–1479), rewarded with the Garter for his military skill at Agincourt and elsewhere, possessed 'ij lyttyl Ewers of blew glasses powdered with golde'. These, like the celebrated collection of glass acquired by Henry VIII, were made in the island of Murano, off the coast of Venice. Henry's blue glass included 'foure standing Cuppes of blewe glass with covers to them painted and gilt; oone Bason and oone Leyer [a laving ewer for rosewater] of blewe glasse partly gilt, the Leyer having the Kinges armes upon it; three Bottelles or Flagons of blewe glasse Glasses like Bollis standing upon fete blewe and white partely gilt; oone Cuppe of blewe glasse, the foot, bryme and cover garnished with silver and gilt with a knop of silver and gilt'. Glass cups with silver-gilt stems and feet 'viced on' (screwed on) were a fashionable conceit at that period.

The private account book of William More, Loseley, Surrey, written in 1556, included among the long list of 'glasse in my wyfs closet: a lyttle blewe bereglasse 1j^d', establishing that blue glass was not the prerogative of the nobility. The inventory of John Eden, Windleston, Durham, 1588, included 'ij blewe drinkinge glasse pottes', and similar references are found until the 1620's, various shades of blue being noted. Excavations on the sites of several glass-houses known to have been operating at this period have revealed fragments of English-made blue-glass table-ware.

Not until the discovery of cobalt in the mid-sixteenth century was it possible to make a semi-transparent blue glass, except at the vast expense of using oxide of lapis lazuli, known as ultramarine. A vitreous form of cobalt oxide prepared under the name of smalt was soon in use for tingeing German and Venetian glass at less than one-hundredth the cost of ultramarine. English-made 'smalt glass' was referred to in a patent granted during 1618 'for making the same smaulte heretofore brought from beyond the seas'. Nothing more is heard of the project. In 1642 an import duty of 3s. 4d. per pound was levied on 'smalts to make glasse', and there are references to 'smalt glass' in association with flint-glass during the 1680's. The purity of the smalt was progressively improved until in the eighteenth century a superfine quality was produced capable of imparting to flint-glass the magnificent Bristol-blue.

Cobalt, a greyish-tinted, brittle, slightly magnetic metal displaying a faint tinge of red, was first discovered — so far as Europe is concerned — in Saxony. This state had long been celebrated for rich deposits of minerals, the Saxons believing that their vast underground treasure of silver, copper, and lead was guarded by gnomes or kobalds. When the supply of ores suddenly failed in the sixteenth century, blame for the disaster fell upon the kobalds who were thereupon accused of transmuting the ores into rubbish, which was named cobalt.

The despised cobalt became the subject of a series of experiments carried out during the 1540's by the glass-maker Christopher Schürer of Neudeck who discovered oxide of cobalt to be a highly concentrated blue capable of tingeing glass throughout its fabric, yet preserving its translucency. This oxide he named zaffre. The delft potters of the Low Countries soon found this to be an ideal pigment for decorating their newly evolved earthenware.

A few years later Schürer continued his experiments, producing a much purified cobalt oxide which he added to potassium silicate glass to the extent of 2 to 10 per cent. This substance, ground to flour fineness and stored in bags of white leather, he named smalt. Added to molten transparent

346

glass, it spread throughout the metal which, when vitrified, displayed a strong blue tint: one part of fine smalt to ten thousand of glass gave an attractive hue.

When directing the manufacture of hard-paste porcelain at Meissen during the 1720's, Augustus the Strong, Elector of Saxony, found that Saxon smalt failed to produce a colour comparable with the tone and brilliance of that decorating imported Chinese porcelain. The elector offered a prize of 1,000 thalers for a process by which smalt of equal radiance could be produced. When this had been accomplished, so precious was the monopoly to Meissen that its export was prohibited, severe penalties being prescribed for smuggling. Smalt of somewhat poorer quality continued to be exported, and in 1733 the best of this cost £11 an ounce in London.

The Transactions of the Society for the Encouragement of the Arts in 1754 recorded that 'a *fine* blue glass is frequently made in London from common white flint-glass to which is added foreign smalt'. Cobalt deposits had, of course, been known to exist in England from the time of James I, and in the spring of 1755 the Society offered a premium for its discovery in qualities suitable to warrant development. This resulted in the establishment of a cobalt mine near Helston, Cornwall, where zaffre and smalt were soon in profitable production, the Society recording them to be superior to the Saxon imports. S. More in a letter dated 11th February 1756 wrote: 'Some of this [Cornish] zaffre was given to Mr. Stephen Hall, partner with Mr. Hughes, Glass Maker, at the Faulkon Glass House, Southwark, who a few days later gave me a small piece of glass of a most excellent Blew Colour and which had been coloured with this Zaffre, and he told me that two parts of this Zaffre could Colour as much glass as three parts of that actually sold [from Saxony]. A considerable quantity of this glass was made and a vase sent to the Society of Arts.' This letter, with much other relevant information, is preserved in the Society's library.

Supplies of Saxon cobalt products ceased from early in 1756 when Saxony became involved in war with Prussia. The Prussians seized the mines, mills, and workshops associated with all forms of cobalt production and when the war ended in February 1763 they were in possession of the Royal Saxon Smalt Works. A group of merchants trading in goods seized from Saxony acquired the stocks, and a considerable amount of superfine smalt was sold to a Bristol warehouse, believed to have been owned by William Cookworthy, the wholesale druggist who later founded the Plymouth and Bristol porcelain factories. He sold this smalt at the unprecedentedly low price of 15s. an ounce to glassmen and potters. The glassmen used it to charge flint-

347

glass with an intense dark blue colour which, when held to the light, displayed a tinge of royal purple in thick sections, and almost sea-blue where thinly blown. When fresh supplies of smalt were needed in London, Stourbridge, Sunderland, Warrington, or elsewhere, the call was now invariably for 'Bristol-blue', to distinguish this from the harshly blue smalt associated with the period of the Seven Years War when only English-mined cobalt had been available.

Thomas Dossie in his *Handmaid to the Arts,* 1764, recorded that 'some parcels of fine smalt or vitrified oxide of cobalt brought from Saxony has not long been available in England. Its goodness consists of being dark, bright and cool although it always verges on the purple, but the less so the better.' After further emphasizing its exceptional hardness and dark hue, he noted that 'Bristol-blue' was used for many purposes for which the common smalt was unsuitable.

Bristol-blue flint-glass was prepared in small covered pots measuring 6 inches across and 12 inches deep. Known as piling pots, these were placed on the ordinary pots and were used only for 'metal fit for the nicest works'. This glass was improved by keeping the crucible in the furnace for a considerable time after vitrification seemed complete, thus making it harder and freer from specks and bubbles.

Although Bristol-blue glass was made in fairly considerable quantities there is little evidence to associate Bristol glass-houses with its manufacture on a large scale. Production was necessarily limited owing to the small size of the piling pots. There is adequate proof, however, that it was in continuous production at Bristol from the early 1760's until the end of the eighteenth century. A few examples of the 1790's are recorded bearing the signature 'I. Jacobs Bristol' in gold script. These were made by Isaac Jacobs, Temple Street, Bristol.

It was made also at Stourbridge, Warrington, Sunderland, and later at Sheffield and Birmingham. The *Newcastle Journal,* 16th September 1769, printed the announcement : 'To be sold, at the New Glass Houses, Sunderland, all sorts of Double Flint Glass, White Enamel, Fine Blue, and Green Glass.' At the same time it was also advertised by Abraham Hawkes, Dudley.

The Napoleonic wars blocked supplies of Saxon smalt and artificial ultramarine was evolved, but this does not appear to have reached the glass industry until 1804. Its price was negligible in comparison with zaffre and smalt, but it gave a harshly blue tint suitable only for some of the inexpensive blown-moulded ware made with the aid of Chubsee's open-and-shut mould. When Saxon smalt was available once more towards 1820, dark blue

272   Girandole-candlesticks with candle-shades, 1820's

273–276 Tumblers dating from 1772 to *c.* 1800

350

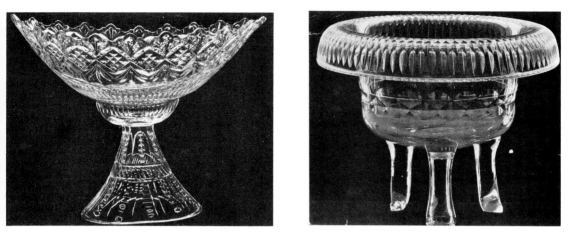

277, 278   Irish cut-glass fruit bowls: *left*, with hollow pedestal stem; *right*, with three feet

279, 280   Irish cut-glass fruit bowls with boat-shaped bodies and square feet

281–283   A collection of stemmed fruit bowls

284 Taper decanter enamelled in colours with the owner's initials in gold

285 A wineglass cooler with gilded key-fret border, signed 'I. Jacobs Bristol', in gold

286 Three short taper decanters lettered in gold

BRISTOL-BLUE GLASS

287 Celery glass

288 Vase candlestick

289 Butter-dish with prism cutting

290 Covered butter-dish with stand

IRISH CUT-GLASS

291   Water-jug, cut with a band of large relief diamonds and horizontal prisms

292   Cream-jug, with round foot cut with radial motifs

293   Fruit bowl with pinched radial foot

294   Fruit bowl with kettle-drum body

295 Cut-glass rummer with wheel-engraved coaching scene

296 An Irish decanter engraved with the vesica ornament

297 Wine fountain with silver tap

298 Footed decanter on a square base, engraved with flower and foliage motifs

glass was again in production and termed smalt glass to distinguish it from the synthetic colour.

Post-1820 blue glass displaying, when held to the light, the royal purple tinge peculiar to fine Saxon smalt, may be dated to the George IV period. Purifying treatments afterwards given to the cobalt oxide for the removal of copper, lead, iron, nickel, and so on affected the resulting hue given to glass, so that little, if any, king's glass may be dated after about 1840.

Because of its high refractive power, its lustre, and sparkle, this type of glass, possibly coloured with genuine ultramarine and thus displaying no trace of purple, was used for jewellery, for smelling-bottles, and other 'toys'. A pendant might have a centre of thick Bristol-blue glass set with a mono-gram or other motifs in diamonds, and miniature frames might be backed by ovals of the same material. Smelling-bottles measuring from 2 to 3 inches in height might be lavishly gilded or painted in enamel colours with motifs that included pastoral figures, exotic birds, flowers and foliage, diaper patterns, and scrollwork. Many had flat-sided rectangular bodies, round shoulders, and all-over facet-cutting: others had flat-sided oval or square bodies. They were fitted with ground-glass stoppers concealed beneath repousse caps in gold or gilded silver.

Although usually called scent bottles by collectors they were referred to in glass-sellers' advertisements as smelling-bottles. An advertisement of 1768 referred to such bottles as 'neat-cut smelling bottles', and at a sale of blue-glass at Christie's in 1788 they were catalogued as 'Etwee Smelling Bottles'. The majority date from about 1770, but Francis Buckley dis-covered a reference in the *Bristol Journal*, 15th October 1763, when two blue and gold toilet bottles, of the stoppered kind, were sufficiently valued to be included in a list of stolen property. Similar trifles for feminine use included snuff-boxes, sponge boxes, and bodkin cases.

Blue flint-glass had been made already in the form of vases, but when Bristol-blue appeared glass-sellers were faced with a demand for sets of mantel ornaments in this colour. Such handsome jars and beakers no doubt were considered inexpensive counterparts of the Derbyshire blue john chimney-piece ornaments then newly fashionable. Sugar-bowls, cream pails, and drinking-goblets were also made in imitation of blue john. Goblets in several sizes soon appeared in the form of drinking-rummers with drawn stems and plain feet.

The ledgers of Michael Edkins, a Bristol free-lance decorator of glass and delftware, were inspected by Hugh Owen and quoted in *Two Centuries of Ceramic Art in Bristol*, 1873. These recorded several entries regarding

Bristol-blue glass, the earliest being on 19th July 1763 when Edkins gilded '4 blue Jars and Beakers with mosaic borders' for 2s. and a '1 pint Blue Cannister with gold and letters' for 8d. Other articles in blue glass recorded by Edkins include tea-canisters, basins, hyacinth glasses, wall cornucopias, and cans, the latter being handled mugs.

Silversmiths soon realized that rich Bristol-blue glass was the ideal lining for the newly fashionable pierced ware, forming an exquisite background for intricate openwork designs in silver. Salts, sugar-baskets, and mustard pots bearing the London hall-mark for 1764 have been noted containing undoubtedly original Bristol-blue glass liners with hollowed bases.

The earliest reference to table-ware in blue glass noted by Frank Buckley was an advertisement in the *Bath Chronicle,* 1766, when the celebrated glass-seller and designer, Christopher Haedy, first announced 'blue stands for pickles'. These were circular dishes with wide-spreading rims such as were made in silver for pickles.

Decanters in Bristol-blue flint-glass were made, at first of the shouldered type (fig. 215) with a spire-finialled stopper fitted into a slightly tapering lipless mouth. With undecorated decanters the spires were smooth; otherwise they were cut into pyramid form. Label decanters (fig. 286) might be ornamented in gold, the lettering being enclosed in a cartouche design composed of scrollwork with vine-leaves and grapes. A gilded chain added to the illusion that the label was hanging from the neck. Others were painted in oil colours which were mixed with a dessicator so that they dried hard (fig. 284). Still others were enamelled with coloured frits, vitrified in a muffle. In 1765 Edkins was decorating for Williams, Dunbar & Co., who had established a flint-glass house at Chepstow in the previous year. His ledger records '2 quart Decanters blue' and '2 blue Decanters'.

Taper decanters in blue glass, their flat vertical lozenge-stopper finials, sometimes with lunar-cut edges, fitting into mouths with slightly everted lips, date from about 1770. These continued to be made well into the nineteenth century. Prussian-shaped decanters with neck-rings, sometimes facet-cut, were also made and might be fitted with either target or pear-shaped stoppers.

There was in the 1820's a fashionable vogue for serving wines and spirits from blue decanters and squares accompanied by drinking-glasses in matching tints. A Victoria and Albert Museum pattern book dated 1812 illustrates sets of taper spirit decanters with gilded labels painted below shoulders which display a greater curve than the eighteenth-century series. These were usually in sets of three (fig. 286) labelled rum, gin, and brandy.

Their target or pear-shaped stoppers are shown ground with concave printies and edges bevelled or notched. The printies on such a stopper were lettered in gold with the initial named on the decanter below, thus securing its return to the bottle for which it had been specially ground to ensure an air-tight fit. Each side of the bevelled edge was gilded with a chain motif matching that on the body.

Label cruet sets, gilded with lettering and scrollwork, were advertised in 1764, soy and sauce bottles shortly afterwards. Cruet frames in Sheffield plate were fitted throughout with Bristol-blue oil and vinegar bottles and three castors, and soy frames with three to six gold-labelled bottles. They continued in production until the 1830's, little variation being found apart from the colour of the metal and the spread of the mouth.

There was a fashionable conceit between the 1770's and the end of the eighteenth century for finger-bowls to be of gilded Bristol-blue glass, whilst the remainder of the glass equipage was in cut flint-glass. That the Bristol-blue actually made at Bristol was more desirable than that made elsewhere is suggested by the fact that in 1784 William Cowper commissioned a visitor to Bristol to buy some blue glasses (*see* page 309). Finger-bowls and double-lipped wineglass coolers (fig. 285) were made in various qualities of blue glass until the 1850's.

Loving-cups cover a period of about sixty years from the 1770's. They are to be found in all qualities of Bristol-blue, ordinary blue, and synthetic blue. To ensure stability in early examples, the lower half of the waisted bowl was thickened and pressed with twisted gadrooning to which the lower terminals of the handles were welded.

Reference has been made above to the blown-moulded flint-glass shaped by means of an open-and-shut mould forming a series of inexpensive hollow-ware with fire-polished finish. Such pieces were decorated with elaborate designs, the earliest being geometrical, and the most common motifs consisting of encircling ribbings; flutings, motifs composed of concave circles and ovals; diamond motifs and diamond diapers in combination with ribbing and fluting. Seldom found in king's blue, examples have no more than a curiosity value to collectors.

Figures 284–6

Bristol-blue glass, the name being applied in the sense of a generic term for dark blue transparent glass made in England.

(284) Tall taper decanter of rich smalt blue painted in oil colours with grape and vine-leaf motifs with the original owner's initials in gold.

In the collection of Mr O. T. Norris

(285) Wineglass cooler with gilded key-fret border, signed 'I. Jacobs Bristol' in gold beneath. Isaac Jacobs was glass manufacturer to George III; 1796–1800.

In the Victoria and Albert Museum

(286) Set of three short taper decanters with lozenge stoppers. Decorated with gold representations of wine labels with chains encircling their necks. Each stopper is lettered in gold with the initial of the spirit named on the decanter below, thus ensuring its return to the correct bottle for which it had been specially ground to secure an air-tight fit. Similar decanters are illustrated in a pattern book dated 1812.

In the Victoria and Albert Museum

CHAPTER TWENTY-TWO

IRISH GLASS

THE EARLY HISTORY of glass-making in Ireland is unknown. That glass was used by the early Irish is proved by an old manuscript in which the illustrious sixth-century St. Columcilla stresses not only the transparency of glass but also its purity. Approaching days less ancient, there still exists an Irish deed dated 1258 recording the name of a glass-maker; a similar reference occurs in 1319. Thenceforth until the end of the fifteenth century a small amount of glass was made in Ireland, mostly for glazing purposes. The entire productions of these early years have perished.

The industry is known to have existed in 1575, when the privilege of operating a glass-house was granted only after earnest petition to the English monarch. In the Patent Rolls for 1588 appear lengthy documents written by Captain Thomas Woodhouse, who had established furnaces for making drinking-glasses. He made humble suit to Queen Elizabeth I for the sole rights of manufacturing glass in Ireland; early in the following year he was granted an eight-year monopoly of the Irish glass industry. This monopoly was apparently sold to George Longe a few months later.

Longe, writing to Lord Burghley, promised Queen Elizabeth not to keep 'more than two glass-houses in England, but will set up the remainder in Ireland, whereby the woods of England would be preserved and the super-fluous woods of Ireland wasted, which in time of rebellion Her Majesty has no greater enemy there'. Longe offered, should the patent be granted, to repair free of charge and with superior glass any of Lord Burghley's buildings. He also suggested that every glass-house operating in Ireland would be the equivalent of twenty men in garrison. Longe continued in business for some years, occasionally granting licences to others. It is due to this master craftsman that glass-making became an established craft in Ireland.

During the reign of James I, glass-making continued intermittently until 1622 when a glass-house was built at Ballynegery. The following year the small town of Birr was supplying Dublin with drinking-vessels and table-ware. Sir Percival Hart obtained a twenty-one-year licence in 1634 giving

361

him a monopoly for making black glass drinking-vessels in Ireland. Forest wastage was so extensive that in 1641 the Government prohibited the felling of trees as fuel for the Irish glass furnaces. In 1667 Ananias Henzy, a glass-maker from Stourbridge, erected a glass-house at Portarlington: some of his wineglasses and tumblers still remain.

A glass-house was operating in Dublin as early as 1675, a second, the Round Glass-house, being established in Mary's Lane by that ardent Jacobite, Captain Philip Roche, some time during the mid-1690's. His wares, 'the newest fashion drinking glasses and all other sorts of flint-glasses as good as any made in England', were sold by itinerant hawkers. Roche died in 1713 a rich man, leaving £5 legacies to many of these 'salesmen'. The factory continued in operation and in 1746, and again in 1752, was advertising itself as the only place in Ireland where flint-glass was manufactured.

In the latter advertisement a wide variety of table-ware was announced: 'all sorts of the newest fashioned drinking glasses, water bottles, claret and burgundy ditto, decanters, jugs, water glasses with and without feet and saucers, plain, ribbed and diamond moulded jelly glasses, sillybub glasses, comfit and sweetmeat glasses for desserts, salvers, glass plates for china dishes, pine and orange glasses . . . all sorts of cut and flowered glasses may be had of any kind of pattern, viz: — wine glasses with a vine border, toasts or any flourish whatever, beer ditto with same, salts with and without feet, sweetmeat glasses and stands, cruets for silver and other frames all in squares and diamond cut, sweetmeat bowls and covers'. Although the advertisement added that the glass was sold at much cheaper rates than that imported from England, production soon ceased and Mrs Delany writing from Delville in 1759 comments, 'I send to England for good glass'.

The Round-house had closed by 1755 and between that year and 1764 no flint-glass appears to have been made in Dublin. Then the firm of Richard Williams and Company rebuilt a bottle glass-house opposite to Marlborough Bowling Green and installed a furnace of the Perrott type. Advertisements in various newspapers during 1770 show the firm to have been making 'all the newest fashioned enamelled, flowered, cut and plain wine, beer and cyder glasses, common wines and drams, rummers, decanters, water glasses and plates, epergnes and epergne saucers, cruets, casters, jugs, salvers, jellies, sweetmeat glasses, salts'. The firm operated in a big way and shortly was advertising 'glass lustres, girandoles, chandeliers, and candlesticks'. The glass-house was subsidized in 1784 by the Dublin Society to the extent of £9,000 and during the following decade received nearly £20,000 in additional premiums. The firm made vast quantities of deeply cut table glass during the first quarter of the nineteenth century, closing in 1829, an early victim of the Excise Act extension of 1825.

The Excise Act of 1746 had imposed a duty of 1d. a pound on all raw materials used in the making of flint-glass in Great Britain, but excluded Ireland. The same act prohibited the importation of any glass into Ireland except from Great Britain, and forbade the export of glass from Ireland. As was no doubt intended, the Irish glass trade was virtually destroyed, being permitted to supply only her own very limited market. The excise tax in Great Britain was doubled in 1777 when the American war of Independence was raging and Ireland took advantage of this turmoil to assert a few of her political rights including the boon of free trade. From 1780 all import restrictions were abolished, and within five years the Irish glass industry was booming, new glass-houses being in full production at Waterford, Cork, Dublin, Belfast, and Newry. These were all underselling England yet employing English labour from mixing-room to cutter's wheel. Technique and style were entirely English.

Lord Sheffield, writing in 1785, remarked that the best Irish drinking-glasses were 3s. to 4s. a dozen cheaper than English of comparable quality. He also recorded that most of the Irish glass exported in 1783 went to Portugal. Before the end of the decade, however, almost the entire output of pure-blown cut-work was dispatched to America: a considerable amount of blown-moulded glass, thin in section, was underselling English glass in England.

Irish cut-glass attained its greatest renown during the first twenty-five years of the nineteenth century. Then, in 1825, the Government applied the heavy excise duty to Irish glass, each furnace also requiring an annual licence costing £20. The output of Irish glass was reduced by half during the next five years and in 1833 the duty paid by the entire Irish industry was less than that paid by a single prosperous factory in England. From the early 1830's when machines for pressing glass were introduced to England from America, the decline was accelerated even though in 1835 the excise duty was greatly reduced, being abolished ten years later. During the early years of the excise duty numerous illicit furnaces operated in obscure villages easy of access to large towns.

From 1803, Irish glass in general exploited a clearer metal than hitherto. A splendid prismatic fire was given to this metal by cutting in deep relief, diamond motifs predominating. The metal from a single pot, however, was not all of one quality. Here, as elsewhere, metal taken from the top, and known as 'tale', was sold more cheaply than the lower, finer metal. Best-quality Waterford rummers, for instance, were sold at 6s. a dozen; tale at 4s. 4d. a dozen; and tale fluted at 4s. 8d. a dozen.

For nearly half a century any glass displaying a faintly blue tint in its texture was deemed to be of Waterford origin and its value enhanced accordingly. Many a collector acquiring costly, elaborately cut-glass displaying this so-called 'distinctive blue tint' was convinced that for this reason it must be Waterford. But, in fact, any Irish glass made between 1783 and about 1810 might have this peculiar depth of tone, as did certain flint-glass issued during the period by Bristol, Stourbridge or elsewhere.

The exclusive association of the blue tint with old Waterford was started in 1897 when Albert Hartshorne made this claim in his monumental work.[1] Dudley Westropp[2] denied this outright by stating 'I have never seen a marked Waterford piece with the blue tint'. Mrs Graydon Stannus, however, lecturing on 'Irish Glass' to a distinguished audience at the Royal Society of Arts in 1925 produced a number of marked specimens for inspection. Every example displayed this blue tint. Those in Westropp's reference were obviously made after the introduction of purified lead oxide in 1810.

The peculiar depth of tone found in much flint-glass — English, Irish, and Scottish alike — made before 1810 is due to the fact that the lead oxide used was manufactured from lead mined in Derbyshire. Makers of flint-glass had found, early in the reign of George III, that lead oxide prepared from Derbyshire lead possessed characteristics which greatly improved the quality of their metal. The lead oxide also contained an impurity, well known to the glass industry of the period, and recognized as a defect which technicians long tried to overcome. In every other respect lead oxide derived from Derbyshire was preferred by glass-makers to any from other sources.

In about 1810 the firm of Blair Stephenson, of Tipton, Staffordshire, evolved a process by which this tint, known contemporaneously as 'Derby blue', was eliminated from lead oxide. The making of purified lead oxide from Derbyshire was a profitable monopoly for a decade, the firm supplying every glass-maker of repute. Then their manager joined the firm of Adkins and Nock of Smethwick. In 1864 Henry Adkins, a member of this firm, communicated these facts to the British Association.

Dudley Westropp discussed the presence of blue with Richard Pugh, the last of the Irish flint-glass makers, who told him that 'the blue tint of the old glass metal was caused by impure oxide of lead having been used in the manufacture'. The Irish glass-houses for long bought their lead oxide from

[1] *Old English Glasses* by Albert Hartshorne.
[2] *Irish Glass* by Dudley Westropp.

Wilson Patten, Bank Quay, Warrington, to whom the Derbyshire miners dispatched their lead ore by strings of pack-mules. Not every consignment contained the impurity responsible for the Derby blue which, it must be understood, was not 'colour' but a tint inherent in the metal itself. There was, therefore, no consistency in the presence of Derby blue in glass during the period concerned and its depth of tone noticeably varies.

It is now customary to believe that Waterford glass has no tint. Mr J. J. Hughes in his foreword to the catalogue of the Exhibition of Waterford Glass held at Waterford in 1952 wrote: 'the statement that Waterford glass has a distinct bluish tint has been disproved by experts. Waterford glass certainly is lovely and has many wonderful qualities, but a bluish colour is not among them.' This is contradicted, however, by the selection of marked examples shown by Mrs Graydon Stannus to the Society of Arts. It is only reasonable to conclude that in Waterford glass, as in contemporary English glass, the Derby blue tint might or might not appear, but that its existence in a specimen indicates a date earlier than about 1810 and its absence, with consequent crystal clarity, makes a post-1810 date more probable. Efforts so far made to reproduce the genuine Derby blue tint have been unsuccessful, but a bogus 'Waterford blue' is frequent.

Irish glass-makers, like the English, were continually experimenting in the hope of securing an absolutely perfect glass and this, according to the Society of Arts, they failed to achieve during the collector's period. Early Cork metal sometimes displays a yellowish tint: a number of marked specimens were shown at the Antiques Exhibition, 1925; early Dublin is apt to have a shadowy black tint such as was seen in marked specimens shown to the Society of Arts in 1925.

The bloom occasionally found on the surface of old flint-glass, English and Irish alike, but wrongly often ascribed to Ireland only, was picturesquely described by Mrs Graydon Stannus as 'rather like the bloom of grapes and if cleaned off it will return'. According to Mr C. J. Phillips[1] this all-over film of opaque dullness was caused by the use of high-sulphur fuels in the leer. Bands of bloom sometimes found encircling hollow-ware a little distance from the rim were the result of reheating at the furnace mouth.

Waterford is celebrated for the magnificence of its cut-glass although there is no evidence that it was highly regarded in England during its period of production, 1783–1851. London, Sunderland, Stourbridge, Birmingham, and Bristol were all producing comparable metal and cutting, using designs that were more or less interchanged. The competing Irish metals made at

[1] *Glass* by C. J. Phillips, 1941.

Cork and Dublin were inferior in brilliance, however, to the Waterford productions.

Flint-glass had been made at Gurteens on the outskirts of Waterford as early as 1729 when the proprietors of a newly established glass-house advertised 'all sorts of flint-glass, double and single'. There is no evidence that this business continued beyond 1739. The now celebrated Waterford glass-house was founded by George and William Penrose, uncle and nephew, who in 1783 built a glass-house on Merchant's Quay, Waterford, at a cost of £10,000. In the *Leinster Journal* of the following year they advertised 'all kinds of useful and ornamental flint-glass of as fine a quality as any in Europe, having a large number of the best manufacturers, cutters and engravers'.

The Penroses, substantial import and export merchants, financed the project, employing John Hill as works manager. John Blades,[1] the well-known glass-cutter of Ludgate Hill, London, described Hill in 1785 as 'a great manufacturer of Stourbridge, lately gone to Waterford and has taken the best set of workmen he could get in the County of Worcester'. John Hill was, in fact, son of a Stourbridge manufacturer in a large way of business. A map dated 1774 showing the parish of Oldswinford marks Hill's glass-house on the main Stourbridge–Wolverhampton road. The proprietor was Thomas Hill, a prosperous industrialist, ironmaster, claymine owner, and brick-maker. The metal and technical processes used at Waterford by his son John no doubt closely reflected styles carried on at the parental glass-house. Within twelve months seventy or eighty work-people were employed. But Hill came under the displeasure of William Penrose's wife Rachael, and in 1786 he left the firm.

First, however, he instructed Jonathan Gatchell, a Quaker and clerk of the works, in all the technical secrets connected with the making of flint-glass. From then until 1799 when both the Penroses had died, Gatchell acted as technician and compounder of materials. The firm then came under the control of a partnership consisting of Jonathan Gatchell, James Ramsey, and Ambrose Barcroft, a nephew of William Penrose.

In 1802 the partners erected a new glass-house in Ann Street, Waterford, on the site of an old tan-yard, retaining a warehouse on their old premises at Waterford Quay. They appear to have replaced their outmoded furnaces by the newly patented Donaldson furnace which produced a glass more crystal clear than formerly and used no more than one-third the amount of fuel. This partnership continued until the death of Barcroft in 1810, when

[1] *Journals of the Irish House of Commons*, 24th January 1786.

366

it was dissolved, Gatchell becoming sole proprietor by mortgaging the glass-house and some land known as Willow Gardens.

With the imposition of an excise tax of 10½d. a pound of flint-glass from 1825, the firm, like other Irish glass-houses, found itself labouring under an intolerable burden, but one that had been borne by the English glassmen from 1745. The tax paid by the Waterford firm during the first excise year was £3,910 7s. 5d., suggesting an output of about 90 tons. Westropp has recorded that the average annual output between 1830 and 1840 was 50 tons of manufactured glass.

An effort was made to speed up production by installing a steam-engine for driving the glass-cutting machines, a method that had been in common use in England from 1805. This succeeded in its object but apparently cut more glass than the firm could sell and in this connection Mrs Elizabeth Walpole, one of the partners, wrote from Exeter in 1832, 'if the steam engine pours out such a flood of goods so that there is no room [to store it] and that sales cannot be effected in self defence, it would seem desirable that the engine should be stopped entirely. . . . I am quite satisfied as to the employing of turners in this way.' The engine continued in use, however, until the firm closed in 1851.

In a further effort to stem declining sales Waterford improved the quality of its metal by the installation of a Wheeley furnace in 1830. This gave a more crystalline appearance to the metal and brought it into line with English quality.

The metal of Waterford may thus be grouped into three well-defined types: Penrose to 1802; early Gatchell, 1802–30; late Gatchell, 1830–51; with the intermittent Derby blue tint pre-1810. During the Gatchell periods Waterford became noted for skilful cutting, most usually in diamond forms, large and small, arranged in various designs.

Cork established its first glass-house in Hanover Street, with access to the Quayside, during 1783, financed by three partners, John Burnett, Atwell Hayes, and Francis Rowe, at a cost of £6,000. Like the Penroses they employed experienced English glassmen, and for the most part used English materials. Their advertisements show them to have made plain and cut flint-glass, and black bottles. Cork became a centre for light-weight blown-moulded hollow-ware and their output of decanters made in this way was considerable.

These were blown in one-piece brass moulds, and as glass stiffens quickly in such circumstances a quick-setting flint-glass was evolved. The glassman gathered molten metal on his blowpipe, then expanded it by blowing until it filled the interior of the mould cut with vertical flutes in intaglio. Inflation forced the glass on the blowpipe into the pattern on the mould and formed a clear impression. The blown glass remained the same thickness so that the flutes on the outside of the finished glass appeared as corresponding ridges on the inner surface. In some examples, not necessarily of Cork origin, a faint mould mark is discernible at the top line of the body of a decanter where the slope of the shoulder begins. These were probably blown by experienced bottle-makers which accounts for the long slender necks characteristic of decanters made by the Cork Glass Company. Flint-glass table-ware of normal section was made, although rather slighter and less heavy than that of Waterford.

Production was continually disrupted by ever-changing proprietorship brought about by financial instability. Substantial subsidies were made by the Dublin Society, such as £1,600 in 1787 and £2,304 in 1794. It is thought that the glass-house was closed between 1788 and 1792 when no applications were made for premiums. The newly patented Donaldson furnace was installed in 1803 under the proprietorship of Joseph Graham and Company.

The new firm obviously issued flint-glass table-ware of a finer quality than formerly, the old furnace continuing to produce the cheaper blown-moulded goods. Some notably fine dessert services were made during this period and gilding became a speciality. The quality of cut-ware manufactured was obviously considerable, for a Cork Glass Cutters' Union was established. Cutting was carried out by hand until steam power was installed in 1817, a contemporary advertisement noting that it drove 'the wheels of the modern glass-cutting machinery of the best description', introduced by the last proprietors, William Smith and Company, in a final effort to ward off disaster. A year later the factory closed.

The stock of glass then included 'cut lustres, Grecian lamps, four-light Grecian lamps, richly set with patent drops, hall globes, side bells, candle-sticks, dessert sets, butter coolers, pickle glasses, sugar bowls, cream ewers, jelly glasses, salt cellars, jugs, decanters, rummers, wine and finger glasses, wine coolers'.

Pure-blown flint-glass was cut with patterns commonly in vogue: blown-moulded work might be further ornamented with the speedily produced vesica pattern, characteristic of Cork (fig. 300 centre). These plain, pointed ovals might enclose an eight-pointed star or a sunburst. Six vesicas usually encircled a decanter body, and where they impinged sprigs were notched above and below the outline. When engraved, the ovals were usually filled with trellis-work lines.

368

Examination of a collection of decanters marked 'Cork Glass C°' indicates the following features to be characteristic (fig. 300). The flutes or vertical corrugations encircling the base of the body do not extend to the lower rim. Cork blown-moulded flutes were poorly produced and extend about two-thirds of the distance towards the shoulder which may be incised with the vesica pattern, often with a double row of regularly spaced short horizontal lines below the lower neck ring. There may be two or three neck rings, usually of the double-feathered type, although plain triple rings square rings, and rings cut with flat facets have been noted. Stoppers may be of the low-domed mushroom type pinched with radial flutes; others are in the pinched target design.

The Waterloo Glass Works Company, established on Wandersford Quay, Cork, towards the end of 1815 by Daniel Foley, appears to have executed some extensive orders for finely cut table-services for military messes, particularly those engaged in the occupation of France. Within a year Foley was employing a hundred men, much of the experienced labour being drawn from the Cork Glass Company. There is no doubt that in some measure this contributed to its closure.

Production appears to have been delayed for a year, however, for on Christmas Eve, 1816, Foley announced in the *Cork Overseer* that his 'workmen are well selected, from whose superior skill the most beautiful glass will shortly make its appearance to dazzle the eyes of the public, and to outshine those of any other competitor. He is to treat his men at Christmas with a whole roasted ox and everything adequate.' No doubt higher wages and improved amenities lost the older factory many of its more experienced cutters; forcing the firm to increase production by installing steam power.

Foley's project appears to have prospered until the imposition of the excise tax. The firm closed down in mid-1830, a few months after advertising that prices had been reduced 20 per cent and that improvement in the annealing process made their glass proof against hot water. The stock sold at this time included ceiling lustres, chandeliers, chimney lustres, decanters, claret jugs, crofts, tumblers, rummers, butter coolers, and pickle urns.

The Waterloo glass-house was reopened in November 1831 by Geoffrey O'Connell, who had entered into partnership with Foley in 1825. He now advertised that he had 'restored one hundred families to employment'. The excise duties were too heavy a burden, however, and in 1835 he was made bankrupt through inability to pay.

Forms and cutting patterns closely followed those of Waterford. Examination of blown-moulded decanters marked 'Waterloo C° Cork' suggests that the majority were prussian-shaped rather than barrel-shaped, with the base very perceptibly narrower than the shoulder. The flutes extend higher up the body than those of the Cork Glass Company in which the sides of the decanter are only slightly off-vertical. The vesica pattern appears and an engraved band of stars between two pairs of feathered lines, with wreaths above and below the lower neck rings; there may be three neck rings of the plain triple variety. Ribbon scroll engraving is also found, and rows of hollows may encircle the shoulders. Stoppers are low-domed mushroom shapes, pinched with radial flutes and sometimes with a knop immediately below. Pinched target stoppers are also found.

Irish blown-moulded hollow-ware sometimes bears a moulded factory mark beneath the base. The lower part of the body — decanter, finger-bowl, wineglass cooler, jug — is encircled with closely spaced flutes, sometimes with a circuit of simple engraving above. These identification marks, which are sometimes faint and indistinct, consist of the name of the firm impressed in raised letters on a flat ring encircling the centre of the base around the rough punty mark. The following marks have been recorded: 'Penrose Waterford'; 'Cork Glass Cº'; 'Waterloo Cº Cork'; 'B. Edwards Belfast'; 'Francis Collins Dublin'*; 'Mary Carter & Son Dublin'*; 'Armstrong Ormond Quay'*; 'C M Co'* (Charles Mulvany and Co., Dublin). Those marked with an asterisk were wholesalers with sales large enough to warrant the cost of special moulds at the glass-house. Such trade-marks are unknown on English glass.

It is impossible to attribute any unauthenticated piece of Irish glass to any particular glass-house, either by metal or by the style of cutting used, although certain characteristics are fairly accurate pointers to period of manufacture, and a few cut motifs may be noted, such as the vesica associated with Cork, the inverted arch with star and splits used by Waterford and the Waterloo Company of Cork, and the pendant arch of Waterford.

Westropp records the activities of more than a dozen flint-glass houses additional to those referred to here. These include the Terrace Glass Works, Cork (1818–41), with a productive capacity comparable with Waterford; Chebsey & Co., Venice Glass-house, Dublin (1787–99), which during its first seven years sold glass valued at £37,849; J. D. Ayckboum, New Venice Glass House, Dublin (1799–1802); Benjamin Edwards, Belfast (1776-1812), among the first of the established glassmen to reap the early fruits of free trade. He was also a maker of cutting machinery. Numerous manufactories were established for the cutting of blanks bought from the glass-houses.

Figures 287–90

IRISH CUT-GLASS

(278) Celery glass, body cut with festoon pattern above vertical prisms; band of blazes encircling neck; fan escallop rim; *c.* 1830.

(288) Vase-candlestick with solid body fluted and notched; scalloped flange with lustres; socket with expanded sconce; square foot with octagonal cut dome; *c.* 1790.

(289) Oval butter-dish with semi-circular handles; body cut with horizontal prisms and rim with vertical prisms; *c.* 1830.

(290) Butter-dish with domed cover and dished stand; *c.* 1800.

All in the Corning Museum of Glass

Figures 291–4

CUT-GLASS OF THE EARLY NINETEENTH CENTURY

(291) Water-jug, body cut with band of large relief diamonds; shoulder with rounded flutes; neck with horizontal prisms; notched rim.

(292) Cream-jug with round foot cut with radial motifs; body cut with band of large diamonds in relief between rounded flutes.

(293) Stemmed fruit bowl with boat-shaped body cut with large diamonds in relief; scalloped rim and pinched radial foot.

(294) Fruit bowl with kettle-drum body cut with wide flutes; shoulder encircled with band of diamonds in relief; rim cut with narrow vertical prisms.

All in the Corning Museum of Glass

Figures 295–8

295) Rummer with outward sloping bucket bowl encircled at base with short wide flutes; band of narrow blazes above, and a wheel-engraved coaching scene. Stem rising from a small solid dome on a flat foot with triple-ring knop and strengthened bowl junction . 1830.

296) Irish decanter made at Cork, with blown-moulded body. Engraved decoration ncludes a wide band of vesica ornament with stars in ovals, between a shoulder band of trawberry diamonds and narrow flutes encircling the base. Three feathered neck rings nd moulded target stopper.

371

(297) Wine fountain with silver tap and highly domed cover, believed to be of Waterford origin. Supported on domed foot with hollow stem attached to the body by a silver joint; 1790's.

(298) Round-footed cordial decanter on square base, with wide fluting encircling base and facet-cut neck; body engraved with flower and foliage motifs; stopper with lunar-cut pear-shaped finial; *c.* 1790.

All in the Corning Museum of Glass

Figures 299–300

IRISH GLASS JUGS AND DECANTERS

(299) Two-quart-size trade jugs intended for ale.

(*Left*) Engraved with two oval medallions of iron-working scenes flanking a monogram, with hop-and-barley motifs.

(*Right*) Blown-moulded with comb-fluting encircling the base, engraved with agricultural motifs including the plough and barley flanking a ribbon bearing the motto 'Success to the Land', and a spray of shamrock.

(300) A pair of blown-moulded quart-size decanters with comb-fluting encirling their bases; incised with pendant crescents and stars, two rows of small ovals encircling their shoulders, three double-feathered neck rings, and mushroom stoppers with plain shanks. Marked beneath 'Waterloo Co Cork' in raised letters.

(*Centre*) Quart-size jug, blown-moulded with encircling flutes and incised with the vesica pattern filled with interlacing lines. Marked beneath 'Cork Glass Co' in raised letters.

By courtesy of Messrs Delomosne & Son Ltd

299 Irish jugs, two-quart size, engraved with iron-
working and agricultural scenes

300 Pair of blown-moulded quart-size decanters and quart-size jug, marked beneath
'Cork Glass Co.' in raised letters

301 Champagne flute and cordial glass
302 Goblet with ovoid bowl

303 Three fluted wineglasses of a type popular between *c.* 1816 and 1840

SCOTTISH GLASSES

304 Leith-made goblet probably engraved by J. H. B. Millar, *c.* 1850

305 Thistle-shaped dram glass with solid gadrooned base

306 Sweetmeat glass

307 Dram glasses: (*a*) with notched bowl; (*b*) with spirally moulded bowl;
(*c*) with funnel bowl

SCOTTISH GLASSES

308–310   Designs from the pattern books of the Edinburgh Glass-house Company,
Leith, on paper watermarked 1811

CHAPTER TWENTY-THREE

SCOTTISH GLASS

G LASS-MAKING IN SCOTLAND is almost three hundred and fifty
years old. The first glass-house was established in 1610 at Wemyss,
Fife, by Sir George Hay, then gentleman of the bedchamber to
James I, later Lord Chancellor and Keeper of the Great Seal, and finally
created Earl of Kinnoull by Charles I. The king granted him a forty-one-
year monopoly for the making of glass-ware in Scotland. Sir George Hay
thus became the Scottish counterpart of Sir Jerome Bowes, owner of the
English glass monopoly, later acquired by Sir Robert Mansell (Chapter I).
There is evidence to show that from 1620 Hay employed at Wemyss a
number of Italian glass-workers highly skilled in the production of
'christall and white glass'. These men had been brought from Murano at
Mansell's expense to work in his Broad Street, London, glass-house
(Chapter 1). It appears that they soon became dissatisfied and deserted to
Scotland, records indicating that the quality of Scottish glass improved.

The Venetian ambassador on 29th April 1622 wrote to his Government
that the greater part of the Italians who had worked in London 'have
betaken themselves to Scotland perhaps in the hope of having flints of the
Picino by the ships which will go from our [Italian] ports'. This suggests
that the silica used at Broad Street contained too many impurities for fine
glass to be produced equal to the Venetian, and confirms the production
of Scottish-Venetian glass. The Wemyss glass-house was unprofitable,
however, for in 1627 it was acquired by Mansell and production ceased
shortly afterwards.

A number of small bottle- and window-glass factories operated during the
next half-century, none of them apparently outliving their founders. In the
1650's Robert Pope established the Citadel Glass-house at Leith where he
made 'all kinds of glass including bottles'. Entry of foreign glass so adversely
affected sales, however, that in 1664 the Privy Council protected the
industry by placing a tariff on imported glass and fixing maximum prices
for home products. Other glass-houses were established periodically in Leith
including one in 1682 by Charles Hay of Kinnoull who made 'a superior

377

quality of metal . . . suitable for clear wine glasses', by which, no doubt, flint-glass was implied. By the end of the seventeenth century Leith employed 'one-hundred-and-twenty glass blowers not counting attendants', suggesting that more than two thousand people were employed in the trade.

The proprietors of the Citadel Glass-house established the Edinburgh and Leith Glass Company early in the eighteenth century where flint-glass was made although the principal trade was bottle-making. Here were blown two of the largest bottles ever seen in Georgian Britain. A 94-gallon bottle was blown in 1747 and the *Manchester Magazine*, 1751, reported that on the 28th December previous 'a globular bottle had been blown to a capacity of 105 gallons by Thomas Symmer, principal director of the glassworks, South Leith. It contains two hogsheads and its dimensions are 40 inches by 42 inches.'

Little is known of the Edinburgh and Leith Glass Company, although the works operated until about 1830. During the last half-century an immense amount of flint-glass was sold, plain, cut, and engraved: a pattern book printed on paper watermarked with the date 1811 is still in existence illustrating a wide range of productions. In this it is noticeable that wine-glass feet are not so high in the instep as those made in England, that the feet may be welted (folded), and the punty scar unground. It surprises many collectors to know that coloured hock glasses or *roemers* (fig. 138) were made here, resembling the Continental pattern with threaded bases and strawberry prunts. Similar glasses catalogued as hock glasses were made in England being recorded in 1829 'threaded and prunted at 1ˢ per pound more than wines'.

Champagne flutes are illustrated (fig. 310) with everted, incurved, and straight rims, with two designs for cut bowls. Small rummers are noted (fig. 308) with folded feet and unground punty scars. Cutting is illustrated in all the well-known English and Irish patterns — blazes, herring-bone, relief diamonds, and so on — but naturally none of the well-known Regency patterns finds a place. Cut water-jugs, trifle-bowls with scalloped and fan-cut rims, and sugar- and finger-bowls with serrated rims are exactly as usually attributed to Irish glass-houses.

Another important flint-glass house was founded by Doctor Colquohoun at Verreville, near Glasgow. A newspaper advertisement of the period announced that 'the Verreville Crystal-work is carried out on a scale and taste equal to any in Europe'. During the 1780's the firm was acquired by Williams, Ritchie and Company, the partners including two experienced executives from Newcastle, Charles Williams and Isaac Cookson. It is reasonable to assume that methods and patterns followed those of the long-proved Cookson establishment at Newcastle until 1806 when the firm came into the possession of John Geddes who abandoned the bottle-making section and concentrated on flint-glass. His experience had been acquired at the Edinburgh and Leith Glass Company.

Verreville appears to have been a source of magnificently cut illuminatory glass-ware such as chandeliers, girandoles, and candlesticks, as well as supplying branches, lustres, and stems for master glass-cutters to decorate and assemble.

Arnold Fleming in *Scottish and Jacobite Glass*, 1938, lists many items from the Verreville price list of August 1811. Among the undecorated table-ware priced by weight are salvers, candlesticks, and prisms, 3s. a pound; handled syllabubs 2s. 6d. a pound; ringed decanters, 2s. 2d. a pound; bowls, blue or flint with covers, 2s. a pound; rummers, 2s. a pound; with square feet, 2s. 2d. a pound; with pulley bowl, 2s. 6d. a pound. Those priced by the dozen include: ale glasses, purled, 6s. 6d.; feathered, 7s.; custards with handles, 7s.; sweetmeats, footed and oval, 6s.; flutes with welted feet, 6s. 6d.; with square feet, 10s. 6d.; with pulley buttons, 12s. 6d.; wineglasses with welted feet, 5s. 6d.; with square feet, 6s.; with double-button baluster stem, 9s.; with triple-button baluster stem, 9s.; with pulley-button baluster stem, 12s.

At Leith in 1773 James Ranken, a lapidary, established a flint-glass house which by the end of the century was specializing in cut illuminatory glass, some of it outstandingly beautiful. The output of the Verreville and Ranken glass-houses must have been tremendous and much of their finer cut ware — particularly Ranken's — has no doubt been attributed to Ireland.

A traveller visiting Dunbarton in 1785 noted the quality of the flint-glass issued by the Dunbarton Glass Company, established in 1776. His comments, quoted by Fleming, recorded its 'beautiful manufacture in the finest manner, the metal equal to any made in Britain. Over three hundred operatives are employed and fifteen hundred tons of coal consumed in the furnaces, eighty-eight bales of hay and straw are needed for packing purposes, and twelve hundred tons of kelp. They afford employment to over ten thousand tons of shipping and have contributed hitherto £40,000 of Excise Duty yearly'. Here, as in the other late-Georgian glass-houses mentioned, cutting was carried out on the premises for a plan of the glass-house preserved in Dunbarton Public Library shows such a shop.

Excellent wheel-engraving was executed, both in the glass-house and by outside engravers. Fleming mentions John Smith of Bangor Road, Leith, as a heraldic engraver and notes the high cost of this ornament. He also records the work of J. H. B. Millar, a Bohemian who set up as a glass engraver at Norton Place, Leith: 'his favourite style was classical, such as copies from the Elgin Marbles, Mercury, Jupiter and goddesses, Cupid's Triumph, etc. One of his most admired pieces was a claret jug with a picture of the "Sleep of Sorrow" and "The Dream of Joy". We have also sporting scenes of his, such as a spaniel chasing a stork, with water and foliage. An exquisitely executed vase, three feet high, representing the Battle of Inkerman was displayed at the International Exhibition of 1862 where it was sold to the Duke of Cambridge for 160 guineas: it took several months to engrave.'

There is little to differentiate between Scottish and English glass of the same periods for the larger glass-houses in both countries did their utmost to follow improvements in manufacturing techniques and fashionable designs in form and decoration. In the Royal Hotel, Inverness, is a collection of about one hundred examples of flint-glass accumulated during the last two decades of the nineteenth century from houses and cottages in Northern Scotland. The assumption may be made that most of these were of Scottish manufacture.

Several examples resemble illustrations in the pattern book of the Edinburgh and Leith Glass Company. These include a dram glass with ribbed and notched bowl, knopped stem, and plain foot with punty scar beneath (fig. 307a); a champagne flute cut with long flutes, round cut knop, and plain foot (fig. 303c); a wineglass with fluted bowl, bladed knop, and welted foot (fig. 304); and a pair of thistle-shaped dram glasses with gadrooned moulding encircling the bases of trumpet-shaped bowls supported on plain disc feet (fig. 305).

Mr. Fleming referrs to Reid Merret, son of the translator of Neri's *L'arte Vetraria*, the first textbook on glass manufacture to appear in the English language. Reid Merret was English representative of the Edinburgh and Leith Glass Company. In his ledger, dated 18th November 1745, Merret wrote: 'His Majesty's [Prince Charles's] army has returned here again, and this day our homes and churches are filled with them. I know not when we shall get any time to do any business again'. The use of the term 'His Majesty' suggests Merret to have been a Jacobite. Edinburgh was the headquarters of Prince Charles's propaganda department, controlled from 1741 by two Cardinals. It is interesting to speculate whether these two dignitaries placed orders with Merret, perhaps at his inspiration, for drinking-glasses engraved with Jacobite emblems.

380

Figures 301–3

SCOTTISH GLASSES

(301) Champagne flute with air-beaded knop and air-twist stem, on plain foot; four-piece structure on such glasses is rare. Height 9 inches; mid-eighteenth century.

(*Right*) Cordial glass with bucket bowl, the lower part encircled with very shallow flutings, on square silesian stem and plain foot. Height 7 inches; 1730–45.

(302) Wineglass with ovoid bowl, compound white opaque-twist stem: a fine lace-twist within a single spiral; plain foot. Height 6 inches; 1760–80.

(303) Three fluted wineglasses of a type popular between *c.* 1810 and 1840.

(*Left*) Lower part of bowl cut with shallow flutes, merese at top of stem, beaded knop, plain foot. Height 7 inches.

(*Centre*) Plain bowl, merese, knop, and folded foot. Height 6½ inches.

(*Right*) Bowl cut with long flutes, round cut knop, plain foot. Height 8 inches.

By courtesy of Trust Houses Ltd

Figures 304–7

SCOTTISH GLASSES

(304) Deep-bowled goblet wheel-engraved with an all-over design composed of vine-leaves and grapes wreathed around bacchantes in the form of satyrs, and a panther. This engraving is probably the work of J. H. B. Millar, a glass-engraver of Leith who specialized in classical scenes (*see* page 380).

In the collection of Lady Bromet

(305) Thistle-shaped dram glass with trumpet-shaped bowl, solid gadrooned base, plain foot. Height 4¼ inches; *c.* 1805.

(306) Sweetmeat glass such as is illustrated on confectioners' trade cards of the late eighteenth century. Ribbed trumpet bowl with flattened knop and moulded domed foot.

(307) Dram glasses:

(*Left*) With ribbed and notched bowl, knopped stem, plain foot with punty scar beneath.

(*Centre*) With spirally moulded body, drawn stem with plain central knop and lower knop with air tears, on folded foot with punty mark beneath, mid-eighteenth century.

(*Right*) With funnel bowl, the lower part cut with flutes, with ball-knopped stem and plain foot.

All by courtesy of Trust Houses Ltd

Figures 308–10

Designs from the pattern book of the Edinburgh and Leith Glass Company, Leith, printed on paper watermarked 1811.

(308) Rummers with solid, square, stepped feet and knopped stems. (*a*) Toddy rummer, ogee bowl with incurved rim, illustrating two methods of cutting strawberry diamonds. Stem with spherical knop, plain and cut. Height 8 inches. (*b*) Toddy rummer with hemispherical bowl encircled by a band of triangles cut with strawberry diamonds, alternating with a fan and leaf pattern: four encircling rings cut below. Stem cut with flutes, knop encircled with diamonds. Height 7 inches. (*c* and *d*) Rummers in which the bowl base is cut with wide hollow flutes: above is a band of ornamental cutting. Height 6 inches.

(309) Four cut sugar-bowls. (*a*) Triangles cut with strawberry diamonds above triple rings, with fan escallop edge. (*b*) Cross-hatched circles with swirl-cut base, and fan escallop edge. (*c*) Band of fine diamonds cut on large diamonds above triple rings, with fan escallop edge; (*d*) Strawberry diamond arches above double rings, and fluted rim.

(310) Four tall champagne flutes with (*a*) everted, (*b*) incurved, (*c*) straight bowl rims with short knopped stems. (*d*) Illustrates two designs for cutting the lower part of the bowl; short stem with two cut knops.

GLOSSARY

GLOSSARY

ACORN KNOP. A tooled motif in the form of an acorn and sometimes inverted: found in stems and as a lid finial. Fig. 37c.

AIR-TWIST. Threads of air spiralling within a stem: formed by the extension of air bubbles Fig. 69.

ANNULAR KNOP. A round-edged flattened knop, placed horizontally. Fig. 179.

ANNULATED KNOP. A flattened knop, sandwiched between two, four or six thinner. flattened knops, each pair progressively less in size. Fig. 233.

ARABESQUES. Intertwined scrollwork of leaves and flowers, usually engraved on bowls. Fig. 41.

ARCH AND SPRIG. A repetitive cut motif encircling sweetmeat glass bowls. Fig. 231.

BALL KNOP. A large spherical knop often found immediately above a silesian stem. Fig. 47b.

BALUSTER. Stem of pure baluster form (fig. 61) or inverted (fig. 39): also stem consisting of a baluster combined with knopped motifs. Fig. 40.

BATCH. A mixture of raw materials prepared for melting.

BELL BOWL. A deep-waisted bowl with an incurved profile and wide mouth. Fig. 43.

BLADED KNOP. A thin sharp-edged flattened knop placed horizontally. Fig. 145.

BUCKET BOWL. A bowl with almost vertical sides and horizontal base. Frontispiece.

BULLET KNOP. A small spherical knop breaking the line of a stem: formerly known as the olive button. Fig. 52.

COLLAR KNOP (*see* Merese).

CORDS. Slight striae felt on the surface of flint-glass and similarly caused. Frontispiece.

CRIZZLING. Loss of translucency caused by excess of borax which leads to impermanency in glass. Fig. 18.

CULLET. Broken flint-glass added to the batch.

CUSHIONED KNOP. A large spherical knop with narrow cushion top and/or bottom. Fig. 37a.

CUSP. A point at which two branches of a curve meet and stop. A centrally placed stem knop shaped by cutting. Figs. 90a and c.

CYLINDER KNOP. A knop in the form of a cylinder, often containing a tear.

CYST. A rounded protuberance in the base of a wineglass bowl.

DIAMOND-POINT ENGRAVING. A pattern hand-inscribed on glass with the point of a diamond. Figs. 8 to 12.

DOMED FOOT. (*a*) Domed and folded. Fig. 40. (*b*) Terraced dome. Fig. 256. (*c*) Flat dome. Fig. 254.

DRAWN STEM. Stem of a footed vessel made by extending a gathering of metal at the base of the bowl: called also the straw stem. Fig. 57.

DROP-KNOP. A knop resembling in shape the frustum of an inverted cone and usually placed $\frac{1}{2}$ inch to 1 inch above the foot. Fig. 254.

ENAMEL TWIST. Enamel threads spiralling within the stems of drinking-glasses. Fig. 84.

ENGRAVING (see Wheel-engraving; Diamond-point engraving).

FIRE POLISHING. Reheating of finished ware to obliterate marks left by tools and produce a smooth even surface.

FLINT-GLASS. Originally glass in which the silica was derived from calcined flints; glass in which lead oxide forms the flux. Lead crystal is the twentieth-century term.

FLUTE. A drinking-glass with a tall, deep bowl, fig. 157; a vertical groove cut or moulded into a bowl surface. Fig. 222.

FOLDED FOOT. The rim of a circular foot on a stemmed vessel folded under while hot, giving extra strength to a part most liable to be accidentally chipped. Figs. 47 to 50.

GADROONING. Borders of moulded deep convex flutes forming a decorative band, or ribbing impressed on a second thin layer of applied glass. Fig. 134.

GATHER. A blob of molten metal secured on the end of a blow-pipe.

GOBLET. A drinking-glass: at first bowl-shaped without handles, sometimes mounted on a foot and fitted with a cover.

HERRING-BONE FRINGE or BLAZE. Delicately cut parallel mitres, vertical or slanting, encircling early-nineteenth-century glasses. Fig. 295.

HOLLOWED. Punty scar ground smooth.

KICK. The pyramidical dent to be found in the base of early bottles and decanters. Fig. 211.

KNOP. A protuberance or knob, other than a baluster, either solid or hollow, breaking the line of a stem. Shapes are too numerous to list.

KNOP-AND-BALUSTER. A simple inverted baluster surmounted by a knop. Fig. 45.

LEAD GLASS (see Flint-glass).

LEER. Tunnel in which flint-glass is annealed and cooled, thus toughening the metal and lengthening its working life.

LIME GLASS. Metal in which soda and lime are used as a flux producing a glass as clear as flint-glass but not so heavy or resonant: invented 1863.

MERESE. A sharp-edged, flattened glass button connecting bowl and stem, or between foot and stem of a wineglass. Figs. 34c and f.

METAL. Glass either molten or cold.

MOULDED GLASS. Blown glass ornamented or given its final body shape by the use of moulds.

MULTIPLE KNOPS. Knops of a single shape repeated in a stem. Fig. 97a.

MUSHROOM KNOP. A mushroom-shaped protuberance found in stems, associated with incurved and funnel bowls.

'NIPT DIAMOND WAIS.' Diamond-shaped network made by pinching together vertical threads or ribs of glass.

OPAQUE TWIST (see Enamel twist).

PINCHED TRAILING. Applied bands of glass pinched into a wavy formation. Fig. 206.

PONTIL (*see* Punty).

POTASH GLASS. Glass fluxed with unrefined vegetable ashes.

PRESSED GLASS. Glass shaped mechanically in moulds.

PRUNT. A glass seal, with surface plain or tooled, such as strawberry, and applied to the stem or bowl of a drinking-glass. Figs. 14 and 15.

PUNTY or PONTIL ROD. Long solid iron used principally to hold a vessel during the finishing processes after removal from the blowpipe.

PUNTY MARK. The scar left on a glass when the punty rod is snapped off. Usually found on the base of a glass, latterly ground and polished.

PURLED ORNAMENT. All-over diaper with small round or oval compartments. Fig. 239.

QUATREFOIL KNOP. A short knop pressed into four wings by vertical depressions, the metal being drawn out with pincers. The wings may be upright or twisted. Fig. 34.

RETICULATED. Moulded pattern in diamond-like formation: also called expanded diamond.

RIB or DIAMOND MOULD. Straight or twisted lines forming diamonds or other patterns and impressed on the surface of a bowl. Fig. 15.

RIGAREE. Applied ribbons tooled in vertical lines forming tiny contiguous ribs.

ROUNDED FUNNEL BOWL. A long tapering bowl maintaining its convex curvature throughout. Fig. 40.

SCALLOP. A rim outline cut in the form of a series of semi-circles or cyma outlines. Fig. 266.

SEEDS. Minute air bubbles in the metal, indicating that the glass-house could not raise furnace temperature high enough to eliminate all air bubbles trapped among the raw materials. Fig. 17.

SODA-GLASS. Glass in which the principal flux is carbonate of lime, usually the second alkaline base.

STEP. A flattened button connecting the stem of a rummer with its foot. Fig. 138 top left.

STONES. Red and black specks within the fabric of early flint-glass, the result of imperfect fusion between oxide of lead and silica.

STRAIGHT-FUNNEL BOWL. A straight-sided bowl shaped like the frustum of an inverted cone. Fig. 39.

STRAW STEM. A plain stem drawn directly from the base of the bowl. Fig. 57.

STRIAE. Apparent undulating markings within the metal, perfectly vitrified and transparent, showing the metal to be of uneven composition because insufficiently molten before working.

STUCK SHANK. A drinking-glass stem made from a separate gather of glass welded to the base of the bowl. Frontispiece.

SWELLING KNOP. A slight protuberance in the stem containing an air tear. Fig. 42.

TEAR. A bubble of air enclosed in the metal. Shape may or may not be intentional: usually in stems or finials for decoration. Fig 39.

TERRACED FOOT. A foot tooled in concentric circles. Fig. 259.

THISTLE BOWL. A waisted bowl in which the lower part is a solid or hollow sphere of glass.

THREAD CIRCUIT. A thin trail of glass applied around the rim of the bowl or decorating the neck of a vessel.

TINT. A residual colour tinge inherent in the ingredients of which the metal is composed.

TRAILED ORNAMENT. Looped threads of glass applied to the surface of a bowl or foot. Fig. 24.

TRUMPET BOWL. A waisted bowl of incurving profile merging into a drawn stem. Fig. 57.

VERMICULAR COLLAR. A wavy trail of glass encircling a stem or decanter neck.

WELTED FOOT (*see* Folded foot).

WHEEL-ENGRAVING. A pattern cut into the surface of a glass by pressing it against the edge of a thin, rapidly revolving wheel. Figs. 114 to 115.

WING KNOP (*see* Quatrefoil knop).

'WORMED GLASSES.' Drinking-glasses with stems containing spiral twists of air or enamel.

WRITHING. Surface twisting or swirled ribbing or fluting on stem or bowl.

SELECTED
BIBLIOGRAPHY

SELECTED BIBLIOGRAPHY

BATE, PERCY. *English Tableglass.* 1905.

BEATSON, CLARK AND COMPANY. *The Glass Works, Rotherham, 1751–1951.* 1951.

BLANCOURT, H. *Art of Glass,* 1699.

BLES, JOSEPH. *Rare English Glasses of the 17th and 18th Centuries.* 1926.

BOWLES, W. H. *History of the Vauxhall and Ratcliff Glasshouses and their Owners.* 1926.

BUCKLEY, FRANCIS. *History of Old English Glass.* 1925.

BUCKLEY, WILFRED. *The Art of Glass.* 1939.

ARTHUR CHURCHILL LTD. *History in Glass.* 1937.

DILLON, E. *Glass.* 1907.

DOWNEY, ALAN. *The Story of Waterford Glass.* 1952.

ELVILLE, E. M. *English Tableglass.* 1951.
　　　　　　　English and Irish Cut Glass, 1750–1950. 1952.

FLEMING, ARNOLD. *Scottish and Jacobite Glass.* 1938.

FRANCIS, GRANT R. *Old English Drinking Glasses.* 1926.

HADEN, H. J. *Notes on the Stourbridge Glass Trade.* 1949.

HARTSHORNE, ALBERT. *Old English Glasses.* 1897.

HAYNES, E. B. *Glass Through the Ages.* 1948.

HONEY, WILLIAM BOWYER. *Glass.* 1946.

HUGHES, G. BERNARD. 'Enamel and Milk-white Opaque Glass.' *More About Collecting Antiques.* 1952.
　　　　　　　'Old English Bottles.' *More About Collecting Antiques.* 1952.
　　　　　　　'The Glass Blower.' *Living Crafts.* 1953.
　　　　　　　'English Glass.' *The Concise Encyclopaedia of Antiques.* 1954.

HUGHES, G. BERNARD AND THERLE. 'Blown-moulded, Pressed, Cased, Flashed, Stained Glass.' *After the Regency.* 1952.

PERCEVAL, MCIVER. *The Glass Collector.* 1918.

POWELL, H. J. *Glassmaking in England.* 1923.

THORPE, W. A. *English and Irish Glass.* 1927.
　　　　　　　A History of English and Irish Glass. 2 vols. 1929.
　　　　　　　English Glass. 1935.

WESTROPP, M. S. D. *Irish Glass.* 1920.

WILMER, DAISY. *Early English Glass.* 1910.

Wine Trade Loan Exhibition of Drinking Vessels Catalogue (Edited by Andre Simon). 1933.

YOUNG, S. *The History of the Worshipful Company of Glass-sellers of London.* 1913.

YOXALL, J. H. *Collecting Old Glass.* 1916.

391

INDEX

INDEX

The numerals in *heavy type* denote the *figure numbers* of the illustrations

403